TRUST YOU ENJOY THE STORY

Sincerely

Son of Sister Maria

MICHAEL PARLEE

authorHOUSE®

AuthorHouse™
1663 Liberty Drive
Bloomington, IN 47403
www.authorhouse.com
Phone: 1-800-839-8640

First published by AuthorHouse   7/5/2011

ISBN: 978-1-4567-2457-3 (sc)
ISBN: 978-1-4567-2458-0 (e)
ISBN: 978-1-4567-2459-7 (hc)

Library of Congress Control Number: 2011901542

Printed in the United States of America

DEDICATION

To the Foster Children of this world, who through no fault of their own were deprived of the love and care of their biological parents.

To their birth mothers, who because of circumstances beyond their control were unable to care for their child and forced to endure the pain of giving up their own babies.

ACKNOWLEDGMENTS

As in my first book, Tanya, I owe much to two ladies: Barb Baer my editor and Pauline, my wife. It never ceases to amaze me how Barb's professional tweaking can so improve my writing. Pauline is my proof reader and sounding board. Without question, 'Son of Sister Maria' has evolved for the better because of their assistance.

INTRODUCTION

Son of Sister Maria begins in a small coal mining town in southwest Alberta. With a chronically depressed, bedridden mother and an alcoholic father there is no question that sixteen year old Maria has a most dysfunctional home life. Maria's life changes for the better when she meets Andrew, a twenty-two year old service man. For the first time in her life she feels true love and support. Ominous clouds soon begin gathering though. It's in the midst of World War II. Andrew is posted overseas and isn't expecting a leave for eight months. Shortly after he leaves, Maria finds out she is pregnant. When she breaks the news to her folks, her mom attempts suicide and has to be permanently institutionalized. There is no support from her father as alcohol rules his life. In desperation, Maria phones her boyfriend's folks for support. Her world further shatters when she learns to her horror that Andrew's folks have just received word that Andrew has been killed in action. Throughout her pregnancy, events force Maria to make the painful decision that she must give her baby up for adoption.

Baby Andrew is adopted by a young couple who soon divorce. In the divorce the adoptive mother is awarded sole custody of wee Andrew. Unbeknownst to the adoption agency, Andrew's adoptive mother has as an addictive personality. She becomes addicted to heroin and baby Andrew is again made a ward of the government. We follow Andrew as he goes from foster home to foster home. Some of the homes are good and some horrible. Throughout his troubled life, Andrew longs to find his biological parents. Will he ever find them?

CHAPTER ONE

A raw northwest wind was lashing Coalberg, a small mining town in the coal branch of southwest Alberta. Maria braced herself against the wind, the driving snow stinging her cheeks. School was out for the day. As she slowly trudged the three blocks from the school to the doctor's office, fear was gnawing away at her. Maria was trying hard not to break down as she approached the receptionist desk.

She slumped down on a chair in the waiting room, sick with apprehension. "Maria Turnbull," the receptionist called out. Maria slowly got to her feet and followed the nurse into the examination room. "The doctor will be with you in a few minutes," she said, showing Maria to a chair.

As the nurse closed the door, fear again welled up inside Maria. Panic had been her constant companion for the last three weeks her period was late. Doctor Corey examined her two days ago and she would get the test results today. She looked up, her heart beating wildly as the stocky, white-bearded doctor entered.

"I'm sorry, but your tests were positive, Maria," he began, placing his hand on her shoulder. "I'm afraid you're pregnant."

Maria sat in stunned silence. The doctor's voice seemed to be coming from a distant room. Finally, she forced herself to focus.

"How can that be?" she blurted out. "Andrew and I only had sex three times and we used condoms."

"Well as you probably know, they do occasionally fail. I'm sorry Maria. I know you weren't planning a pregnancy."

"What can I do?" Maria whispered, tears streaming down her pretty face. "You know Mom and Dad. They won't be able to handle this."

"I'm aware of the problems you have with your parents," Dr Corey responded, nervously tapping the desk with his pen. "Your mom's been my patient since your birth. That's when her depression started."

"What we need to do now is look for some help for you. Considering your dad's drinking problem, I suppose he's out of the question."

Maria nodded. "Dad never gives me a hard time like Mom does, but the last year or so it seems he's spending pretty well all his free time in the beer parlour."

As the doctor looked at Maria's chart he thought back over his involvement with Maria's folks. Jennifer, Maria's mother, had been his patient for many years. She'd spent as much time in the psychiatric wards of the hospitals in Lethbridge and Calgary as she did at home and although presently not hospitalized, seldom left her bed. From what he'd gathered, the only time she spoke to either her husband or daughter was to demand something or lash out at them. Doctor Corey felt for Maria's dad, but recognized that over the last few years, Clyde was letting alcohol rule his life.

"I just can't take it," Maria sobbed. "Mom will be impossible to live with and Dad will probably go on a three day drunk. What's going to happen if he gets fired? He's already had two warnings from the mine. They have him working on the surface now because of his drinking."

The doctor shook his head. "Even though your dad's a kind sort, I guess we have to face the fact that he's an alcoholic."

The doctor glanced down again at Maria's medical chart.

"Let's see. You say you and Andrew were intimate sometime in mid-January. Based on that, your baby should arrive in middle to late October. By that time you'll be seventeen, right?"

Maria nodded.

"I know this news is pretty shocking. It will no doubt take you some time to think your situation through, but let's try to look for some options for you. What about your boyfriend? If that's a no go, are there any friends or relatives other than your folks you could turn to?"

"The only relative I have is my aunt who lives in the United States," Maria replied, her voice trembling. "She's pretty well off. If it all comes apart at home, I suppose that's a possibility, but she's a cold one. She's always acted stuck up with our family."

"And the baby's father, Andrew. It's not my intention to pry into your affairs, but what about him?"

"Andrew and I met three months ago. He's in the Air Force and is overseas right now. He left about three weeks ago and mightn't be back for another seven months or so."

"Well I guess he's out of the picture for now. Do his folks live nearby and would there be any chance of support from them?"

"I guess that's a thought. I've been at their place a few times and they always treated me well. They live in Lethbridge. Andrew's dad is a high school teacher. His mother died years ago and his grandmother Rose lives with them. Before I try to contact them though, I should tell Mom and Dad. I just know they'll be torn up with me, Mom anyway."

"Well keep me informed," the doctor concluded, putting his hand on Maria's shoulder again. "If your folks get too uptight, just give me a call, day or night." Doctor Corey quickly wrote out his home phone number on a card and handed it to her.

As Maria got up to leave, her feet felt leaden. "Why couldn't I have normal parents?" she moaned. "Why did this have to happen to me?"

She slowly shuffled her way home through the storm, the driving northwest wind biting at her tear-stained cheeks. Coming to the corner, Maria gazed up at their old house, a grey unpainted two-story shanty much like the other colourless company houses in Coalberg.

Climbing the rickety porch steps, she whispered, "Why can't Andrew be here for me?"

Maria pushed the snow from the doorstep with her foot and stepped inside. It was cool in the living room. Almost in a trance, she took the half-full coal scuttle and emptied it into the old upright coal furnace. Putting the pail down, she kicked her winter boots off and slouched down in the easy chair.

"Dear Lord, I need your help so badly," she moaned.

As she sat there in a daze, Maria's troubled past flashed through her mind.

Her mother's horrible words, 'I was forced into marrying that drunken dad of yours because I was pregnant with you,' hurt so much. "Why does Mom have to keep saying that? I've heard those words so many times it seems they're carved right into my heart. Every time I hear them again, they just cut a little deeper."

Maria's mother's mental health steadily deteriorated throughout her pregnancy with Maria and only got worse after the birth. Jennifer resented her baby and was incapable of bonding with her. The negative feelings she harboured towards both her husband and daughter only intensified with time.

Throughout her formative years, Maria longed for the love and approval of her mom, but it was not forthcoming. There was never a kind word. She couldn't remember a hug. Maria was forced to build a shield around her inner self to keep from being destroyed by her mom's negative feelings towards her.

If it hadn't been for her dad's half-sister, Sharon, Maria and her dad couldn't have managed during the early years of Jennifer's illness. Sharon moved in with them shortly after Maria was born and became Maria's surrogate mother. Although Sharon had a learning disability that kept her from getting much schooling, she had a big heart and helped keep the family together.

There was always tension between Jennifer and Sharon. The summer Maria turned twelve it came to a head when Jennifer accused Sharon of stealing some of her jewellery. In the brouhaha that followed, Sharon left and the responsibility of running the household fell on Maria's shoulders. Looking after the household was a heavy burden, but made much heavier with a mother who spent all day lying on her bed staring blankly at the wall. Maria could not remember her mother ever thanking her.

Having to cope with a father who drank too much didn't help matters either. Even though she loved her dad, Maria realized he was weak and ineffectual. She learned not to expect too much from him with the household chores. Years of scorn from his wife had quashed what little self-esteem he had. Alcohol was the tool he used to cope with a cold, indifferent wife who either wouldn't or couldn't show him any affection. For the last ten years of their marriage there had been no intimacy between Clyde and Jennifer. If it hadn't been for her dad's strong Catholic background, the marriage would have dissolved years ago.

Clyde's drinking problem was starting to interfere with his job and the mine boss had him on probation. To make matters worse, the money he spent on liquor made for tight economic straits at home. Maria had never been on a holiday. She welcomed the odd babysitting job as it gave her the chance to buy a few clothes for herself.

Maria met her boyfriend, Andrew, at a dance in Lethbridge where he was taking his air force basic training. It wasn't long before they were going steady.

Driving home from a date one night, Maria snuggled close to Andrew. "When we're together I feel so warm and complete. For the first time in my life, I'm feeling real love. It's almost like it's too good to be true."

Andrew held Maria close. "I've never felt this happy before either. Just remember, after this damn war is over we'll be spending the rest of our lives together."

They did make a handsome couple. Maria was petite, blonde, blue-eyed, had beautiful features and as Andrew put it, "a figure that a man would die for." At twenty-two, Andrew was nearly a foot taller than Maria. He was dark, physically fit and in Maria's view, the most handsome man she'd ever met.

Maria and Andrew had not become sexually intimate until a couple of weeks before he was shipped out. As with many young couples in war time, the possibility that death could separate them tended to alter their old thinking.

Maria recalled the last time they made love. "I've never been so happy and content in all my life," she whispered. "It feels so wonderful being here in your arms. I don't want this moment to ever end. I'll remember it as long as I live."......

"I'm cold! Bring me another blanket," a harsh voice called out from the bedroom.

Maria leapt to her feet and headed to her mom's bedroom.

"This will keep you warm till the house warms up," Maria said as she draped a blanket over her mom. "I filled the heater with coal. It won't be long before the house warms up."

Jennifer made no reply as she turned her face to the wall again.

Even though she was feeling very down, Maria got started on supper. She opened the cellar trap-door and got some potatoes. Climbing back up the cellar stairs she noticed frost on the inside of the footing walls. Over the last few weeks she'd told her dad several times that the house needed to be banked up with snow. "I guess I'll have to do it myself or everything in the cellar will freeze."

Though it was over an hour since her dad's shift ended, he was still not back from work. Usually Clyde would stop at the local beer parlour for a few drinks and be home around eight. Maria thought it wise to wait till he returned before breaking the news of her pregnancy. The fear of her folks' reaction had her stomach churning. Despite feeling nauseous, Maria re-stoked the coal heater and took her mom's supper in to her on a tray.

For several years now, Jennifer had eaten her meals in her room. As usual, she did not acknowledge her daughter, keeping her face to the wall. Only after Maria left did she sit up and eat.

Ever since Aunt Sharon had left, Maria had made a practise of waiting to have supper with her dad.

At eight-thirty, Maria's dad stumbled in with a fair shine on. Clyde was short, balding, red-faced and had developed quite a beer belly. As they ate, Maria was so on edge she had no appetite. Finally she could take it no longer and leapt to her feet.

"Dad, we have to talk," she cried out, her voice quivering. "Let's go to Mom's room."

Clyde dutifully followed his daughter into Jennifer's bedroom, a puzzled look on his face.

"Mom, Dad," Maria began, on the verge of tears. "I've got some bad news. I just found out this afternoon that I'm pregnant." Neither her mom nor dad made a reply so Maria continued. "It was with my boyfriend, Andrew Carpenter. I guess one of the condoms must have broken."

Deathly silence ensued.

"Oh my God, Maria," Clyde finally responded. "What will the neighbours say?"

Before Maria could reply, her mother turned over and focussed on her with a disdainful stare. Jennifer had only picked at her food for the last few years and was very emaciated. Her face was thin, her eyes cold. "I wish you hadn't been born," she hissed, her voice full of venom. "You never were any good." Then turning to Clyde she continued with sarcasm. "Really though, it doesn't surprise me. What more can you expect with a drunk for a father?"

It was too much for Maria. She broke into tears and rushed upstairs to her bedroom.

"How could she say such a mean thing? She was pregnant with me before she and Dad got married."

A few minutes later Maria's dad tapped on her door, came into her room and placed a hand on her shoulder.

"It will all work out, Maria. I don't know how, but I'm sure it will."

There was a loud crash from downstairs. "Good Lord, what's happening?" Maria cried out. She and her dad raced for the stairs. They found Jennifer collapsed on the bathroom floor, blood splattered everywhere. There were two gaping slashes on her wrists that were spurting blood with every heartbeat. While Clyde attempted to keep pressure on his wife's wrists, Maria phoned for Doctor Corey. The coal company's ambulance arrived a few minutes later and raced Jennifer to the local hospital.

Maria and her dad followed the ambulance in their car. Doctor Corey was unable to put Jennifer under as she'd lost so much blood. Using local freezing, he sutured her wrists and started a blood transfusion. After attending to her, the doctor conferred with Clyde and Maria in the waiting room.

"That was a close one. She did a good job on her wrists. It was only your quick actions that saved her life, Clyde. A few minutes more and it would have been too late. I've patched her up so she's not bleeding anymore and we've started her on a blood transfusion. We'll be sending her to the Lethbridge hospital by ambulance shortly. With your permission, I think we have to consider having her committed indefinitely to the psychiatric ward in Lethbridge. In all likelihood she'll attempt suicide again if she has the opportunity. It's just too risky with her being home alone during the day. It will be a long drive for you to visit her, but I don't think we have any other options."

Clyde nodded without replying. Still in a daze, he signed the appropriate papers and they left.

"It's all my fault," Maria moaned as they drove home from the hospital. "If I hadn't gotten pregnant, this would have never happened."

"Now don't start blaming yourself for what Mom did," her dad replied, putting his arm around her. "Good God, she was pregnant with you before we married. Talk about the pot calling the kettle black. You'd think she'd understand. Guess we've got to remember that she's not in her right mind."

Once Clyde and Maria got home from the hospital they sat at the kitchen table in silence, both feeling drained. Maria kept rubbing her finger back and forth on the red and white checkered tablecloth, trying to wipe out an old stain. She was deep in thought, overwhelmed with what had transpired in the last few hours. Her dad took a chew of snuff and sat staring off into space, tapping his snuff box nervously on the table. Finally Clyde got up, went to the cupboard and returned with a bottle of whiskey.

"I hope it don't bother you too much if I take a drink or two," he started hesitantly. "I imagine you're kind of mixed up pretty bad and I'm in the same boat. Right now I just don't know how to handle it all. Maybe we could talk a bit more about it in the morning."

"I suppose so," Maria replied sadly. "It sure would help me a lot if we could talk about it. I guess we could do it in the morning."

"Yeah, then we'll talk in the morning. I promise not to drink too much."

Slowly Maria got to her feet and once again climbed the stairs to her bedroom.

Clyde sat at the table, the past sixteen years passing before him. "It's all been a proper bitch what with the Mrs being out of her tree and so down on Maria and me," he whispered, taking a healthy swig from the bottle. "What a price to pay for getting someone knocked up." He sat there until well past midnight sipping on the bottle and repeating over and over again, "Oh my God, what will we do now?"

Maria lay in bed, trying to sift through the day's events, tears glistening in her eyes.

"I don't know what hurts more, finding out I'm pregnant, Mom saying I was no good, or her trying to kill herself."

Her mom's words, 'you never were any good,' kept repeating themselves like a stuck record. "I'm glad it's Friday.

As crummy as I feel, I couldn't bear the thought of going to school tomorrow." Finally Maria fell into a deep sleep.

CHAPTER TWO

Maria had breakfast on the table by the time her dad came downstairs. She could still smell liquor on his breath and by the way he walked she knew he was far from sober. They ate in silence.

Maria wanted desperately to talk her problem out, but was waiting for her dad to take the lead.

"Thanks for breakfast," Clyde finally said, getting to his feet. "Last night I said I'd talk things over with you, but first I've got to go out for a bit. I kind of got to work things out of my system if you know what I mean. I promise we'll talk later."

"Yes, I know very well what you mean," Maria muttered under her breath as her dad headed for the door, "a weekend drunk."

Her dad doffed his greasy cap and then turned to Maria, his eyes glistening. "I just want you to know that what your mom said about you last night was dead wrong. You've always been a good daughter. You've had to put up with so much crap what with Mom always being so out of it. Thanks for jumping in and looking after things when Sharon left." After a long pause he continued. "I don't know what else to say. I kind of feel stumped. Remember I do care for you and I know that somehow it will all come out in the wash."

Maria felt numb as she hugged her dad. With a heavy heart she watched him walk unsteadily out to the sidewalk and then head in the direction of the beer parlour.

"Dear Lord, Mom's out of the picture and with Dad drinking what can I do now?" Maria sat at the kitchen table trying desperately to sort her problems out. The more she tried to resolve them, the more convoluted they became.

When she couldn't bear the pressure anymore she phoned her friend Sofia and asked her to come over. Sofia's folks immigrated to Canada from the Ukraine just before the start of the war. Maria helped Sofia integrate into the school and they became close friends. It helped so much to have a friend to pour out her heart to. After a couple of hours discussing Maria's problem over a pot of tea though, the only resolution they had come up with was to somehow contact Andrew and see what he could offer in the way of advice.

"I promise to keep all this to myself," Sofia said as she hugged Maria goodbye. "I'll be praying for you and remember, if you have to talk just give me a phone call. I'll keep in touch."

Once Sofia left, Maria phoned the Catholic priest and walked over to the rectory for a talk. Father Patrick was a very caring gentleman in his late sixties. Physically he was a big man. He stood over six feet, was well-built and getting a little rotund. His acquaintances used to say his heart was as big as he was. Compassion for his fellow-man was the driving force in his life.

Father Patrick led the way into his little kitchen. It was sparse, but neat.

With tears streaming down her face, Maria spilled out the news of her pregnancy and her mom's suicide attempt. She finished by asking for forgiveness for engaging in sex outside of wedlock.

"Your sin is forgiven," Father Patrick responded quietly. "As you know you both didn't exercise enough self-control. It seems to me that at times this horrible war drives people to do things they wouldn't ordinarily do."

Over a cup of tea he continued, "I am very much aware of the problems your mom and dad have. One thing your dad is right about. You are a good girl. I know that you have kept the household going pretty well single-handedly since your Aunt Sharon left. I commend you highly for that."

"Now let's try to find a solution to your problem. You say your boyfriend will be overseas for many months, so marriage for now is out of the question. You could possibly contact him, but realistically with the war on, Andrew's hands are tied. Unfortunately, I don't think you can count on much help from your folks. Until your dad comes to grips with his drinking problem, he'll be of no help to you whatsoever. There are church-run homes for unwed mothers, but it would be less traumatic for you if you had some relative or friend you could go stay with."

"If I remember correctly, both your parents' folks are in England. Are there any other relatives near?"

"I have an aunt in New York, but she and Mom had a run in years ago. She's always been snooty with our family and I'd only contact her as my last resort."

"What about Andrew's folks? Is that a possibility? Would you feel comfortable with them?"

"That's a real good idea. Come to think of it, Doctor Corey mentioned them yesterday. I've been so flustered I completely forgot about his folks. I've been at their place a few times and they've always treated me well. They live in Lethbridge. Andrew's dad is a high school teacher there. His mother died a few years back and his grandmother lives with them. I guess I should be talking to them anyway. As things look now they may be my only help. I'll phone them tonight."

As soon as Maria got home she started a letter to Andrew.

Dearest Andrew,

It's 5 PM here. I hope my darling is doing all right tonight. As for me, I'm feeling pretty rough. I have some really scary news. I found out yesterday that I'm pregnant. So you're going to be a Dad. It's kind of strange. I don't know if I should be happy or sad, so I'm just really scared. It would help so much if you were here, but I guess that's out of the question. Anyway, as you could have guessed, my folks are no help. Mom tried to kill herself and Dad's on a drunk. This all upsets me something awful and I've been doing a lot of bawling. I'm going to phone your dad in another hour. Somehow it will all work out I guess. I'll add some more after I've talked to your dad. All my love for now.

After supper Maria phoned Andrew's place. Andrew's father, Alvin, was having difficulty controlling his emotions when he answered the phone.

"I've got horrible news, Maria," he finally blurted out, fighting desperately for control. "We've just been notified by the Air Force that Andrew's plane was shot down by enemy fire last night somewhere over the Atlantic. They were on a bombing mission. No survivors were found."

"Oh God help us all!" Maria cried out hysterically. "I can't take anymore. I found out yesterday that I'm pregnant. Last night Mom tried to kill herself and now my darling Andrew's dead. I just can't handle it. Oh dear God, please let me die too. I just want to go be with my Andrew so badly."

"Promise me you won't do anything foolish," Alvin implored, recognizing that Maria was in great peril. "I'm on my way."

"Okay I promise," Maria whispered.

"I should be there in an hour and a half or so. Just give me directions how to get to your house."

After giving Alvin her address, Maria hung up the phone and dropped to her knees. "Forgive me, Lord, for thinking of taking my life. I now have part of Andrew in my body. I must do everything in my power to protect our baby."

When Alvin came to the door, Maria was startled. Alvin resembled his son so much that in her muddled state, for an instant, she thought he was Andrew. Alvin embraced Maria and held her until she stopped crying.

"I think for now you should come and stay with my mother Rose and me," Alvin suggested after talking Maria's situation over with her. "We'll have to make some decisions about your schooling and the baby that's on the way."

Maria accepted Alvin's offer and they were soon on the road. On the trip back to Lethbridge they shared their pain.

Grandma Rose met them at the door. She was a white-haired old lady with an open kind face. Osteoporosis had left her stooped. She hugged Maria and they both cried. It helped Maria immeasurably to be able to share her anguish with Alvin and his mom. Their reaction to the news that she was pregnant was a far cry from what Maria had experienced the previous night.

"God saw fit to call our Andrew home, but has blessed us by leaving part of him with you," Rose said, her voice breaking. "I just hope I can live long enough to see my grandchild. My heart is none too good. I've had two heart attacks and God alone knows how much time I've got left."

"As I mentioned to you before, I think it would be very unwise for you to try to stay at home by yourself," Alvin continued. "Obviously you can't count on the support of your family. You said your only relatives were in the states?"

"The only relative I have is an aunt in New York, but I don't think she has a heart. The rest of the family is back in England."

"I think I can speak for Mom when I say you're welcome to stay with us till the baby is born. You can sleep in Andrew's room."

Alvin's face crumbled. He collapsed in a chair at the kitchen table, buried his face in his hands and broke down.

Rose went over and put her hand on his shoulder. She then turned to Maria. "As far as I'm concerned you're as welcome to stay as Andrew was. He told us a lot about you. He said you were a wonderful girl."

"Thank you so much for the offer. It's most kind of you. As you probably know, I'm not used to being looked after like this. I'll check things out with Dad once he sobers up. If I do come to stay, you can count on me pulling my own weight."

Maria retired to Andrew's room and sat on the edge of his bed. "My whole world is falling apart," she whispered, tears glistening in her eyes. "On the positive side, I have the support of Alvin and Rose."

Although it was a comfort to be sleeping in Andrew's bed, she would again cry herself to sleep. Just before she fell asleep, she whispered, "Dear Lord, please send Andrew to me in a dream."

Maria awoke at eight, but there were no dreams that she could recall. In the dim light she noticed Andrew's high school graduation picture on the dresser. "I love you, Andrew," she whispered. Maria was soon asleep again. She dreamt she was in a beautiful meadow. As she approached an old gnarled pine tree in the centre of the opening, Andrew suddenly appeared.

"I'm very happy here, Darling, and doing just great," Andrew said. "Read the letter." He smiled and disappeared.

Maria awoke with a start.

Even though the dream was very brief, seeing her lover again and knowing he was doing well was a great comfort to her. At breakfast she weighed whether or not to share the dream with Alvin or Rose. "For now I think I'd best keep it to myself," she mused, "but what on earth did Andrew mean when he said, 'read my letter?'"

Once they had breakfast, Rose took Maria on a tour of the house. Although just an average-size bungalow, Maria thought it a mansion compared to their house in Coalberg. After she'd seen the house, Maria got on the phone. Several phone calls later she located her dad at Fred Low's place. Fred was one of Clyde's drinking buddies.

"Fred and your dad have really been tying one on," Mrs Low began. "There's no sense in trying to talk to either of those idiots now because they're still drinking. Once your dad sobers up, I'll get him to call you."

After dinner Maria contacted her high school principal and updated him about all that had transpired in the last couple of days. He was aware of Maria's troubled home life and quite relieved that she would be moving in with the Carpenters. The principal was a professional acquaintance of Alvin's and knew that he and his mother would treat Maria well.

Sunday afternoon, Alvin and Maria were on the road back to Coalberg. A Chinook had blown in and the roads were bare. As the miles slipped by, Maria's apprehension kept building.

"I can't thank you and Rose enough for all the help you're giving me," Maria said, "but going back to Coalberg is kind of scary for me. You know, having to meet the principal and then looking up my father who will still probably be drunk."

"It will all work out," Alvin replied. "I know that pulling out of Coalberg and starting over again in Lethbridge is going to be hard for you, but in the long run it will be best for you and the baby."

The principal met them at the school and once Maria picked up all her books, they went to her house to get her clothes and all her personal things. It was cool in the house so with Alvin's help she got the furnace going again and filled it full of coal. On their way out of town, Maria stopped at the Low's place to check in on her dad.

The Low's abode was even starker than the Turnbull's company house, but Mrs Low did her best to keep it neat. Like Maria's house, it had never seen a drop of paint. They had to watch their step as the wooden sidewalk up to the house had many boards missing.

"Your dad passed out an hour ago," Mrs Low said, meeting Maria at the door. "You're smart to be pulling out now. I should have left my old man years ago. The bottle has got the best of him too."

Maria gave Mrs Low the Carpenters' phone number and address and asked her to give them to her dad when he sobered up.

As they pulled out of Coalberg, Maria glanced back with mixed emotions. For her the sun was figuratively setting on the grimy little mining town.

"I'm leaving some happy memories," she mused, "but after all that's happened in the last few days I have nothing to keep me here."

"I've been trying all weekend to get a hold of you," Maria began when she got her dad on the phone the next day. "I was at Low's yesterday, but you were passed out. I have horrible news," she continued, fighting for control. "The day after Mom tried to kill herself I found out that my boyfriend was killed in action. I know you never met Andrew, but he was a wonderful guy. I talked things over with Father Patrick and I've been staying at Andrew's folks' place. They've told me I could stay with them until after the baby is born and I think that's best."

"Sorry to hear about your boyfriend's death. Life sure can be a bitch at times. You've had a rough go of late. It's going to be pretty lonely here without you, but maybe it will be best, for now anyway. I guess I got to smarten up and get off the booze. Try to stay in touch with me. I'll send you a few dollars when I can."

The phone call was the last contact Maria had with her dad for some time. With Jennifer in the hospital and Maria being cared for, what little resolve he had left was soon gone. Rather than stay by himself, he asked a couple of his drinking buddies who were down on their luck to move in with him. Within a couple of weeks Clyde lost his job when he was found drunk at work.

Maria started school on Tuesday. It was a much bigger high school than the Coalberg School and she was able to take all her courses. Getting adjusted to a new home and a new school with new classmates and teachers was very stressful for Maria. Alvin advised her it might be best not to make her pregnancy known to the other teaching staff or her classmates. The love and support of Alvin and Rose helped her through the first trying days.

Three weeks after Andrew's death, a small parcel containing his personal effects arrived from the Air Force. It was another evening of tears. As they went through the package there was an envelope with Maria's name on it. Maria opened it. With tears in her eyes she stared at the picture of Andrew and her taken just before he left for overseas. It would remain her treasure for the rest of her life.

Later, as Maria sat on her bed looking at the photo, she was sobbing. She was just going to set the photo on her end table when a piece of paper that was between the photo holder and the picture fell out.

Maria unfolded the note, her heart beating wildly. It was a letter addressed to her from Andrew.

Dear Maria,

I have been at my posting less than two weeks.
I miss you something awful. I wish this damned war
would end so we could be together. I want so badly
to spend the rest of my life with you. I hope that
you're holding up okay. It's been pretty boring.
As you know, I'm the tail gunner and we're on bombing
runs. There's been no enemy planes shooting at us and
just the odd bit of anti-aircraft fire. Before I sign
off I must tell you about the dream I had last night.
I was standing by your bed. You were lying there
holding a baby. You said, 'Andrew, this is our baby,'
and then the dream ended. I don't have a logical
explanation for this, but ever since the dream I have
a very strong feeling that the baby you were
holding was a boy. I love you so, Maria. I have to
report for duty in fifteen minutes. Will finish
the letter tomorrow.

"Oh my God; this is what Andrew meant in my dream
when he said, 'read my letter.' By the date on the letter it must
have been written the day Andrew's plane was shot down.
That's the day before I found out I was pregnant!"

Although the letter brought many tears, it comforted
Maria to know that somehow, miraculously, Andrew had a
premonition about her being pregnant even before she found
out.

CHAPTER THREE

Maria was adjusting well to both her studies and the care Alvin and Rose were providing. Alvin and Rose thought Maria was taking over too much of the housework and were constantly after her to ease up a bit.

On a Saturday in early May, Maria got Alvin to drive her back to Coalberg so she could visit her dad. It was a perfect spring morning. The pastures along the highway were getting new growth and the bluffs of trees were starting to get a faint hint of green. Farmers were out in full force cultivating the fields. Here and there you could see their palls of dust.

When she saw the front yard of her folk's house she was taken aback. There was garbage strewn everywhere and scads of empty beer and whiskey bottles. She looked inside the house through the open kitchen door and gasped. It was a total pigsty. There were dirty dishes stacked sky-high and clothes and empty liquor bottles lying all over the place. Swarms of flies were buzzing around the open garbage. She could see that the floors hadn't been washed since she left.

Maria's dad greeted her at the door, dishevelled, two weeks of stubble on his face and smelling rather high. "I'm sorry for the mess," he began without making eye contact. "I've kind of given up without you or Mom around." Still staring at his feet he continued in a dejected tone. "I went to see Mom a couple of times, but she wouldn't say anything to me. She wouldn't even look at me. That really hurts. I guess you know I lost my job. I get the odd day's work down at the mine and they still let me stay here. So far I make enough to get by on, but barely. That's why I haven't sent you any money. Ted and Stan have moved in with me. They help a bit if they can. I know I've got to smarten up, but it's awful hard. How are you doing?"

"I know what it's like visiting Mom," Maria replied, shooing flies from the open butter-dish. "I've been to see her a few times myself. It's so hard to take when she lets on that she doesn't even see you. I guess we both know what it's like to be hurt by her. Come to think of it, nothing really has changed since she was here. Still, you always hope. As for me, I'm managing not too bad. Andrew's folks are very good to me."

Maria sat at the kitchen table, staring off into space, trying not to dwell on the stench of the room. As she glanced over at her dad her heart went out to him. "It's sad," she mused, "but there's really nothing I can do for either Mom or Dad. With Dad there still is a glimmer of hope, but I can't get him to turn his life around. He'll have to do it on his own."

There were no tears this time as Maria hugged her dad goodbye.

"I feel so bad, so disappointed," she commented to Alvin as they headed out of Coalberg. I know that Dad and I still care for each other, but until he changes his ways there's no way we can live together again."

Maria was managing well in the new school. She had the urge to share at times, but continued to follow Alvin's advice and kept the news of her pregnancy from her classmates and teachers. She was hoping she wouldn't show too much before school was out in June.

Maria and Rose got along admirably. Rose was the mother and grandmother that Maria never had while Maria was the daughter and granddaughter Rose had so longed for. When Maria thought of all the warmth, love and support she got from Alvin and Rose, it made her realize how wretched her home life really was.

One day when they were alone, Maria asked Rose about Andrew's mother.

"Lilly passed away the winter Andrew was six. They were a very close-knit family and both Andrew and his dad had a rough time adjusting to her death. Alvin's dad died of cancer a year later and I came to live with them. Alvin has been a wonderful son, but I worry how he'll manage when I pass on. He's the kind of man that can't seem to cope well by himself. I guess worrying won't help any though."

By the middle of June, Maria's pregnancy was starting to show, forcing her to wear loose-fitting clothes. She was quite relieved when the school year ended.

With Alvin away at the University of Alberta in Edmonton completing his master's degree, Maria and Rose were spending the summer by themselves. Rose's health was steadily deteriorating and Maria was pretty well running the household. Although not confined to bed as of yet, Rose had to spend most of her time resting.

"What are your plans for the future?" Rose asked Maria one day. "I'd love to be well enough to look after the baby while you finish school, but unless a miracle happens that will be out of the question."

"I've been doing a lot of thinking about what I should do. I'd love to keep the baby of course, but I don't know how I'd manage. Alvin told me that come September he'll help me home school until the baby arrives. I know that both of you will help me in any way you can, but I guess the decision about what I do when the baby arrives has to be mine. It tears at my heart to think of it, but I guess adoption is something I've got to consider."

"If you decide to keep the baby you can rest assured you'll be welcome to stay with us until you get all your thinking straight. After all, the baby will be Alvin's grandchild and my great-grandchild. Why do I have to be so sick? As you say, adoption is an option, but like you I hate the thought of it. I guess we have a few months to think it through. Just remember, Dear, whatever decision you make, Alvin and I will back you all the way."

Alvin returned for a weekend in mid-August with some surprising news. He had accepted a position as a principal in a small school in a suburb of Calgary. The position would come open after the Christmas break.

Maria got her driver's license in July. The Saturday before school started she borrowed Alvin's car and drove out to Coalberg to see Father Patrick. It was a sunny fall day and as she pulled out of Lethbridge she noticed the high Chinook arch over the mountains to the west. Driving along she said aloud, "It's all so beautiful, Lord. Why does my life have to be so complicated?"

Father Patrick answered Maria's knock and greeted her with one of his big bear hugs. "So good to see you again," he began, sitting Maria down at the kitchen table. Soon he was pouring the tea.

"I'm kind of betwixt and between as to what I should do,"

Maria began. "I value your wisdom so that's why I've come. I'd love to keep my baby, but without help from my folks, with Rose's health so poor and Alvin moving to Calgary, it doesn't look good. I wonder if I'll be forced to give the baby up for adoption. Right now I'm just trying to look at all my options."

After a long pause Father Patrick responded. "I would like to offer you my sympathy, Maria. It must be heart-breaking for a mother-to-be to have to think of the possibility of giving up her baby. I want you to know I've been praying for you over the last few months. It sounds like you've already done a lot of soul-searching. I imagine you've talked things over with Andrew's folks and now you want my advice."

Maria nodded.

"A number of years ago I had a young girl in my parish in similar straits. However, she did have the full support of her family. With the help of her folks she managed to raise her child. Although she loves her son dearly, it's been a real burden on her and her folks. To date it has stymied any chance she's had of a career or marriage. As you know, the family is sacred. After pondering your dilemma ever since you left last winter, it seems to me that you should give adoption serious consideration both for your good and the good of your child. If Alvin's mother, Rose, was able to look after your child while you finished your education and found work, that would be one thing, but it seems that won't be the case. You must face the reality that there's a lot of uncertainty with your support. If you were to keep your baby, the chance for both of you leading normal lives would be questionable. There are scores of couples unable to have children of their own who'd give your baby their full love and support. Regardless of what decision you make, I'll try to help you in any way I can. I'll keep praying that you make the right choice."

"Thanks for your advice, Father. It's starting to look more and more like I'll have to consider adoption."

"Maybe we could talk about something a bit more cheerful," Maria continued after a long pause. "What's going on in Coalberg?"

Over another cup of tea Father Patrick brought Maria up to date on the local comings and goings. Maria tried phoning her friend Sofia, but she wasn't home.

"Stay in touch after you have your baby," Father Patrick said as Maria was leaving. "Anytime you need to talk, day or night, you have my number."

In mid-September Maria started her home schooling, with Alvin tutoring her in the evenings and on weekends.

Towards the end of the month, Alvin had another surprise for Rose and Maria. Joy Courtly, a teacher from Edmonton he'd met in summer school came to spend the weekend. Joy was in her late forties and although she was good-looking, her face was drawn. Maria thought it charitable to say she was a little overweight. Joy went through the motions of being pleasant, but Maria felt her coolness.

Sunday evening Alvin took Joy to the bus station to catch the bus home. Maria wasn't feeling any too sprightly as she made Rose and herself a cup of cocoa.

"You look a bit down," Rose began, turning to Maria. "Would it help you to talk things out?"

"You're right. I am down. It sure doesn't look good for me keeping my baby. After I talked to Father Patrick it wasn't looking good, but now with Joy on the scene it's looking even worse."

"Yes, she does seem a bit of a cold fish. Although she's polite, I couldn't help but get the feeling she thinks that if both of us were out of the way, her chances of snagging Alvin would be better."

As Maria was feeling none too chipper, she turned in early. "Dear God, I've pretty well given up on keeping my baby," she prayed. "Help give me assurance that it would be the right thing to do."

Maria would never know whether it was a vision or a dream, but sometime in the night she suddenly felt the strong presence of Andrew in her room.

"Don't be frightened," he began quietly. "I know how torn you are over whether or not you should keep our baby. My mission is to advise you that though painful, it would be best for our baby's welfare and yours too if you give him up for adoption. I say 'him' because our child will be a boy. I will be our son's spirit guide throughout his life. I must go now. Remember I love you and am waiting for the day when you'll join me."

Maria awoke with a start and sat up in bed. As she reflected on Andrew's message, she knew now that she must give their baby up for adoption. "Thank you, Lord, for sending Andrew to me," she whispered and drifted off to sleep again.

Maria shared her dream with Rose after Alvin left for school in the morning.

"There's no question in my mind that you were visited by Andrew's spirit. A month after my husband Frank died, he came to me. I was having a very rough time and spent most of my waking hours crying. That evening I was lying on my bed, sort of half asleep, half awake. Suddenly there seemed to be a flash of light and there he stood, smiling down at me. He said he was in a wonderful place and not to grieve for him. As suddenly as he came, he was gone. I'm sure Andrew's spirit knows of the heartache you're going through and wanted to help you with the decision you have to make."

"I'd pretty well decided on adoption before, but now Andrew's visit gives me the confidence I need to go through with it. I know giving up our baby will probably be the hardest thing I'll ever have to do, but at least I can prepare myself for it now."

That night as they were eating supper, Maria turned to Alvin. "This afternoon your mom and I were talking about what I should do when I have the baby. I know it will be painful, but the more I think on it, the more convinced I am that it would be best for all of us if I give my baby up for adoption."

"I can appreciate the anguish you've had to go through to make that decision," Alvin replied, a relieved look coming over his face. "I'll support you in any way I can. You're welcome to stay here after the baby is born. Mom and I won't be leaving for my new teaching position until after Christmas."

After a pause Alvin continued nervously. "I recognize that it might not be the best time to bring this up, but Joy and I have gotten pretty serious. We're planning on getting married next summer."

"I'm happy for you, Son," Rose replied in measured tones. "I just hope I can last long enough for both the birth and the wedding."

Like Rose, Maria was shocked with the news. As she thought of Joy coming into the family, she was more convinced than ever that her decision to give the baby up for adoption was the right one.......

In early October Rose's heart began acting up again and she had to be hospitalized. Maria missed the companionship of her surrogate grandma. She and Alvin visited Rose most evenings.

Maria was at the kitchen sink when her first contraction came. "Oh my God!" she cried out, clutching her stomach. "I didn't think I was due until next week." She had been feeling a bit under the weather so hadn't accompanied Alvin to the hospital to visit his mother. Fighting back panic, she tried to remember the coaching Rose gave her. "I've got to time the contractions," she whispered hoarsely, "or maybe I should phone the hospital first."

Maria had just dialled the hospital when Alvin pulled into the driveway.

"I've just gone into labour," Maria called out, meeting him at the door. Maria packed her bag and within twenty minutes they were in the labour room. Alvin stayed with her for a couple of hours, but Maria's contractions were quite erratic.

"If I were you, Mr Carpenter, I'd go home and get some sleep," the nurse suggested. "When a woman is having her first baby, the labour can sometimes take a lot of time. It doesn't appear that Maria's labour is going anywhere fast. We'll give you a phone call if the labour starts to get down to business and we move her into the delivery room."

"Yes you might as well get some rest," Maria added. "You have to teach tomorrow."

The labour room was Spartan. As Maria stared at the dull green walls and ceiling, her thoughts went back to the day she met Andrew. "Why can't he be here with me, Lord?" she whispered, tears filling her eyes. "Why did he have to die?"

Maria's labour was erratic until noon of the next day. Finally they moved her into the delivery room and Alvin was notified.

"Push," Nurse Hampton called out, "push. Really bear down. Now push again."

"I'm doing the best I can," Maria cried out. "Why does it have to hurt so much?"

"One more time," the doctor encouraged. "We're just about there."

With one last cry of pain, Maria pushed with everything she had and the baby's head emerged.

A few moments later the doctor called out, "Congratulations, Maria, it's a boy."

"I knew it would be a boy," Maria replied weakly. "I just hope he's healthy."

Nurse Hampton took the baby, cleaned him up, weighed and measured him, then brought him to Maria when she was back in her room.

"Your baby appears normal and healthy, Maria," the nurse said. "Would you like to hold him?"

As Maria cradled the baby to her bosom, she felt her heart would burst with love. "My little Andrew Junior," she whispered. "You sure look like your dad."

Turning to the nurse she implored. "Do you think it would

be okay if I tried to nurse him? My breasts are so full and he's trying to find them with his mouth."

"I know how you're feeling," Nurse Hampton replied tenderly. "I've had two babies of my own. It will only make it more painful for you if you start breastfeeding him when you have to give your little fellow up. My heart really goes out to you, Maria, but I think its best you don't."

As the nurse took the little baby boy from Maria, his little hand was gripping his mommy's finger. Maria was sobbing uncontrollably.

"Why does it have to happen this way?" she moaned, turning to the wall. "Why did my precious Andrew have to die? Why couldn't I have normal parents? Why can't I keep my darling baby? I just want to be with Andrew so badly."

"We saw your baby," a soft voice called out. Maria rolled over. It was Rose in a wheelchair. Alvin had just wheeled her in. "He looks so perfect," Rose continued. "He looks so much like his dad."

As the tears slipped down Maria's cheeks she whispered, "I love him so much. Why do I have to give him up?"

All three held hands in silence and wept.

Rose finally gained some control. "God only knows how I'd love to help you look after the little fellow, but that's not possible. My doctor wants me admitted to an extended care hospital. We'll have to have faith that God will look out for little Andrew. All we can do is pray."

Over the next few days, visits from Rose, Alvin and Father Patrick helped Maria immeasurably. Painful though it was, she was becoming more assured with each passing day that she was making the right decision about adoption.

On the day before Maria was released from the hospital, baby Andrew was brought to her for their last visit. "Your baby's adoptive parents will be picking Andrew up within the hour," the nurse said. "Yesterday the Child Welfare caseworker handling the adoption told my supervisor she was confident your baby will be going to a very good home."

"I'm happy to hear that," Maria replied disconsolately. "Please have your supervisor tell the new parents what happened." With tears in her eyes she handed her baby to the nurse for the last time. "I love you, Andrew," she whispered. "I'll pray for you every day as long as I live." Turning to the nurse she continued, "Make sure the new parents know that I love him and that I'd be so happy if they could name him Andrew, after his dad."

A few minutes later when Alvin wheeled Rose into the room, Maria blurted out, "the new parents are picking Andrew up in a few minutes. Oh dear God, I hope they'll take good care of my baby. I guess it's for the best, but sometimes I feel I'm horrible for giving him up. God only knows how it hurts."

No one made a reply. Rose and Alvin just held Maria's hands as tears streamed down their faces.

CHAPTER FOUR

Ron and Rita Perkins were teachers living in Red Deer. Though they longed to be parents, after three years of marriage they were still childless. When Rita was checked out by a gynaecologist, they learned the sad news that she would never bear children.

"I guess our only option now is to adopt," Rita said with resignation as they were leaving the doctor's office.

"I don't know," Ron replied unenthusiastically. "I'd still much prefer to have our own."

Rita kept up the adoption lobby until Ron finally gave in. A short time later they put their names in for adopting a new-born. After reams of paperwork and a couple of interviews they were put on a waiting list.

Close to a year later, their caseworker notified them that a baby boy had just been given up for adoption at the regional hospital in Lethbridge. If all went well, they could pick him up in a week.

On Friday afternoon, Ron and Rita met with their caseworker, Mrs Chaplin, a greying lady in her mid-fifties.

"Well this is your day," she began, smiling broadly. "I imagine you have everything ready for the baby."

"We're ready," Rita replied, her face aglow. "Our little boy has his own room all fixed up. I'm so excited I hardly slept a wink last night."

Ron smiled, but didn't say anything.

Mrs Chaplin glanced up at the parents-to-be. She always tried to envisage what kind of parents her clients would make. Rita had refined features and was just a little overweight. Mrs Chaplin liked her exuberance. "She'll make a good mother," she thought. Her glance turned to Ron. He had a pleasant bland face and though of average height, was slight to the point of being scrawny. Mrs Chaplin thought him weak. The fact that Rita had done almost all of the talking in their interviews only added to her suspicions of him. "I wonder what kind of a dad he'll make. Only time will tell."

Rita was all smiles when the nurse handed her their baby.

"What about honouring the birth mother's wishes and naming our boy Andrew?" Rita said to Ron once they were inside the car. "I really feel strongly that we're obligated to do at least that for her."

"I don't see why," Ron snapped back. "The baby's ours now. The birth mother lost all control over the baby when she gave him up for adoption. If she wanted him named Andrew, then why didn't she keep him?"

"Don't be so infantile and selfish," Rita replied acidly. "You know very well she would have kept her baby if it had been possible. I'm well aware that we have the right to choose any name we want, but I still say the only decent thing to do is to at least consider that wish of the birth mother."

Rita held their sleeping baby boy close all the way back to Red Deer. She had booked off work for the next two weeks and was never far from her boy.

The discussion over selecting a name for the baby was a heated one and went on over several days. Finally they arrived at a compromise. They named their baby Andrew Ron Perkins.

When Mrs Chaplin did the follow-up with Andrew and his parents, she was happy to see her original assessment of Rita was on the money. She was bonding well with Andrew and becoming a very good mother.

Conversely, Ron was having real difficulty in accepting Andrew as his son. He was still fixated on having his own biological child.

"Ron, it's almost as if you're sulking over us getting Andrew," Rita said one day. "You're not even trying to get acquainted with him."

"That's just not so. I am trying, but I'm still having problems over the fact that we're not the real mother and father."

"Nonsense, pure nonsense," Rita retorted. "Regardless of your hang-ups, we are Andrew's real parents now. All I can say is you're going to have to try harder. If you don't, not only will the three of us suffer as a family, your and my relationship will suffer."

A month after the adoption had been finalized; Mrs Chaplin received a letter from Dr Renner, Rita's old family doctor. By the date on the letterhead she noted that it had been written six months ago.

"This would have to be one of the reference letters for Rita Perkins," she thought. "It must have been written when we were doing her request for adoption. I guess it got lost in the mail."

Dear Mrs Chaplin,

Further to your enquiry for a character reference
for Rita Perkins. She grew up in this community and
I was her doctor from her birth until her second
year of college. I wish her and her husband well if
they do get a child, but I must be honest and site
one reservation that I have. Although Rita was a
conscientious student and from what I observed
lived a moral upright life, my professional view is
that she had an addictive personality. From thirteen
to fifteen she suffered from bulimia. During that
time I had to hospitalize her a number of times.
Once in college she had a bad bout with alcohol.
She lost her first year as she had to go to a
detoxification centre. On the positive side, she
always seems to be able to fight her way back to the
top. To my knowledge, she's had no problems for the
last few years. As I mentioned before, if she and
her husband are awarded a child, I wish them the
best.

Yours truly,
Dr M.A. Renner

"Good grief," Mrs Chaplin muttered. "It would have helped to have had that letter six months ago. It's a little too late to do anything now though. The adoption is already completed. I guess all one can do is hope for the best."

As time passed, the relationship between Rita and Ron was becoming more and more strained. Rita had an insatiable need to spend all of her spare time with Andrew and the moment she got home from school, baby Andrew was in her arms. Ron was used to being the centre of the household and resented this. He now often spent the evenings at school doing his class preparation rather than bringing his work home. Ron was convinced that Rita's lack of attention towards him was her way of punishing him for not readily accepting Andrew as his own son. Their bedroom life, which never had been all that grand, was now pretty well non-existent. Most nights Rita slept with Andrew.

Since Rita still worked full-time, June Cox, an older widow in the other side of their duplex looked after Andrew Monday to Friday in her home. She noticed the coolness that was developing between the couple and was convinced that Rita's doting over Andrew was excessive. When June mentioned this to Rita, she denied it and became quite upset. Within two weeks of their talk, Rita left her teaching position so she could devote all her time to Andrew.

Things finally came to a head one afternoon when Ron got home from work. "What's this?" Rita screamed, handing him a note. "I found this in your suit coat pocket, you low-bred bastard. It's from your friend Elsie. The bitch signed it, 'Love Elsie.' You didn't even have the brains to cover-up for yourself."

Ron didn't have much to say in his defence regarding his affair, not that he was given a chance to explain. After a week of ranting, raving and copious amounts of tears, Rita was at wit's end and asked Mrs Cox to drop by to talk things over. After a lengthy discussion, Mrs Cox finally convinced Rita to give their marriage another try.

"I'm willing to give our marriage another chance," she began when Ron returned from work that afternoon. "There's one condition though. You have to promise never to have anything to do with Elsie again."

"I suppose I can live with that," Ron responded without making eye contact.

Mrs Cox was relieved when Rita dropped by with Andrew later that evening and told her of the development. June desperately hoped that their marriage could now be renewed.

That night as they were lying in bed, Rita turned to her husband. "Before we're intimate again, there has to be a trial period to prove your fidelity. Remember, before and after this trial period is over, absolutely no contact whatsoever between you and this woman."

Ron took insult from Rita's demands. Rather than trying to prove to Rita that he was being true to her and attempting to interact more with his son, he retaliated by becoming more distant from both of them. In the interim, Rita was becoming more fixated than ever on Andrew.

Several weeks later the final dislocation came. "We have to talk," Ron began, his voice shaking. "Things aren't getting better between us. In fact they're getting worse. It's been three months since we supposedly turned over a new leaf. In that time we haven't had sex once."

"And whose fault is that?" Rita countered, raising her voice. "It's not easy being intimate with a self-centred ogre. I can't remember the last time you held your son. The only one you think of is yourself."

"I refuse to get into a hollering match," Ron shot back,

"but I want out of this marriage. Up until last week I kept up my end of the bargain and cut off all contacts with Elsie, but that's all changed. Now I'm seeing her again."

Rita screamed a volley of obscenities at Ron and slapped him hard across the face. Ron did not hit Rita back. Without a word, he grabbed his coat and headed out the door.

"You'll pay for this, you low-bred scum!" Rita called out after him. "I'm going to take you for everything you've got and then hit you for all the law allows for child support."

Andrew was crying so Rita went over and picked him up. The little fellow sensed something was not right. For the rest of the evening Rita did her best to comfort her son despite her inner turmoil. She knew that tough days lay ahead.

As Rita promised, the divorce was messy. When the divorce finally went through, Ron was left with not much more than the clothes on his back and was shackled with hefty child support payments.

Ron had been born in the southern states, attended university there and was in Canada on a work permit. Still having contacts in the states, he left enough money in the bank to cover the first month of child support and then quit his job. With his girlfriend Elsie, he headed to a new teaching position in Florida.

Rita discovered too late that she had been taken to the cleaners. She contacted the government agencies that policed spousal support in Alberta. Because Ron was an American citizen, they put her in contact with the proper agencies in the states. After a couple of months of enduring mountains of red tape, she gave up.

Rita tried desperately to keep her head up, but before long

her resolve started to slip and her old nemesis alcohol became a part of her life again. Up until now she had taken excellent care of Andrew, but that soon started to change.

Mrs Cox was becoming fearful for Andrew's welfare. Seeing Rita wasn't getting any financial support from Ron, she offered to look after Andrew at no cost so Rita could go back teaching. Rita declined her offer. Even though she brought Andrew over to be looked after when she went on her benders, Rita seemed unable to accept the reality that she must pull up her socks and provide better care for her son.

Bad went to worse when Rita met up with Walter, an old college boyfriend. Back in their drinking days they had a brief fling. Walter had never been motivated. He dropped out of college and over the years never managed to find work. Although he no longer had a serious drinking problem, he was now addicted to heroin. He came from a wealthy family who had given up on him. Walter and his folks had an unwritten understanding. He didn't publicly embarrass the family by getting into trouble and they kept him supplied with money for his habit.

Within a week Walter moved in with Rita and soon had her on heroin. With Rita's addictive personality, getting another fix became the driving force in her life, even supplanting her strong mothering instinct. Without question, Andrew's care was slipping badly.

Up until now June Cox had kept mum about the deteriorating situation between Rita and her baby. Finally one morning, Rita brought Andrew over, hungry, dirty and crying. June couldn't take it anymore.

"Rita, you're falling to pieces," she began sternly. "Just look at your little guy. Look at all the sores on his bottom. You used to be a wonderful mother, but you're not giving him good care anymore. I can't stand back and watch Andrew suffer. I've been forcing myself to hold off for some time now with the hopes that you'd turn around. I'm sorry, Rita, but even though I care for you a great deal, if things don't improve, I'll have no choice but to report the kind of care your giving Andrew to the authorities."

"I'm sorry June," Rita replied without making eye contact. "I'm living in hell. I know I'm not giving Andrew proper care anymore, but I'm so mixed up, so confused. Though part of me still wants to look out for my boy, I hate myself because I've lost all control. All that drives me now is this horrible need I have to get another fix." With tears running down her cheeks she finally made eye contact with June. "If you do have to report me I'll understand. I know you'll be doing it for Andrew's welfare. Thank you so much for caring for him, but I'm so out of it I can't promise you anything. Please believe that I love my son dearly."

Shortly after Rita left, Mrs Cox contacted the government agency by phone and told them of Andrew's sad plight. The agency asked her to keep them abreast of the situation and promised to send a social worker out to do an investigation.

Early the next morning, Rita brought Andrew over to Mrs Cox. "I'll try to get back to pick Andrew up tonight," she said unconvincingly. Although it was warm in the house, Rita was shaking like a leaf.

Needless to say, Rita didn't show up that evening. Two days later a social worker came out to check on Andrew. June told her that Rita hadn't returned in two days. The social worker examined Andrew carefully and then turned to June. "I can appreciate your concern. There certainly are some signs of neglect here. We must remember though that this is not a foster care case. Rita is the legal parent and in the divorce settlement was awarded sole custody of Andrew. We have to proceed carefully. You mentioned when you last talked to Rita that she told you she was having a serious problem with drugs. If she would admit that to us, or if we had strong proof of her addiction, we would certainly take action." As the social worker was leaving she added, "As of today, we'll be compensating you for looking after the young fellow. Please keep us abreast of the situation and thank you so much for looking out for Andrew."

A week later, Rita and Walter still had not shown up to get Andrew. When June again contacted the welfare department they sent out the caseworker. As Andrew was doing well with his step-mom, the caseworker offered to continue to pay her for looking after Andrew until either they could locate his mother or he would be made a ward of the government.

"I'll do my best," June said, "but it's heavy on me. I'm getting up in years and my health is none too good. My doctor has advised me not to baby-sit anymore on a full time basis."

Three weeks later the welfare department still couldn't find a trace of Rita. Sighting abandonment, the officials made Andrew a ward of the government. Even though Andrew was only twenty months old he had been traumatized by the events of the last few months and cried whenever June was out of sight. Having lost his adoptive mother had been extremely upsetting for him and now he was just getting used to his nanny.

On Friday morning the child welfare worker contacted June. She would be out in the afternoon to pick up Andrew. When she took Andrew from June's arms he cried hysterically and made a desperate attempt to hold onto his nanny. Finally the welfare lady had to physically restrain the little boy. As she carried him to the car, Andrew's sorrowful sobbing would be forever etched in June's mind. The last glimpse she had of him, he was standing up on the car seat reaching his arms out expectantly to her. Giving Andrew up to the welfare worker would haunt June for as long as she lived.

Little Andrew cried all the way to the orphanage. When the matron, Beth Chatkins, saw the caseworker coming up the walk-way with him, her heart went out to the little fellow. She was all too familiar with that heartbroken sob and the look of hopeless bewilderment on those sad little faces. It was not a good day for little Andrew, first losing his mommy and now his nanny.

Staff Lizzie offered to help Andrew out for his first few hours in the orphanage and was at the door to take him from the caseworker. Lizzie was from Romania and since none of the kids in the orphanage could pronounce her last name, it just stayed Aunt Lizzie. Like most women, Lizzie was blessed with a powerful mothering instinct. She was the night mother and officially worked from eight in the evening till six in the morning. She was as often seen in the orphanage during the day in her off hours as during her night shift. Lizzie was single, stayed in the staff quarters and thought of the orphanage as her home. Years ago her supervisor had given up on trying to keep her from working several hours a day without pay. When a small child needed mothering, that's what they got from Lizzie. Hours of work were the last thing on her mind. Her simple philosophy was that the child's needs always came first.

Lizzie was a large woman with a kind strong face. It helped Andrew that she was on the plump side like June. Within an hour, Lizzie had Andrew calmed down and they had dinner together. She had a couple of carrying cradles she sewed out of denim with a strap attached that she could put over her shoulder. The one for the older kids had leg holes. Hand-in-hand she led Andrew around the orphanage. When he got tired she put him in his pod and carried him everywhere she went. In the late afternoon she took him to her room and they slept for a couple of hours. Lizzie knew Andrew would have trouble sleeping that night, so carried him till he fell asleep. Once in the night Andrew awoke crying for his new nanny. Back into the pod he went for the rest of the night and off and on for most of the next day. A few days of this type of care and Andrew calmed down enough to start fitting into the routine.

The next week, the matron called Lizzie into her office. As she looked across her desk, little Andrew was sitting contentedly on Lizzie's lap playing with her wristwatch.

"Well you did it again," Beth began, smiling. "At times like this I don't know how we'd manage without you. When we pick up these little tykes they desperately need to bond with a mother figure. Just look at the little guy. You've got him well on his way to adjusting to his new home. These little ones don't need someone to analyse them. All they really need is loving, mothering and a feeling of security. You've supplied all of these things to Andrew. It would be nice if we could pay you for the extra time you invest in your little friends, but we've been that way before. I know you do it because you care for these little people and have a heart bigger than all outdoors. You may have to wait until you're in the next world, but I know you'll be richly rewarded for your kindness."

Within a month's time, Andrew was getting along with the other staff and starting to make friends. Of the staff, without question, "Aunt Wizzie" was his favourite.............

CHAPTER FIVE

The day after Andrew was picked up by his adoptive parents, Maria was discharged from the hospital. A week later she borrowed Alvin's car, drove back to Coalberg and stopped in to see Father Patrick.

"I just wanted to drop by and thank you for all the concern and prayers you've had for me and the baby," she began, tears slipping down her cheeks. "It's been so hard giving up my baby, but I guess it's for the best."

"Yes I believe so," Father Patrick replied softly. He led Maria into the kitchen. "God will see you through this rough time. None of us know why we have to suffer, but God has told us that at times he lets trials come to those he loves to make us stronger. I guess the trick is to learn from our trials."

"Yes you're right," Maria said, pulling herself together. "I'd also like to talk over my plans with you. I would first like to finish high school and study to become a teacher. I'd like to join the church and teach somewhere in a parochial school."

"My, my, my, that's most commendable," Father Patrick responded as he made a pot of tea. "If you'd allow me to give you a hand, I think I could help you with that. I'd like to suggest a small convent in the village of Morning Dale, just a little north of Edmonton. I learned last month that Sister Agnes is in charge of the high school at the convent. You'll remember her. She taught you here in the Coalberg Catholic Elementary School a few years back."

"Yes I recall," Maria said enthusiastically. "She was my favourite teacher."

"We also have a program that might be of assistance to you. If your intent is to join the church, our diocese has a special fund set aside to help needy students attending high school at a convent. Of course after you finish high school and are studying to become a sister in the church, all your expenses will be looked after."

After her visit with Father Patrick, Maria stopped at her old house. The front yard, if anything, was dirtier than it was on her last visit. Getting no response from knocking, Maria opened the door. The smell was overwhelming. There her dad and his two drinking buddies were, sprawled out on the chesterfield and easy chairs, sleeping off a drunk. Maria counted fifteen empty beer bottles and a couple of spent wine bottles. With a heavy heart she closed the door, climbed into Alvin's car and headed out of town.

When Maria told Alvin and Rose of her talk with her priest, they were very supportive. "You'll be less than a day's drive from Mom and me," Alvin said. "You can drop down for some weekends and on holidays."

Maria and Alvin spent Christmas with Rose in the extended care hospital in Calgary and then everyone was on the move. Maria was accepted by the convent in Morning Dale and would be starting her studies the first week in January. Alvin bought a house in Calgary.

Father Patrick drove to Lethbridge to see Maria off. "I've known you for so many years it's almost like I'm losing a family member," he said, his voice breaking. "I of course never had children of my own. If I were a married man though, I'd be so proud to have you for a daughter. I have faith you'll do well."

When Maria arrived in Morning Dale late in the afternoon, it looked like a winter wonderland. It was in a rural setting that was quite wooded. All the trees were decked in thick hoar frost. The convent properties bordered the North Saskatchewan River. The small village of Morning Dale was downstream a half mile.

Sister Agnes met Maria shortly after she arrived and helped get her oriented to her new home.

"Father Patrick has written me a letter of recommendation on your behalf. Of course I remember you as one of my best students when I taught in Coalberg. He indicated that your plans were to stay on after finishing high school, take teacher training, join the church and possibly teach in church schools in the northern part of Canada."

"Those are my plans," Maria replied quietly. "As Father Patrick no doubt told you, I had to give up my baby boy. I know I'd love teaching and of course I will never marry. Father Patrick had a long talk with me before I made out an application to attend here. He said to make sure I had the right motives and that doing penance for my mistakes wasn't one of them."

"That's good advice. Both Father Patrick and I have seen young people join the church as nuns or priests for the wrong reasons. It always ends in misery for the individuals."

Maria's room was small and somewhat Spartan. Her

roommate, Flo Bourassa, was a petite Métis girl from northern Alberta. The first few weeks were very hard for Maria as she was still grieving the loss of her baby. Like Alvin, Sister Agnes suggested that for the immediate, it might be easier for Maria if she didn't share this news with too many. Flo proved to be Maria's salvation. She was a girl who was all heart.

"I have this feeling that something's bothering you, Maria," Flo began one night after the lights were out. "If you ever want to talk about things I promise to keep it a secret. I have some painful experiences from my past. If you'd care to listen, it would help me if I could share them with you."

"That would be fine," Maria replied nervously, "Go ahead."

"Well when I was ten, a horrible thing happened. I was staying at my cousin's place and my uncle did something awful to me. When everyone was out of the house he exposed himself to me and forced me to do some disgusting things with him. I think they call it oral sex. He threatened me with a terrible beating if I ever squealed on him. When I got home I went straight to my father and told him what happened. Although Dad was a very strong man and had a bad temper, he was always fair with us. Dad and I rode over to my uncle's place on horseback. My uncle denied doing anything wrong with me and said I was lying. I told my uncle that I had noticed that he had a strange birthmark on his lower stomach. When he heard this, he turned red and said that he was sorry. Sorry or not, Dad gave him a fearful beating right on the spot and told him he'd kill him if he ever bothered any of us kids again. I was so terrified I cried my eyes out. After Dad gave Uncle the beating, he helped my aunt patch him up."

"When we got home I asked Dad if I was to blame in some way. He said it was nonsense to think that way. He said some men are like dogs and even though he didn't like beating on his brother that he had it coming. It still makes me feel mixed up about the sex thing."

"Thanks for sharing that with me. It must be hard to live with that memory." After a long pause, Maria continued. "You're right. There is something that's really weighing heavy on me. You see, two months ago I had to give my baby up for adoption." With tears streaming down her face Maria told of her dysfunctional family, of getting pregnant, the death of her boyfriend, the birth of her son and finally feeling forced to give up her baby boy. "All I can do now is pray for my son's welfare," she concluded sadly.

Flo hopped out of bed, went over and hugged Maria. "I feel so honoured that you'd share your pain with me. I'll pray for him every day too."

This sharing was the beginning of a beautiful friendship that was to last all their lives. Maria and Flo prayed together each night and without fail always remembered young Andrew's welfare.

Despite her loneliness, Maria was enjoying her studies.

In late winter Alvin sent her a bus ticket and when the Easter break came, she went to see them in Calgary.

The evening she arrived, Alvin took Maria over to the extended care hospital to visit Rose.

"I'm so thankful the Lord has spared me long enough to see you again," Rose said, taking Maria's hand. "Thank you so much for your letters. It's so good to hear that you're doing well."

"Yes I'm really enjoying being in the convent. I do miss

you and Alvin and my little Andrew, but other than that I'm managing fairly well. How's your health, Rose?"

"Oh I'm getting by," Rose sighed. "The doctor tells me I'm holding my own, but I know I'm living on borrowed time. On the positive side, being an invalid gives me plenty of time to pray for all of the family, especially little Andrew."

"I was talking to Mrs Chaplin last week regarding an orphan who had been placed with a family in the area and would be attending our school," Alvin interjected. "She remembered my involvement with Maria and the baby. She said she was limited in what she could tell me, but that your baby was adapting well to his new family and getting excellent care."

"Hearing that takes such a load off my mind," Maria whispered. "I'm constantly praying that he'll be okay. Thank you so much for praying for him too, Rose."

The following day Alvin had Joy over for dinner. Everyone was on edge and conversation didn't come easily. Maria was giving an overview of her studies when Joy interjected, "I trust all your teachers at the convent are certified and that your studies will lead to a university entrance. There are some religious schools whose standards aren't up to much."

"Morning Dale Convent has exceptionally high standards," Alvin shot back testily. "I personally checked out the Convent's accreditation when Maria told me of her intent to attend. Their academic standards are higher than most schools in the Calgary area."

"I'm happy to hear that," Joy continued, her face showing colour. "You'll have to pardon me. My father was an Orangeman and of course quite anti-Catholic. I was brought up to distrust Catholics. I know now that for the most part the Orangeman beliefs are all rubbish. I try hard not to be prejudiced, but I'm afraid my childhood bias occasionally shows through. I'll just have to try a little harder."

If conversation had been difficult before, it became nigh unto impossible now. Regardless of saying she'd have to try harder, Joy was still putting her foot into it. "How's the food at the school?" she asked Maria. "You look like you could stand to add a few pounds."

"The food is excellent. I eat like a horse."

Alvin glanced over at Joy's very Rubenesque figure and then across to Maria's attractive, athletic build. "Yes Joy," he thought. "At least Maria doesn't eat like two horses."

Sensing the conversation was going nowhere, Alvin got out the Crokinole board. Even when playing parlour games, Maria was aware of Joy's aggressive stance towards her.

"If you have it in your heart, Maria, please excuse Joy's behaviour," Alvin said in the morning when he and Maria were alone. "Between the two of us, she has two big problems. First, her former husband abandoned her for a younger woman making her suspicious of young women in general. Second, as you witnessed last night, regardless of what she says, she's still very suspicious of anything to do with the Catholic religion. Both Mom and I have to make allowances for her. Despite her hang-ups, she's really a good woman and in time I'm sure she'll warm up to you. In the interim, I'd be so grateful if you could look the other way occasionally."

"That's no problem. Having to put up with my mother, I know what it's like living with someone who's suspicious. I owe you and Rose so much. If it ever gets so that Joy can't handle me being around, I'll understand."

Alvin walked over and put his hand on Maria's shoulder. "Joy is a very decent person. I'm trying to help her build up her self-esteem, but she has lots of scars from the past. Thank you so much for being so understanding. You'll always be welcome here and that's that. You will always be family, always be my daughter-in-law. With your understanding, I'm sure we'll all manage."

"I'm so overjoyed to hear that little Andrew's doing well," Rose began the next afternoon when Maria visited her. "It makes a person realize how powerful prayers are."

"Yes you're right. Thank you so much for your prayers for both Andrew and myself."

"How are things going between you and Joy? At times she can be pretty prickly, especially when it comes to religion. I've had my go-rounds with her, but I'm sure at heart she's a good sort."

"Yes, that's what Alvin told me. Things got a little ticklish the other night, but we all managed. Alvin figures she'll feel less threatened once they're married."

"Yes I suppose that's possible," Rose replied without conviction. "I'm hoping that things will work out well. I constantly pray that they will."

Just before the end of the school year, Sister Agnes met with Maria. "I'm very pleased with your progress. You should have no problem graduating with honours. The compassion you show to others also warms my heart. It's so rewarding to see young folk who really practice their religion rather than just mouth it. What are your plans for the summer, Maria?"

"I guess I'll have a three month break before teacher

training begins. I'd like to visit Mom, look up my dad and then I suppose get a job until school starts up again."

"There are opportunities for girls of your calibre for summer work in our church outreach mission in native communities in the north. The pay isn't very grand, but the experience would be invaluable for you if you plan on making your life's work teaching in parochial schools. Give it your prayerful consideration. I would highly recommend you."

A few days later, Maria stopped in to see Sister Agnes and accepted a position. Once school was out, she would visit her folks and friends in Coalberg for a couple of weeks and then head to her new posting...............

When the bus pulled into Coalberg, Maria noticed that not much had changed. It was still the dirty little mining town she'd left several months before. There was no new construction and the houses still remained as they were, unpainted and weather-worn. Old man Switzer's shed door was still banging in the wind as it had done for years. On reflection, she thought Coalberg looked quite scruffy. The sharp acrid smell of the coal hadn't changed either. Maria would be staying with Sister Nora in the church residence. Maria had thought of staying with her friend Sofia, but she had joined the Army. Father Patrick offered her the use of his car.

Maria could have cried when she saw her old house. There was no improvement from her last visit. If anything, the yard was even more cluttered and there was waist-high grass. Beer bottles and garbage were still scattered everywhere. A couple of broken windows were covered with cardboard. Maria knocked repeatedly before someone hollered out in a drunken slur, "Yeah, save the damn door. Who the hell is it?"

"It's me, Maria. I want to see my dad." Slowly the door opened and Maria's very inebriated father staggered out onto the porch step. He was filthy and smelt rather rank.

"Dad," Maria said sternly, "you're still drinking."

"Yeah I guessh so," he mumbled, not making eye contact. "I'm shorry. I shid know better. I'm shorry, so shorry."

"Your phone is cut off, but I've written you several times. Did you get my letters?"

"I guessh so," Clyde replied still looking at the ground. "I'm shorry."

Maria realized it would be fruitless to try to talk to her dad anymore. With a heavy heart, she turned and left.

Maria was on the road early the next day to visit her mom. When she got to her mom's ward, the nurses warned her not to expect too much. "Your mom's condition has remained static and we have to keep her heavily sedated."

Jen was half-propped up in bed, looking even more emaciated than she had before. She was looking off into space when Maria walked in.

"Hello, Mom," Maria began, her chest growing tight. "I've come for a little visit. I finished school for the year and thought I'd look you up."

A flash of recognition played in Jen's eyes and then the cold stare returned. She slid down in bed and turned to the wall.

"I had my baby boy last fall. I went through some hard times. Just after I told you and Dad about being pregnant, I found out my boyfriend was killed in action. I had no other choice but to give my baby up for adoption. Anyway, I hear the baby is doing well. I just finished my grade twelve in a convent near Edmonton."

Maria was having a difficult time as there had only been that one flicker of recognition. She was so hoping for a smile, even a nod of approval. Slowly Jen turned over, set a cold stare on Maria and mumbled, "I don't want to see you. Just leave me alone."

Maria managed to control herself till she got out of the room. Once in the hallway she broke down.

"Looks like you need a big hug," a nurse said, coming up to Maria and holding her tight. "My heart goes out to you. Try to remember your mom's very ill. I know it's hard, but one can't take the way she acts personally."

"Thanks, I needed that," Maria whispered. "Even if she'd get angry it would be easier, but you're right. I have to remember she's very sick."

Over the next few days, Maria visited some friends. Early one morning she dropped in on her dad once more. Although not drunk, he still smelled strongly of liquor. Maria pushed some of the litter into the centre of the kitchen table and sat down on a beer stained chair. Her dad sat across from her.

"I used to go to see your mom," he started disconsolately. "She doesn't give a damn for me anymore it seems. Maybe she never did give a damn. She sort of looks right through me. She's never said a word to me. I can't take it, so I just won't visit her no more." Clyde covered his face with his hands and cried.

"I know, Dad, I know," Maria said, getting up and laying

her hand on his shoulder. "I dropped in on her the other day. It hurts something awful doesn't it?"

"I should tell you a bit about my baby. My son was born healthy. As I had little support I was forced to give him up for adoption. It was a very hard decision to have to make."

"I'm so sorry for you. Life can be hard at times. You probably did the right thing. I've just got to get off the booze."

Over the next few minutes Maria attempted to make conversation with her dad. Sadly, she recognized how far he had slipped.

As Maria drove back to Sister Nora's house she felt numb. "Trying to visit Mom and Dad has been heavy sledding," she thought. "I've got to face it. Nothing has really changed since my last visit."

The next day Maria was on the bus for Calgary. "It's sad, but I really don't have anything keeping me here anymore," she whispered as the bus pulled out of Coalberg onto the highway. "It's no longer my home."

Maria spent a few days visiting Alvin and Rose before heading back to Morning Dale.

A week later, Maria arrived at the small Indian village of Caribou Crossing. Maria would be working as an aid with the twenty-odd native children in the St. Mary's Hospital. The hospital was run by the Sisters of Mercy. Although Maria recognized that she was more of a babysitter than a teacher, her association with the native children was preparing her for her life's work.

A couple of weeks after arriving at the hospital, Maria met Warren, an 18-year-old boy from Vancouver. He was working for the summer in the Hudson Bay store. As they got to know each other, she wondered at times if his interest in her was a bit more than platonic. They were sitting on the lakeshore one beautiful, still evening. The water lapped at their feet and the western sky was turning crimson. Suddenly Warren reached over and took Maria's hand.

"We should talk," Maria said, slowly pulling her hand away. "I feel I owe it to you to tell you a bit of my past. You see, two years ago I had a relationship with Andrew Carpenter. He was twenty-two and in the Air Force. A couple of weeks after he was posted to Europe, I found out I was pregnant. The next night we got word that he was killed in action. It was horrible. I had no support from my folks and ended up having to give my baby up for adoption. I'm sure I'll never have another relationship or marry. I'm going to go back to the Morning Dale convent in the fall to study to become a nun. I want to teach in church schools in the north. You're a good friend, so it's only fair that I tell you a bit about myself."

Warren was big enough to understand where Maria was coming from. Their friendship continued on a platonic level for the rest of the summer.

When Maria returned to the convent, a letter from Alvin was waiting. Joy and he had married in August. Alvin extended an open welcome to Maria to visit them anytime she was able to.

In early winter, Alvin sent Maria a return bus ticket. Once school was out for the Christmas break, she was on her way to Calgary. Alvin's hope that Joy would become less prickly to Maria once they were married did not materialize. Maria did her best to show Joy kindness, but despite all, Joy remained suspicious and cool towards her.

Rose's health had taken a turn for the worse and she was

now confined to bed. Despite her grave condition, Maria had a number of good visits with Rose before returning to the convent.

In mid-January, Alvin phoned Maria. "I have sad news," he began. "Mom passed away in her sleep last night. I've been trying to prepare myself for this, but I'm still finding it hard to accept. She's been such a good mother to me."

"I've also been doing my best to steel myself for this news," Maria replied. "She was like a mother and grandmother to me. I'm writing exams, but I'll be there for the funeral."

The day after the funeral, Maria returned to the convent. With Rose's passing Maria felt a large part of her life had been taken away from her.

Every night, Maria prayed for her son. One morning in class, twenty months after Andrew's birth, Maria felt a sudden very strong need to pray for the welfare of Andrew. Her teacher, Sister Louise, was a godly lady. When Maria told her of her heavy burden, Sister Louise excused her from class. Maria went to her room to pray. After praying for many hours the burden left as fast as it had come. It would not be the last time Maria would feel the sudden need to pray for her son's welfare.

That night when Maria wrote in her diary, she noted feeling the sudden urge to pray for her son.

As time slipped by, Maria tried to stay in touch with Alvin and Joy by letter. Alvin was always slow to reply. Finally Maria's last letter was returned unopened with the notation that they had moved without leaving a forwarding address.

Maria finished her teacher training and took her vows of chastity. She accepted a teaching position at a Catholic

Michael Parlee

school in Wasp Lake, a small native community in northern Alberta................

CHAPTER SIX

Shortly before Andrew's third birthday, Mrs Lena Smyth and her two foster sons, Ron and Ralph, spent a couple of afternoons at the orphanage visiting Andrew. Lena was a wisp of a woman, outgoing and full of snap. Ron and Ralph were native twins from a broken family. They were small for their age and had been with Lena and her husband Jack for a year. Although Andrew was somewhat younger than the twins, the three got along admirably. As they were leaving on their last visit, Lena asked Andrew if he'd like to come and visit them the next day. Without a pause he replied, "I go ask Wizzie." Lena followed Andrew over to talk to Aunt Lizzie and then made arrangements with the matron to pick him up the following morning.

The Smyth house was right on the outskirts of Stoeler, a town in central Alberta some fifty miles from Red Deer. The house was small, but Lena kept it neat. There was a fairly large garage in the backyard. Abutting the backyard were twenty acres of parkland and then the cultivated fields. Andrew and the twins had a gay old time and played for several hours. On the way back to the orphanage Lena asked Andrew if he'd like to live with her, Jack and the boys. Andrew seemed very excited. After a pause he said, "Ask Wizzie."

Mrs Chatkins, Aunt Lizzie, Lena and Jack met the next

week. After talking with all of them, the matron was confident that having the Smyth's take Andrew as a foster child would work out well. Aunt Lizzie took great pains to explain the move to Andrew. She assured him that he would have fun with Ralph and Ron and told him that she would come to visit him.

Andrew's move to the Smyth's went well and he was quite enjoying his new playmates. The government caseworker was pleased with how Andrew was adjusting to his new home and reported that he was a happy little boy. When Aunt Lizzie dropped in for her unofficial visit, Andrew didn't cling to her as he once had. After sitting on her lap for a few minutes he was off again to play with his new brothers.

Since Lena and Jack couldn't have a family, they had taken Ron and Ralph to raise as their own. The Smyth's were poor and although Jack had a bit of a drinking problem, Lena kept him in line. With the few dollars Lena got from the government for looking after the boys and Jack's small wage they managed to get by. Lena and Jack longed to adopt the boys, but recognized that if they did so, the government's help would be gone and Lena would have to find outside employment to make ends meet.

Six months after coming to his new home, Andrew was fitting right in and developing a real closeness to his new brothers. Though Jack was good with the boys, for the most part he was more of a pal to them than a father. Andrew loved his new mother, but learned that though Lena loved him and his brothers, she was boss. It would always be she who corrected them if they misbehaved.................

The years slipped by and soon Andrew was in school and doing well. When the government caseworker visited the Smyth's in early August she wrote in her report: Andrew certainly appears to be a happy, well-adjusted boy. My observation is that the Smyth's, Ron, Ralph and Andrew are a close-knit family.

By the time Andrew was in grade three, he was already bigger than his brothers. Having more of an assertive nature, he was becoming the leader of the pack.

It was an early October morning in Stoeler. The day dawned sunny and warm. The poplar and birch along the village streets and the trees and shrubs in the woodlots of the surrounding farms had turned every shade of yellow, orange and scarlet. Fall was in the air. The smell of freshly threshed grain from the surrounding farms mingled with the acrid aroma of the high-bush cranberries from the wooded lands. The three boys were headed for school, relishing the pleasant Indian summer morning. They meandered along, stopping now and then to throw rocks at telephone poles to see who had the best aim. Andrew, Ron and Ralph were in grade three.

There was a group of boys hanging around the south side of the school having a contest to see who could spit the farthest. Andrew joined the group, while Ralph and Ron held back. They were quite familiar with the sting of racial prejudice and knew it was best not to be too eager to interact with the other boys unless invited into the group.

"Look at this," Andrew shouted, running up to the starting mark and spitting for all he was worth. "Come on Ralph. See if you can beat that."

Ralph hesitantly stepped up to the piece of board that was the starting line.

"No Indians allowed," Len Ferrier sneered, stepping up to the board and giving Ralph a shove. A few of the boys tittered while the others nervously scraped at the loose dirt with their toes.

"I'll bet your old man still scalps people," Len leered with a smirk. "Why don't you savages go back to the reserve?"

A sick, frightened look came over Ralph's face as he scuttled back to the outside of the group.

"How about picking on someone your own size?" Andrew shouted, striding up to Len and stopping just a few inches from him.

"You're nothin' but a dumb orphan too," Len shot back. "Know what everyone? Andrew's an Indian-lover."

Len was also in grade three, but was bigger than his classmates as he'd failed a couple of times. He had black matted hair and ill-fitting clothes. If he wasn't scowling, he had a mean, sarcastic look on his dirty face.

Andrew still had a fairly large stone in his pocket from their throwing contest.

"Look out behind you," he hollered at Len, recalling a fighting trick he'd learned from Jack.

Andrew was gripping the stone in his right fist. As Len turned to look behind him, Andrew smoked him a dandy on the side of the head. Len's legs buckled and he bit the dust. The blow stunned Len, but not for long. In a moment he was on his feet and the fight was on. Although Len was a bit bigger than Andrew, he did not have the fierceness of his rival. They were soon down on the ground, working each other over with real fervour.

One of the grade six girls witnessing the fight ran for the

teacher. Within a few moments Miss Noreen was pulling the combatants apart and ushering them into the classroom. The class had just begun when Rob Parks, the principal came striding into the room with the strap in his hand. Although a very fair man, Rob was a firm believer in the necessity of corporal punishment.

"Len and Andrew, up to the front," he barked. "You know our rules on fighting on the school grounds!"

Both boys gave a nervous nod and keeping their eyes glued to the old oiled floor, headed to the front.

"You, Leonard, do you have anything to say in your defence?"

Len shrugged without making eye contact.

"Alright then, hold out your hand."

Len hesitantly moved his hand in Mr Parks' direction.

When Rob grasped Len's hand, the poor boy didn't look nearly as cheeky as he did when he was giving Ralph a hard time. He stared at the principal's knees and Parks continued. "It will be two on each hand. I hope this will be a lesson to you and the rest of the class."

The trauma of the moment was too much for one small grade one girl and she started to cry. Miss Noreen went over to her, squatted down by her desk and put her arm around her shoulder.

Smack! Smack! Len was able to hold on for the two licks on his right hand, but broke down when he held out his left hand. By now quite a few of the grade ones were in tears.

Len ran for his desk, covered his face with his hands and made a futile attempt to control his sobbing.

"Now to you, Andrew," Parks snapped, "what do you have to say in your defence?"

"I was just sticking up for my brother, Sir," Andrew replied, on the verge of tears. "Lenny said Ralph's old man probably still scalps people and for him and Ron to go back to the reserve. Then he pushed Ralph and said I was a dumb orphan."

"Class, I don't ever want to hear another nasty comment from any of you about anyone's racial extraction!" Parks roared, "nor for that matter, whether we're orphans or not! Do I make myself clear?"

There wasn't a peep from the students, but they all nodded gravely.

"Now, back to the unpleasant task still at hand," he said in a subdued tone. "Step up here, Andrew."

With tears in his eyes, Andrew took a few steps forward and bravely held out his right hand.

A bewildered hush came over the class as Mr Parks laid his hand on top of Andrew's. The principal brought the strap down with much more force than he had used on Len.

"The other hand now," the principal called out. Andrew stuck his left hand out. The principal again covered Andrew's hand with his and gave himself another two hard licks.

The class stared at Mr Parks in shock, mesmerized by what they just witnessed.

"I hope you children have learned something this morning," he stated quietly.

"You can take your seat now, Son," Mr Parks concluded, gently laying his hand on Andrew's shoulder. Grasping the strap in his swollen left hand he strode out of the room.

As Miss Noreen called the class back to order, there were tears in her eyes.

"Thanks a lot for sticking up for me," Ralph said to Andrew on their way home from school that afternoon. "You didn't have to do that."

"Us guys have to stick together. At least we got the principal on our side. It was good to see Lenny get a good strapping."

"Yeah it sure was. He deserved every lick he got. Boy you caught him a good one on the side of the head. I sure wish I could punch that hard."

"This here helped," Andrew said, showing Ralph the rock he had used in the fight. "Jack said it makes your punch a lot harder if you put a small rock in your fist. I guess he's right."

Miss Noreen phoned Lena at noon and filled her in on what happened at school. Jack returned from work at three and got an update from Lena. When the boys returned from school, Jack listened with great interest to their version of the adventure.

"Andrew, I'm sure proud of you for sticking up for Ralph. It looks like the old 'rock in the fist trick' paid off. I know your mom doesn't think much of fighting, but it's time you boys learned the basics of boxing. I used to be pretty good at it. The minister in our church taught me. He was an amateur boxer when he was young. I'll buy you boys a couple of pairs of boxing gloves and we'll start practising."

After supper Lena sat the boys down on the couch. "Miss Noreen phoned me and told me everything that happened at school today. I'm very proud of you for looking out for Ralph, Andrew. Even though I hate fighting, I suppose sometimes we can't avoid it. I'm so happy you boys stick together."

Lena had not given the boys dessert yet. As she handed them each a giant twenty-five cent chocolate bar, there was lots of cheering.

Back at school, for the most part Lenny and Andrew were managing to get along. Without question, they didn't care for each other, but for now, a truce had been called. Miss Noreen was happy with that development.

"I wonder if in the future there's going to be friction between the boys?" she mused. "Only time will tell I guess."

CHAPTER SEVEN

Andrew was eleven and doing well. Although their finances were tight, Jack and Lena always took the boys on a camping trip for ten days in July or August. It was the highlight of the year for the boys. Jack had a friend who let them use his small cabin on a lake a hundred plus miles northwest in the foothills. Jack borrowed a canoe and he and the boys fished every day. This year their holiday was the calm before the storm.

On Saturday afternoon a week after they got back from their camping trip, the boys were out on the country roads picking beer bottles.

"Have you noticed Mom acting kind of strange?" Ralph began when they stopped for a rest.

"Yeah, lately she's been awful quiet," Andrew replied. "I've noticed her eyes are always red, like she's crying a lot."

"I saw both Mom and Dad crying the other night," Ron added. "I had to go out to the toilet and they were sitting at the kitchen table. Dad had his arm around Mom. I wonder what's wrong."

A feeling of uneasiness prevailed as the three boys threw

their sacks over their shoulders and carried on down the road.

The following Monday, Lena gathered the boys around her. "I've some bad news, boys," she began in a husky voice. "You may have noticed that I've been a bit down of late."

The boys nodded, fear reflecting in their eyes.

"I've always had a bad heart. I had rheumatic fever when I was a little girl and that damaged my heart. Over the years I've managed to get by not too badly, but then about three months ago I started to feel run down. I'm always tired now. Last week the doctors in Red Deer told me I've got to have an operation as soon as possible."

"Will you be okay?" Ralph asked, his voice distraught.

"Only the Lord knows that. We'll just have to pray that it will all work out. The doctor wants to operate on me sometime this fall."

Jack came off shift at ten. When he came into the boys' room they were still awake. "Mom says she told you about her heart problem. It looks like she'll have her operation in six weeks or so. I'm feeling pretty much like crap. How about you guys?"

"It's pretty bad news alright, but I guess I'm okay," Andrew replied, his voice shaking. "Is the operation going to fix Mom up? God, I sure hope so."

"We have no guarantees, but I'm sure she'll pull through," Jack continued without conviction. "We'll just have to keep our fingers crossed."

The boys talked for some time after Jack left and had difficulty in getting to sleep.

As the days slipped by, Lena's condition continued to deteriorate. Jack booked off work for her operation. The boys offered to batch. Jack stayed with a friend in Red Deer and each day spent many hours with Lena in the hospital. The doctor felt the operation was successful and five days later she was discharged.

By early December her strength had improved remarkably and she was able to do most of the housekeeping again. The boys were relieved that their mom was making a good recovery.

With Lena's health improving, Christmas was a joyful time for the family. "I'm sorry we weren't able to get you boys as many presents as we'd have liked to," Jack said as they were unwrapping their gifts. "Mom's operation took a lot of money. We still owe the doctor a fair bit and it's going to take us a while to pay it all off."

"That's okay," Ron replied. "Just as long as Mom's fixed up."

"Yeah, that's a good enough Christmas present for us," Andrew continued. "We don't need any more presents."

"I had an awful dream last night," Andrew said as the boys were walking to the skating rink the next morning. "I was standing by a coffin in the church. I couldn't figure who had died cause the coffin wasn't open. Anyway, I noticed that Jack and you guys were in the front bench, but not Mom. I couldn't sleep anymore and I still feel kind of shaky."

"That is sort of scary," Ralph replied. "I sure hope it's not for real and just a dream."

"Yeah, probably just a scary dream," Ron interjected, a frightened look crossing his face. "Sometimes if a guy thinks too much about things, then he dreams about them. That's what they say anyway."

There was a nasty wind from the northeast with the temperature around Zero degrees Fahrenheit and the boys had to scrape an inch of new snow off the ice.

"I think maybe I'm going to head back home," Andrew said after batting his puck around for fifteen minutes. "I feel kind of rough. I can't seem to get that dream out of my head."

"Yeah, maybe we should go back home and play Snakes and Ladders or something," Ron added as he started untying his skates. "I feel a bit crappy myself."

The second of January Jack returned from his nightshift to a quiet, cool house. Usually Lena was up making breakfast for him.

"She's probably catching a bit of extra sleep," he muttered. "God knows she needs all the rest she can get. It's strange though. The fire's just about out." He walked over to the coal heater and threw in a scuttle of coal. "Lena usually keeps the heater stoked up. I guess she must be sleeping pretty heavy."

As he was making a pot of tea, a feeling of panic was building in his gut. "Nothing to worry about," he whispered. "She's just sleeping heavy." Jack put the teapot and two cups on a tray and headed into the bedroom. He set the tray on the floor and lightly placed his hand on Lena's shoulder. Fear was welling up in his chest. "I'm home dear," he whispered. "I made us some tea." Getting no response, he laid his hand on her cheek. It was ice cold.

"God Almighty," Jack cried out. "Lena, are you alright? Answer me, Dear." Suspecting the worst, he rolled his wife over on her back. In the dim light he saw to his horror that Lena's eyes were glazed.

"Oh my God! Oh my God!" he cried in agony, dropping to his knees and holding Lena close. "My darling wife's gone."

Jack woke the boys up and they all broke into tears. "Why did this have to happen to her?" Andrew cried. "She was such a good Mom."

"I thought she was going to be okay," Ralph whispered, trying hard not to break down. "Who's going to look after us now?"

"We'll just have to do the best we can," Jack replied, wiping the tears from his eyes. "We don't have any other choice."

Over the next few days the community rallied around Jack and the boys, bringing over meals and helping with the housekeeping. It was a hard time of adjustment for all of them.

Father Sebastian, Jack, the boys, a few relatives and friends gathered at the church the evening before the funeral. The church looked cold and uninviting to the boys.

"I'm going to leave you now for a spell," Father Sebastian said. "Those of you who feel comfortable in viewing the body may do so. Perhaps we should let Jack and the boys have a few minutes by themselves. I'll be back in an hour to close up the church."

"You boys want to look at Mom?" Jack asked, fighting to keep control. "It's up to you. If it'll bother you, you sure don't have to. Mom would understand."

"I'd kind of like to see Mom one more time," Andrew replied, wiping his eyes with the back of his hand.

"Me too," whispered Ron. Ralph was crying too hard to reply, but he nodded his head.

The boys wept uncontrollably as they stood by the open casket.

"Looks like she's just sleeping," Ralph finally blurted out. "She looks so good, almost like she could sit up. God, I wish she weren't dead."

"I love you so much," Jack cried out in anguish, bending over and kissing his departed mate. Gaining some control, Jack held his grieving sons.

Aunt Jean was with the others who viewed the body after Jack and the boys left. She told Jack that she would stay with them for a few days.

"I'm kind of scared about the funeral tomorrow," Andrew blurted out as he, Ron and Ralph lay in bed that night. "I hope I don't make a fool of myself and blubber too much."

"I was thinking the same thing," Ron replied. "Aunt Jean said it would be alright to cry, but I think we should try not to for Dad's sake."

The church was packed. As Jack and the boys took their place, Andrew, Ralph and Ron were fighting hard to keep a stiff upper lip. The three little men's best resolve not to cry only lasted until the soloist began singing, 'It Is Well with My Soul.' Jack broke down and the three boys couldn't hold back the tears.

"I'm sure glad this day is over," Ron commented to Ralph and Andrew as the boys lay in bed that evening.

"Me too," Andrew replied. "I kind of wish we didn't cry so much."

"Yeah it was pretty hard alright," Ralph added. "I guess we did the best we could."

It was a busy time at the mill where Jack worked, but his boss had a big heart and gave him two weeks off with pay.

As the boys were foster children, child welfare was responsible for their care. Shortly after the funeral, Rosanne, their caseworker dropped in. Although Lena and Jack had always been responsible, she was aware of Jack's weakness for liquor.

Aunt Jean stayed on for a week after the funeral to help out. The day before she left, Jean phoned the caseworker and told her that Jack hadn't drawn too many sober breaths since the funeral.

One evening, a week after Jack returned to work the caseworker dropped in.

"My heart goes out to you and the boys, Jack. How are you fellows making out?"

"We're managing I guess," Jack replied, glancing up at the ceiling. "I imagine you knew that when Jean was here I was kind of hitting the sauce pretty hard. Now that she's gone and I'm back to work, I've laid right off on the booze. It's been hard on all of us, but I think we're kind of holding our own."

"It's not my intent to put too much pressure on you, Jack, but with Lena gone it's imperative that you get a housekeeper to help you out. You often work night shifts and the boys are still a bit too young to be by themselves, unsupervised."

Jack promised he'd hire a housekeeper as soon as he could and Rosanne left. Two weeks later, the boys and Jack were still managing on their own. The boys did their best to keep the house in order and made do for meals when their dad was on shift. Jack did the majority of the cooking and washed clothes on his days off, but it wasn't long before he started to slack off.

"I wonder what's going to happen to us guys," Ron began one evening after the boys were in bed. "Dad quit drinking for awhile, but I think he's at it again. When Aunt Jean left he said he wouldn't drink no more."

"Yeah, I've smelled beer on him for the last week or so," Andrew replied. "The other day I was helping him take groceries out of the car and a beer bottle fell out on the ground. He picked the bottle up and said, 'it's hard for me with Mom gone.'"

"Sure hope he doesn't drink too much," Ron continued. "I wish he'd stop again."

"I do too," Andrew added. "Maybe on Saturday we should try to clean up some and maybe try to wash the clothes if Dad doesn't show up."

The boys' wish for Jack to quit drinking did not come to fruition. With Lena gone there was no strong influence to keep Jack off the bottle. Soon, Jack's drinking was reaching the crisis point. Although he still held his job, he was spending much more of his free time in the beer parlour. On some of his days off he wouldn't come home.

On Friday evening, a few weeks after the caseworker talked

to Jack, Miss Noreen dropped in to check on the boys. None of them had been in school for several days and measles were making the rounds. She knew that Jack had started drinking again and was concerned for the boys' welfare. Ron answered the door and invited her in.

"Ralph and Andrew got the measles. I have to look after them, so that's why I didn't come to school."

"That's very kind of you, Ron. Where's your dad?"

"I don't know. He's on days off and he hasn't been here since Monday."

Once inside, Miss Noreen noticed that the housekeeping left something to be desired. "How are you managing? Do you guys have enough to eat?"

"Not really," Ron replied looking at his feet. "All there's left is tomato soup and a bit of macaroni. Ralph and Andrew are getting pretty sick of that."

Miss Noreen went right into rotation and helped Ron tidy up the house. Once the house was cleaned up, she drove home and returned with a plate of hamburgers for the boys. As Jack still wasn't home by noon Saturday, she stopped in and took Ron shopping for groceries. After she got home she phoned the boys' caseworker, informing her of the situation.

Monday morning things came to a head when the caseworker dropped in. She'd learned from Jack's employer that the mill was on spring shutdown and he would be back to work on Tuesday. She finally located him that afternoon in a beer parlour in a neighbouring town. As Jack was far from sober, their conversation went nowhere.

Monday night with Jack still away, Child Welfare was on

the move. The caseworker asked Miss Noreen if she would look after the boys on a temporary basis until the issue with Jack could be resolved.

When the boys' caseworker next met with Jack, he was sober and quite contrite. He said he'd hire a housekeeper right away and promised to get help with his drinking problem.

Once the housekeeper, May Peacock, was hired, the boys went back home. May was an eighteen year old who had dropped out of high school. Although very friendly, she was totally unmotivated. She got along well with the boys, but her housekeeping skills were poor to non-existent.

Jack's moratorium on drinking lasted a week and then he was back on the sauce. With May there to look out for the boys, Jack no longer felt obligated to do housework and again was spending long hours in the bar. When payday came for May, Jack had no money for her. She paid no heed to his excuses and promises. May contacted the caseworker and told her what had occurred. After supper she packed her bags and left.

Friday after school, Rosanne was there when the boys got home from school. This time the die was up for Jack. The boys would be removed permanently. Rosanne and the boys had everything pretty well packed up by the time Jack arrived. Although not drunk, he had been drinking.

"I'm sorry boys," he cried. "I hope you guys can forgive me someday, but with Mom gone I'm going through hell."

Andrew tried hard to think of something appropriate to say to his dad, but finally turned away.

All of the boys' earthly possessions were in the trunk of

the car. Slowly the boys followed Rosanne out to her Ford Coupe and crawled into the back seat.

"I sure hope you'll let us guys stay together," Andrew began as they pulled out of the driveway.

"Yeah, we got to stay together," echoed Ralph. "We've been together so long we're really brothers."

"I'll do my level best. For the next few days you'll be together. I'm taking you to the orphanage. Before we make any moves we'll talk things over with all of you."

Andrew had a sick feeling in his stomach as they pulled up to the old sprawling brick Wild Rose Orphanage. Being back in the orphanage was a real downer for him.

Monday morning Rosanne met with the three boys. "I'm sorry, but I'm afraid I have some bad news. We won't be able to keep you fellows together. My supervisor contacted Ron's and Ralph's Aunt Elaine in northern Alberta. She wanted to look after Ron and Ralph before you boys went to the Smyth's, but was unmarried at the time. She's married now and I'm sure she and her husband will provide a good home for the two of you. My supervisor asked her if there would be any way she could care for you, Andrew. She said it hurt her to have to break you boys up, but her health wasn't all that good and her doctor advised her that looking after three boys would be too heavy for her."

Andrew bowed his head and covered his face with his hands. He fought hard to keep control, but was soon sobbing. With tears in their eyes, Ron and Ralph rushed over to their brother and each put a hand on his shoulder. Rosanne went over to the boys and put her arms around them.

"I know life seems unfair at times," she finally whispered,

"but I guess we have to make the best of it. Elaine and her husband will be here later today for Ron and Ralph. I know this is hard for all of you, but I'm confident all three of you will see each other again in the future. For now you could write letters. I'm sorry boys. I did the best I could. I'll be back in a few days to see you, Andrew."

Their parting was hard. Ron and Ralph slowly walked with Andrew to Aunt Elaine's car. The boys were fighting with their emotions, trying desperately to be men. Ron and Ralph extended their hands to Andrew. As he shook their hands goodbye he covered his face with his left hand and tried in vain to hold back the tears.

"Life's just not fair," Andrew moaned to Lizzie as Aunt Elaine's car pulled away from the orphanage. "First my new mom dies and then Jack is so drunk he can't look after us. Now I've lost my two brothers. I don't know if I'll ever see them again."

"I know some of your pain," Lizzie replied, holding Andrew close. "I lost both my parents when I was fifteen. That was many years ago and I've had to look after myself ever since then. I'm sure you'll see your brothers again. At least you can hope for that."

"You probably won't be in here all that long. Miss Cathy, the new matron tries to put the children in homes as soon as she can. It's some stupid new Government brain wave that Cathy is in charge of. Rather than trying to be so efficient, I think they should be more concerned with looking out for what's best for the kids, but that's government for you. Anyway, I know you're feeling pretty rough. My heart goes out to you. Anytime you want to talk I'll either be in the orphanage or over in my room. Remember, Andrew, there'll be better days ahead."

CHAPTER EIGHT

Tuesday morning, Andrew, Aunt Lizzie and Andrew's caseworker met with the administrator, Miss Cathy, in her office. The office was so neat one could have eaten off the floor. There were several small Bible verse motto plaques on the desk. Back of her big oak desk on the wall hung a big picture of a peaceful mountain scene. Under the picture was the Bible verse:

ALL THINGS WORK TOGETHER FOR
GOOD TO THOSE WHO LOVE GOD

"I'll bet the guy who wrote that was never an orphan," Andrew muttered as he looked up at the picture.

"Thanks Lizzie and Rosanne for helping Andrew out," the administrator began. "I'm Miss Lillian Cathy. You must be Andrew," she continued, extending her hand. Andrew nodded and shook her hand. Lizzie and the caseworker left. Lillian showed Andrew to a chair, then sat down at her desk and opened a folder.

"Your caseworker, Rosanne, told me you've had some rough breaks with your foster mother's death and your foster father's drinking problems."

Andrew stared at the floor and nodded.

The administrator busied herself again in Andrew's folder, flipping her way through the file. "I see you spent some time here when you were a youngster. Rosanne mentioned that you were feeling down after your foster mother's death and weren't able to attend school for a few days."

"Yeah, I was feeling awful. I tried to go to school, but I felt so horrible I couldn't hack it. The doctor finally gave me some pills and that helped some."

"I see," Lillian replied without emotion. "Miss Lizzie or Rosanne may have told you my job here is now two-fold. We are starting on a new government initiative at our orphanage. It's an exciting new pilot project that I designed and am pioneering. In addition to running the orphanage, I now work with Child Welfare trying to find homes for young people like you as soon as possible. If this new pilot project proves successful, the government will be implementing it in all of the province's orphanages."

"We have a young family coming here tomorrow to meet you. They're the Potts family. They've been looking for a foster child and when I heard you'd be coming, I contacted them. I know them personally and they're a very fine family. They have a son, Dieter, who's twelve and Anne, a nine-year-old niece who's staying with them for the year. Rather than getting you started in school tomorrow, we'll keep you here just in case we can place you with the Potts."

"Can I go now?" Andrew mumbled, his voice breaking.

"Why yes. I'm sure you'll be able to find the way to your room."

As he was leaving the administrator's office, Andrew was so preoccupied he nearly bumped into Lizzie.

"By the look on your face there must be bad news," she said. "You sure look like you need a hug. Just remember, its okay for men to cry." Lizzie held Andrew close.

"Sounds to me like she doesn't want me around," Andrew said as Lizzie walked him to his room. "It seems she can't get me out of here fast enough. A family is supposed to be coming for me tomorrow."

"I guess that's the government for you. As I told you a few days ago, they're sort of trying to combine Child Welfare with the orphanage. I hope your family will work out well for you. I'll be praying for you. If you ever get in a bind, just call me on the phone."

Long after Lizzie left, Andrew lay on his bed looking up at the bland yellow ceiling. "Why did you do this to me, God?" he blurted out on the verge of tears. "What have I got to live for?"

The next afternoon Andrew was called to Miss Cathy's office. "I'd like to introduce you to the Potts, Andrew. This is Arthur and Dorothy Potts, their son, Dieter and niece, Anne."

Andrew was feeling very down, but made eye contact with them as he shook their hands.

"I'll show you folks to another room now," Lillian continued cheerily before anyone could say anything. "You'll want some time to get acquainted."

"Lillian Cathy is a fine lady," Arthur began when they

were by themselves. "She goes to the same church we do. Have you ever been to church, Andrew?"

"Sometimes my brothers and I went to Mass with Mom. Us boys were going to start catechism this spring."

"That should be we boys," Arthur corrected. "You'll have to pardon me. I'm an English teacher."

Andrew glanced across the room at Arthur. He was not impressed. Arthur had reddish-blonde hair that was getting very thin on top. He was short, of medium build and starting to get a paunch.

"Let's change the subject," Dorothy intervened. "Tell us a bit about yourself and your family."

"You probably already know my mom died," Andrew replied, his voice strained. "Well after that my dad started drinking pretty heavy. Sometimes he'd be there to look after the house, but Mom's dying really bothered him. When Mom was alive though, he was a really good Dad."

"It sounds like you've had some rough breaks," Dorothy responded. "It must be hard on you being separated from your family."

Andrew bit his lip and nodded.

Dorothy had nice features and was on the plump side. Although she had a nervous titter, Andrew thought her face much kinder than her husband's.

"How old are you and what grade are you in?" Dieter asked awkwardly.

"I'm twelve and in grade six. My brothers Ron and Ralph

are in grade six too. They're twins and a year older than me."

"They must have failed a year," Dieter said sarcastically. "I'm also twelve, but I'm in grade seven. I skipped grade six."

Andrew looked with contempt at Dieter. He was small like his dad, had the same reddish-blonde hair and like his dad was slightly paunchy around the middle.

"Anne is staying with us for the year," Dorothy continued. "Her dad is my brother. Her folks are missionaries. Last spring Anne started having allergy problems so rather than stay in the mission school, she came to stay with us so she could get her allergies checked out. Her folks are coming to get her next summer."

At first glance Andrew thought he could get along well with Anne. She was slight of build, had curly blonde hair and a kind, pretty face.

They strained for over a half hour to make small talk. Finally Miss Cathy rapped on the door. She and Andrew headed to her office and the Potts left.

"Well they're a nice family, aren't they?" Miss Cathy asked expectantly.

Andrew made brief eye contact with Lillian Cathy and gave an unconvincing nod.

"My sister, Brenda, teaches Dieter and Anne in her Sunday School class. "If you go to stay with them, she'll be teaching you too. I'm sure you'd enjoy that."

Again, Andrew gave a half-hearted nod.

"You, your caseworker and I will have a talk tomorrow morning and then I have an appointment to meet with the Potts in the afternoon. What are your thoughts on going to stay with them?"

Andrew shrugged his shoulders. "I don't know. Mrs Potts and Anne seem alright. I'm not so sure about Mr Potts and Dieter though."

"I'm sure you'll get along fine with them all," Lillian quickly replied. "As you no doubt have learned, Mr Potts is an English teacher in the high school. Dieter is a fine young man. His folks are very proud of him. He's always been an honour student."

That night Andrew lay on his bed, unable to sleep, feeling all chewed up inside. He hated himself for breaking down, but he couldn't hold back the tears. "Dear God, what have I got to live for?" he moaned. Finally he cried himself to sleep.

****

Hundreds of miles northeast at a parochial school on a small Indian Reservation, Sister Maria was kneeling at her bedside praying as she always did before retiring. Suddenly, she had a vision of a young boy lying on his bed in a dark room. Years before she remembered having the very strong urge to pray for her son's welfare while she was still in the convent. As on the previous occasion she could not make out the features of the lad, but could hear him sobbing.

"Oh dear Lord," she whispered, "My son must be in need of your help again. Please, Lord, wrap your arms around him." Maria continued praying earnestly for her son till midnight. Again as in the past, the burden suddenly lifted and Maria climbed into bed.

* *

The following day was as traumatic for Andrew as the previous one had been. The Potts were to be there by early afternoon, but car trouble delayed them. Finally at five o'clock they arrived. Andrew helped Arthur and Dorothy load his few earthly belongings into the back of their Chev station wagon and they were on the way to Noka, a small town about thirty miles north of Red Deer.

The Potts house was finished in stucco, a duplicate of all the other houses on the street that were built just after the war. There was a small detached garage and a bit of a garden spot in the backyard. Other than a few small shrubs, the front yard was all lawn. Although Andrew knew he'd miss the open spaces of Lena's and Jack's place, he recognized the Potts had a much nicer house than his folks had.

Anne came to the door to greet them and helped carry Andrew's stuff upstairs into Dieter's bedroom. There were two small beds on either side of the room. Dorothy showed Andrew his bed and then helped him put his things away.

Andrew noticed Dieter practising the piano when they arrived. The pianist didn't stop to greet them. Dorothy, Anne and Andrew had just finished getting his stuff put away when Dieter made an appearance.

"Want to see my stamp collection?" he asked Andrew.

"Yeah sure," Andrew replied and followed Dieter over to the desk.

Dieter opened the binder. "These are from all over the world. You can look through the binder, but please don't touch any of them. The oil on your fingers stains them and they lose their value."

Andrew spent half an hour going through the binder while Dieter gave him a running commentary.

"You got a very nice collection," Andrew said after they'd finished.

"My dad says it's going to be worth lots of money some day, especially if I keep collecting. Did you ever collect anything?"

"Not really. I play hockey though. I was on the Bantam team in Stoeler. Do you play hockey?"

"No, I'm not into that sort of thing. Dad says hockey is too violent."

A week after moving in, Andrew was learning the ropes. Although Arthur was a pacifist and against corporal punishment, he still had reams of rules. It seemed to Andrew that money was very important to the family, or at least to Arthur. Breaking the rules meant a fine, while exemplary behaviour was rewarded with money.

Andrew was a bit behind with his school work and for the first two weeks spent a lot of time in his room after school trying to get caught up. Although Anne would often drop in for a visit, Dieter appeared to want little to do with him and spent most of his spare time practising the piano. When he did his homework, Dieter always worked at the kitchen table.

"I'm sure glad you came to stay," Anne said one afternoon as she and Andrew walked home from school. "And you know what? Since you've come, Dieter doesn't bug me the way he used to. He still does a little though. He was calling me names last night. I told him if he didn't stop, I'd tell you and you'd beat up on him. Anyway he stopped. Before, when Aunt and Uncle were out he was always bugging me. When I'd tell Auntie about it, Dieter would say he was just teasing. He wasn't though. He was really mean to me."

"Yeah, Dieter is a strange one. He's always looking down his nose at me. He got mad the other day because I beat him running home from the park. It was his idea to race, not mine. He said he was going to beat me but good. Anyway, later that night he said if I was any good my real parents wouldn't have left me. That hurt. I'm glad he goes to the middle school, not ours. If he ever gives you a hard time, make sure to tell me. I'll straighten him out."

"That was just horrible for him to say that about you. I know a little bit about what it's like to be alone. I still have my mom and dad, but I hardly ever see them, just on holidays. They say that their work is very important, but I'd be so happy if I could live with them. Sometimes when I get sad, I wonder if they really want me all that much."

Despite Dieter's aloofness, with the friendship that was growing between Anne and him, Andrew was starting to feel better about his new home.

"Today I was talking to Falk," Andrew began one night at the supper table. "He's the Junior Wolves hockey coach. He asked me to join their team. The regular season is over, but the Wolves are in the finals. Falk said there's probably going to be three or four more games left. I was in the junior team in Stoeler. We played the Noka Junior Wolves a few times. Anyway, I'd sure like to play."

"It's proper to refer to the coach as Sergeant Falk, not just Falk." Arthur corrected. "In my view hockey is too violent a sport. I wish you could find another hobby. Mom and I will have to talk it over."

The next morning at breakfast, Arthur picked up on the hockey topic again. "Mom and I still aren't in favour of you playing hockey, but maybe we could make a deal. We were very disappointed you didn't come to church with us last Sunday, so here's our offer. If you'll attend church with us for the rest of the year, we'll allow you to join the hockey team."

"I guess I could go for that." Andrew replied eagerly. "I'll phone the coach and tell him I can join the team."

"There are a couple of conditions though," Arthur sternly added. "For the rest of this season and for next winter your school marks must stay up or no hockey and absolutely no hockey on Sundays."

Andrew nodded and headed to the phone to call the coach.

The final game of the playoffs was held in Noka on Saturday afternoon. Late in the third period, the teams were tied. Andrew caught a pass at the blue line, streaked toward the goal, skilfully pulled the goalie and backhanded the puck into the top right-hand corner of the net. It was the winning goal and his team held on to win the game and the championship. Anne cheered non-stop for Andrew and the Wolves, but was the only family member in the bleachers.

"I'm so excited we won," Anne gushed as she and Andrew walked home from the rink. "You're sure a good hockey player. Man, I wish Dieter, Aunt and Uncle could have been there. Here, let me help you carry some of your stuff."

"Yeah it would have been nice," Andrew replied

disconsolately, handing Anne his skates and hockey stick. "Somehow they've got this idea that hockey is some sort of a savage thing," he added, kicking hard at a chunk of frozen ice. "There's probably nothing anyone can do to change their minds. Arthur told me that playing hockey would make me violent."

"You should have seen Andrew play this afternoon," Anne began excitedly at the supper table. "Andrew scored the winning goal and the Wolves won the championship."

"That's nice," Dorothy responded. "I would have liked to have been there, but Dieter's piano recital was on."

"I got eighty-nine per cent," Dieter boasted. "That was the highest mark of anyone. One of my pieces got special recognition from the adjudicator."

"You did exceptionally well," Arthur beamed. "Mom and I are very proud of you."

As Andrew and Anne started on the supper dishes, Andrew felt raw inside.

"You look kind of sad," Anne began awkwardly as they were putting the dishes in the cupboard. "Is it about them not being at the hockey game?"

"Yeah I guess so. It's sort of hard to take," Andrew mumbled as he headed to his room.

"Why couldn't I have another Mom and Dad like Lena and Jack?" he thought as he lay on his bed. "Not one word from Arthur about my goal or us winning the championship. Anne's the only one who gives a damn about me. Why did Mom have to die?"

Andrew fought hard to keep a stiff upper lip, but tears were soon running down his cheeks. In the background was the grating sound of Dieter at the piano, playing his award-winning recital piece over and over again.

In early May, Andrew got a part-time job working in a local hardware store. Arthur was against him getting the job and only agreed to it as long as his marks stayed up.

Once school was out for the year, Andrew began working six hours a day at the store. Dieter would be going to their church Bible camp for a week and then spend another week with his grandparents in Red Deer, getting special tutoring in piano.

One day when Andrew got home from work, Anne was in tears.

"Something just awful happened this afternoon," she finally blurted out. "Aunty and Uncle were gone to the city and I was home alone with Dieter. He started bugging me really bad again. I was wearing my swimsuit and he started wrestling with me. Well he held me down and forced his hand in between my legs and started touching me. I finally got away from him. I said I was going to tell you on him and went to my room. A half hour later he knocked on my door and said he had something for me. He showed me one of his stamps and said if I didn't tell his mom or dad he'd give it to me. He said it was worth lots of money. I told him that was bribing. After that, I left and went to my friend's place. When I got home, he, Aunt and Uncle were gone, but the stamp was on my dresser."

"That dirty little creep," Andrew shouted. "Where is he? I'm going to give him a damn good licking like I said I would."

"Please don't do that," Anne pleaded. "Aunt and Uncle took him to camp. You've got to promise me you won't tell Auntie or Uncle. Mom and Dad will be here in a couple of days and I don't want to cause a big family fight. Dad and Uncle don't get along too good as it is."

"Alright, I promise not to tell Arthur or Dorothy, but when you're gone and Dieter comes home, I'm still going to work him over."

"But if you do that and nobody knows why you did it, maybe they'll put you back in the orphanage," Anne cried.

"I don't much care," Andrew retorted glumly. "You're the only one here who is really kind to me. With you gone I don't think I want to stay."

After supper Anne and Andrew went over to see Anne's teacher, Miss Pringle. Anne told her about the incident with Dieter.

The next evening, Arthur and Dorothy went to the mid-week church service and Andrew and Anne were home alone.

"Mom and Dad will be here tomorrow morning to pick me up," Anne began. "I guess I'll be gone by the time you get home from work."

"Yeah, I suppose so," Andrew replied sadly, looking off into space. "It's sure going to be lonely for me without you."

"I'm happy to be going back with Mom and Dad, but I'm going to miss you a lot," Anne sighed, coming close to Andrew. "Would it be alright if I gave you a hug?"

"Yeah sure, that would be alright."

They held each other close for a long time.

"Do you think we'll ever see each other again?" Anne asked, on the verge of tears.

"I don't know," Andrew whispered. "I sure hope so. You're the first girl I ever really liked."

"I like you a lot too. I'm going to pray that you'll be okay and that we'll see each other again."

"Me too. When you get home maybe you could write me. I'll give you the address for the orphanage. I'm sure that's where I'll end up at."

"I promise I'll write. I just have this funny feeling we'll see each other again sometime."

"That sure would be nice," Andrew responded as he briefly held Anne's hand. "We'll both have to pray for that to happen."

CHAPTER NINE

When Andrew got home from work the following day the house was empty and there was a note on the table.

Dear Andrew,

We've gone to the evening service at the Bible Camp. We'll be back late. Anne and her folks left this morning.

Dorothy

"I'm sure going to miss Anne," Andrew muttered as he ate his cold supper.

Over the next few days, Andrew was on a real downer and spent all of his spare time lying on his bed. When Dorothy asked him if he was alright, he said he was just tired from work.

The following Monday when Andrew returned from work, Dieter was there. Dieter seemed nervous and quickly went upstairs to work on his stamp collection.

"Your folks not here?" Andrew asked, following Dieter to their room.

"All of us just got back from camp. Mom and Dad went uptown to buy some groceries."

"Do you recognize this?" Andrew flashed the Tasmanian stamp under Dieter's nose.

"Hey, what are you doing with my stamp?" Dieter retorted angrily. "I told you I didn't want you in my stamp collection unless I was around. Give it here!"

"Not so fast," Andrew sneered. "This here is the stamp you gave Anne to keep her quiet. She told me about you playing with her crotch. I'm going to teach you a good lesson."

"She's lying," Dieter cried out in desperation.

"No she's not," Andrew shot back. "You're the bastard who's lying. Anne asked me to go with her to her teacher. Anne told her everything and showed her the stamp. You're in deep shit."

Dieter turned white and started to shake. "Please don't tell Mom or Dad," he implored. "I hope Anne didn't tell. I was just play wrestling with her."

"Bullshit you were," Andrew said, giving Dieter a push. "You're not lying your way out of this one. Anne never told your folks or her folks and made me promise I wouldn't either. Now you got someone your own size to pick on."

Although Andrew was only slightly larger than Dieter when he first came, there was now a great disparity in their size. Andrew was well into puberty, while Dieter's growth spurt hadn't started yet. Andrew's voice was starting to change and he was as tall as Arthur.

Dieter tried to run, but Andrew cut him off and threw a solid right to the side of his face. It wasn't much of a fight. Dieter backed into the corner and tried to shield himself with his arms. Andrew gave Dieter a couple of good shots to both his eyes and bloodied his nose. Dieter was now sitting in the corner, knees drawn up, crying and begging for mercy.

Andrew stopped, went to the bathroom, returned with a washcloth and helped Dieter clean up.

"You can tell your folks whatever you want!" Andrew shouted as he headed for the door. "I don't care anymore. Your dad will probably have a fit and send me back to the orphanage. It doesn't make any difference to me though because I don't want to stay here anymore. Anne was the only one who treated me decent. I'm going over to Sergeant Falk's place."

"Can I come in? I've got to talk," Andrew blurted out when Sergeant Falk answered the door.

Andrew showed Falk the Tasmanian stamp and just finished telling his story when the phone rang.

"It's for you, Dear," Mrs Falk called out holding the phone out to her husband.

Falk was a large man, well-muscled and trim. He had been with the R.C.M.P. for thirty years. He was forthright, fair and brusque to the point of being blunt. After listening for a few moments he interjected, "look, Arthur, I'd like to meet you, your wife and Dieter down at the precinct in fifteen minutes. I'll bring Andrew with me. I can appreciate your concern over Dieter being assaulted, but I'm afraid there's more to it than that."

Twenty minutes later, a solemn party of five sat down at the large oak table in the police office.

"I certainly trust we can resolve this matter without getting the legal system involved," Falk began intently, drumming his fingers on the table.

Arthur's face was red and his beady eyes mean as he countered, "Dieter's assault is just deplorable and I simply won't accept this type of savage behaviour in my house."

"Just a minute," Falk interrupted. "I'll grant you it wasn't wise for Andrew to take the law into his own hands, but Dieter's alleged crime is far more serious."

"Now young man," Falk continued, turning to Dieter. "We'd like to hear your part in this."

"Well, Andrew came home from work at five o'clock," Dieter started uncertainly. "Mom and Dad were out and Andrew started to punch me."

"Hold up Dieter," Falk again interrupted. "Could you tell us what you did to cause Andrew to start the fight?"

"I don't know," Dieter said, staring at his feet.

"Dieter's always been a well-behaved boy," Arthur interjected. "He just spent a week at Bible camp. I'm positive Dieter would never have done anything to warrant the horrible beating he got."

"Hold it," the sergeant barked. "I was asking for Dieter's input, not yours."

After a long pause, Falk added, "it would appear that Dieter refuses to answer my question. Perhaps you don't realise the gravity of your actions, young man."

"You recognize this stamp, Dieter?"

Dieter turned scarlet, but made no reply.

"Alright Dieter; I just got off the phone with Miss Pringle and she substantiated Andrew's account. Seeing you're refusing to co-operate, I'll have to try and piece it together for your folks. Please bear this in mind. If this is true, it's very serious."

Falk turned to Arthur and Dorothy. "Before your little niece Anne left, she and Andrew went to her teacher, Miss Pringle. Anne was very upset and told her teacher that Dieter had fondled her. Anne's account is that Dieter gave her this stamp as a bribe to keep her from telling what he had done."

"Am I right, Dieter?"

"I guess so," Dieter mumbled.

"And?" Falk asked expectantly.

Dieter shrugged his shoulders and kept staring at the floor.

"Okay, seeing you refuse to co-operate, here's the goods. By Anne's account, when you were alone in the house with her, you started to wrestle her. She told you to stop. You pinned her to the floor, forced your hands between her legs and fondled her. Is that what happened, Dieter?"

Dieter laid his head on the table and started crying. His parents sat in stunned silence.

"Miss Pringle told me that Anne made Andrew promise her he wouldn't tell either you folks or her folks. Anne said she didn't want to cause a family fight. From what I understand, Andrew has honoured that request."

"Obviously the young lady will not be pressing charges. We have two instances of assault here. Both are serious, but in my opinion, the sexual assault is of much more concern. Bearing in mind the ages of the Dieter and Andrew though and the reticence of Anne to lay charges against Dieter, I think we'll have to think this through carefully."

"If you'll accept an old cop's advice, I'd suggest it would probably be best to drop everything. Unless my hand is forced to do otherwise, I'll not be making out any report on this incident and the whole thing will die here. What are your views?" Falk continued, turning to Arthur and Dorothy.

"I'm so shocked I don't know what to say," Dorothy finally blurted out. "Dear Lord, where did we go wrong? I feel so horrible that both of these assaults happened in our home. I wonder if we should contact Anne and her parents about this. If we do though, I can't predict my brother's reaction."

"That would be going against Anne's wishes," Falk replied. "I know the young lady is a minor, but I wonder if contacting Anne's folks would do more harm than good. What are your feelings Arthur?"

"Like my wife I'm overcome by all of this," Arthur began uncertainly. "All things considered though, I concur with you. I can't really see any advantage in involving Anne's folks and I think it would do more harm than good for Anne. No doubt it wouldn't be the best for family relations either."

"Well if that's the way we handle it then where does this

leave us all?" Dorothy interjected. "How does Andrew fit into all of this?"

"Perhaps we should ask him," Falk said, glancing at Andrew.

"I don't know," Andrew replied disconsolately. "Dieter and I never did get along that well. I just don't know. Does it really matter what I think? Probably I'll have to go back to the orphanage. Seems no one gives a damn about us foster kids."

"Don't you think we could work things out?" Dorothy asked hopefully. "Really, this is the first time Dieter and Andrew had a scrap."

"I'm extremely upset by Andrew's savage attack," Arthur interrupted. "If Andrew stays, he'll be on probation. It will only be on the condition that he never again uses physical violence in our home."

"Have you no heart?" Dorothy cried out. "As I just finished saying, this is the only time Andrew has ever raised a hand to Dieter. I'm sure that if Dieter hadn't done that horrible thing to Anne, Andrew wouldn't have touched him."

"That may be, but I simply won't abide this brutal behaviour. There's still blood on the bathroom floor. As I said before, I'm not vindicating Dieter, but the more I think on it the more convinced I'm becoming that it just won't work for Andrew to stay on."

It's sad you're such a little man, Arthur," Falk interjected sarcastically. "At any rate, I've phoned Rosanne, Andrew's caseworker. She'll be here tomorrow and should be able to straighten things out. Andrew has asked to spend the night here and I think that would be best. The caseworker said she'd meet at our place with Andrew and then contact you later. I'll brief her on what we've just covered."

The next day, after talking with Arthur it became obvious to Rosanne that he was intransigent. She drove over to the store where Andrew worked and broke the news to him that he'd be going back to the orphanage. She then accompanied Andrew into the store manager's office.

After hearing Rosanne out, the manager put his hand on Andrew's shoulder. "Sorry you've got to leave, Andrew. Without question, you're the best lad I've had in years. Too bad it had to end this way, but that's life I guess. About all I can say of Mr Potts is he's a total waste of skin. I've had my go-rounds with him over school affairs. He's religious on the outside, but meaner than a junkyard dog on the inside."

A light rain was falling as Dorothy, Andrew and Rosanne loaded all of Andrew's belongings into the caseworker's car. Arthur and Dieter made sure they were uptown on an errand.

"I'm so sorry it didn't work out," Dorothy said quietly, as she hugging Andrew goodbye. "I would have liked you to stay, but then, I'm just one member of this family and at times my vote doesn't seem to count. Best of luck."

As they headed out of town, Andrew was trying desperately not to show Rosanne how much he was hurting. He kept looking out the side window so she couldn't see his tears. Every swish of the windshield wiper blades seemed to say: "You're an orphan, you're an orphan, you're an orphan."

Andrew felt sick as they pulled up to the old brick orphanage. A flood of memories came back to him.

"Why do I have to come back here again?" he blurted out. Rosanne wiped a tear from her eye, shook her head and remained silent. After helping him get his few belongings into his room, she hugged Andrew and left.

Being sent back to the orphanage was a real downer for Andrew and he spent several days lying on his bed, only coming out for meals.

One evening Lizzie knocked on his door. "Looks like you're still feeling pretty low," she began. "It doesn't look like you're trying to get to know any of the other kids here."

"What's the use?" Andrew replied despondently. "You only start to make friends and they send you away. That hurts more than being lonely."

Finally Aunt Lizzie got him to help the maintenance man until school started. Working four or five hours a day kept his mind off his woes, but evenings and off days were still hard to bear.

One day after he finished working, one of the staff brought him a letter from Anne. With great anticipation he tore it open.

Dear Andrew,

I'm staying with my mom and dad at Grandma's place. It's out in the country close to Boston. I hope you are doing okay. I have some sad news. Mom and Dad say I have to go to the mission school when school starts again in September. I cried a lot when I heard that. We will be leaving Grandma's in two weeks and will go to Nigeria. Then I'll have to go to the mission school. I'm very lonely for you. I'll write the mission school's address on a piece of paper and send it with this letter.

Your old friend, Anne

Andrew got a warm feeling as he read Anne's letter. After supper he wrote her a reply.

Dear Anne,

I was very happy to get your letter. It's tough you have to go to the mission school again and that makes me sad for you. I gave Dieter a good licking like I said I would. Also, I never told Dorothy or Arthur, but they found out from Sergeant Falk. There was a big argument. I said I didn't want to stay at their place anymore and Arthur said he didn't want me back. So I'm back here at the orphanage, but might be in another foster home pretty soon. I was feeling horrible my first week here, but now I'm doing some work in the orphanage yard and I feel better. I am lonely for you too. You were very kind to me. Write when you can. I'll never forget you.

Your good friend, Andrew

School started and things continued to improve for Andrew. He had a good teacher and despite his resolve not to get close to any of the kids, he was making a few friends both at the orphanage and the school.

One day after school in late September, Miss Cathy again summoned him to her office.

"A lady from a small town out west has contacted our home looking for an older foster child, preferably a boy. I've had Rosanne check on this lady and everything leads me to believe she'd be an excellent foster parent. Her name is Blanche Carp. Blanche lives on the outskirts of Sunbee and works in the local hardware store."

As Andrew lay in bed that evening, his chest was again

on fire. "Dear God, why can't I have real parents like other kids? Miss Cathy says this Blanche woman wants to help me out. I doubt that. She probably wants me for all the work she can get out of me. Maybe she's after the money she'll get from the government for looking after me." Finally, despite his despondency, Andrew fell asleep.

The interview with Blanche made Andrew feel he was on display and being offered for sale. Although she was not all that good looking, Blanche did have a very good figure. Andrew liked her firm handshake, but thought her face seemed on the hard side.

"You're certainly a husky lad for being just short of thirteen," Blanche said. "Miss Cathy tells me you're a good hockey player. My brother played a month or so for the Boston Bruins. He broke his leg in a skiing accident though and that was it for hockey."

Their interest in hockey made for common ground, but he felt just as apprehensive at the end of the interview as at the beginning and was relieved when it ended.

Later that evening Aunt Lizzie dropped in on Andrew. "Just thought I'd see how your interview went with this Blanche Carp."

"I don't know, I just wonder. There's something about her that makes my skin kind of crawl. Maybe it's the way she looked me over, or who knows. For some reason she makes me feel uneasy."

Despite Aunt Lizzie's assurances that everything would probably turn out for the good, Andrew had difficulty getting to sleep. Over and over he could see Blanche looking at him as if he was some farm animal being sized up by a judge at a county fair.

CHAPTER TEN

Notwithstanding Andrew's feeling of uneasiness, Sunday evening he was on the bus heading to Blanche's place. As the miles slipped by, his uneasiness was intensifying.

Finally the bus pulled into Sunbee, a ranching town on the edge of the foothills. Blanche was there to meet him with her car. Andrew felt numb as he rode home with her. Feelings of despair were quite common for him of late. The feeling of not being wanted had been with him ever since he was taken away from Jack and his brothers, Ron and Ralph. He had learned that the only way to survive was to numb his emotions. To love was a guarantee of heartbreak. Although he couldn't think of anything to say, it bothered him that though in Lillian's office Blanche was quite chatty, now she made no attempt at conversation. The closer he got to her house, the more apprehensive he felt.

They pulled into the driveway. Blanche had a small but well-kept house. The front yard was large and all in lawn with the exception of a few small spruce trees. To the back was a garage, an outhouse, a huge woodpile and a small garden.

"Shoes off," Blanche barked cheerily as they got to the back door. "I like to keep things clean." Andrew followed Blanche on a tour of the house, ending up in his bedroom. "This is

108

your room," she said curtly. "I expect you'll be keeping it clean. I'll do the cooking and you'll do the dishes. We'll share on the house cleaning. There's outside work for you to do too. You'll have to carry water from the well, there's wood to split and carry in and the lawn to be cut. I'm being paid to look after you, but I expect you to keep up your share of the chores. I should tell you too that I'm Catholic. I never miss going to Mass on Sundays. I won't be forcing you to go with me, but I expect you will."

All of Andrew's earthly possessions were in two old battered suitcases. As he carried them into his small bedroom he was raw inside. There was a minimum of conversation at supper and as soon as he had finished doing the dishes, Andrew retreated to his bedroom. He lay on his bed, his chest on fire again. He was doing his best to fight back the tears, but it was a losing battle.

"Why can't I have a Mom and Dad like everyone else?" he whispered. "I need them so badly."

Finally Andrew was able suppress his feelings of anguish. That old familiar numb feeling returned and he dropped off to sleep.

By the second week, Andrew was feeling better about his new home. On Sunday morning, Andrew got up early and accompanied Blanche to church. He liked his new teacher and was starting to be accepted by his new classmates. It helped that Blanche and he were getting along fairly well. On Friday evening she even had a small birthday cake to celebrate his thirteenth birthday.

"I've had some pretty rough times," Andrew began after they finished supper. He told Blanche of the problems with Jack, his stay at the Potts and Arthur refusing to take him back after his fight with Dieter.

"Men," Blanche sneered with loathing. "They're all the same. From my experience they're all bastard rats. I was married once to a real loser. I worked my fingers to the bone putting him through university. You want to know the reward I got for all this? On our fifth wedding anniversary, six months after finishing university, the creep tells me he's got a new girlfriend and wants a divorce. I was going to take him for everything I could, but his crooked lawyer, another man, saw to it that I got next to nothing. There may be some half-decent men out there, but I've yet to meet one."

The next morning, Andrew awoke with a start. Blanche was kneeling beside his bed. She had both arms under the covers and was sliding her hand inside his shorts. Despite feeling very uncomfortable, Andrew had an instant erection and began sweating profusely.

"My, my, you have pretty impressive equipment for such a young fellow," Blanche whispered suggestively.

She flipped back the blankets and helped Andrew take his shorts off. Although very aroused, Andrew felt so panicky he wanted to run.

"Here, I'll show you something you've probably never seen before." Blanche untied her bathrobe and let it slide to the floor.

It was the first time Andrew had seen a naked women and he was totally mesmerised.

"Blanche stepped out of her bathrobe, crawled into bed beside Andrew and began fondling him. A few minutes later she whispered, "I'm ready, you're ready, now do your stuff. First though, we'll have to put a safe on you. The last thing in the world I need is to get pregnant."

When it was all over, Andrew felt used. In all his life he'd never felt more numb. Without a word, Blanche rolled out of bed, put on her bathrobe and headed to the door.

"You won't be telling anyone about this," she said sternly, turning back to Andrew. "Just remember, don't get the idea you can get sex from me whenever you want it. I'll come to you when it's time." With that, Blanche headed out the door.

Andrew lay in bed anguishing over what had just happened. "She never even hugged or kissed me," he thought.

In the romantic stories he'd read, there was always love and emotional closeness associated with the sexual encounters. Despite the sensations of arousal and release, he felt dead inside and so alone again.

Andrew soon learned that the weekly sexual encounters Blanche initiated were not without a price. She was now expecting him to do much more of the housecleaning in addition to his other chores. To add insult to injury, Blanche was not above being scornful of him if his performance in bed wasn't up to her expectations.

As each week passed, Andrew was becoming more and more perplexed. Although initially he had enjoyed the physical aspect of their sexual encounters, now with Blanche heaping scorn on him for not satisfying her every sexual whim, he was dreading Saturday mornings with a passion. Emotionally, he felt down, so used, so unclean. Shortly after Blanche and Andrew began their Saturday morning rendezvous, he could no longer bring himself to go to Mass. His conscience told him that what they were doing was wrong and he just couldn't manage sitting in church anymore.

It wasn't long before Andrew's peers at school began

suspecting that something questionable was going on between him and Blanche. Word was going around that Blanche had bought some condoms at a drugstore in a neighbouring town. Soon tongues were wagging. Blanche's comments didn't help matters either. One night she got a bit tipsy at a party and let slip, "Andrew's a good lad to have around for more reasons than you'd think."

Things came to a head one afternoon at recess when Andrew was outside with a group of his classmates. "Know what everyone?" Ed Mullins began. "I hear Andrew's screwing old Blanche Carp, his foster mom."

Andrew turned scarlet and vehemently denied it. His claim of innocence fell on deaf ears. Ed and several other boys continued taunting him.

The next few days at school were torture for Andrew. Cora, a fifteen-year-old girl in grade nine, finally interceded on Andrew's behalf and gave all of his tormentors a sound tongue-lashing. Although Cora's support made Andrew feel better, the teasing didn't abate all that much.

The taunting was only part of Andrew's problems. Blanche tore into him one evening after he got home from school. "There's stories going around town that there's something fishy going on between us," she shouted. "I warned you about blabbing about what we did."

"I haven't told anyone," Andrew replied, his voice breaking. "It's not my fault. Ed Mullins has been telling everyone at school that you and I are sleeping together. He said his mother found out from someone that you bought some condoms at a drugstore in Red Deer. They just keep bugging the hell out of me at school even though I've told them it's all a lie. I don't know how much more I can take. I just hate school something awful now."

"That Alice Mullins bitch," Blanche hissed. "She always was a busybody. Why can't she mind her own bloody business? Anyway, how do I know you're not boasting about what you're doing, not that you've got anything to boast about. If I find out you have, there'll be hell to pay."

"I just can't seem to win," Andrew lamented when he was splitting wood. "At school they're tormenting me and when I get home I catch it from Blanche. Why did I have to come here in the first place?"

Thursday afternoon, Andrew and Cora were walking home from school. It was a blustery late fall day with fine snow being driven by a northeast wind.

"I don't know how much more of this crap I can take," Andrew said disconsolately. "All the guys at school keep bugging me about Blanche. You're the only one who sticks up for me."

"Well why shouldn't I? After all it's all a pack of lies. I mean, isn't it gross imagining you being intimate with that old battle axe?"

Andrew looked at his feet and made no reply.

"Well it is gross, isn't it?" Cora repeated.

Still looking down, Andrew finally replied, "It's just so horrible, Cora. I can't take it anymore. I've got to tell someone."

"Tell someone what?" Cora shot back. "I sincerely hope there's nothing to those rumours."

"Yeah I guess there is. It was all Blanche's idea. I should

have stayed in the orphanage. This is the worst I've ever felt in my life. Everyone except you tortures me at school and when I get home, Blanche lights into me."

"I just can't believe you'd do this to me," Cora snapped. "Here I've made a fool of myself at school defending you and all the while you're having sex with her."

"Please," Andrew pleaded, close to tears. "It wasn't my idea. It was Blanche that wanted it."

"Well did she force you?" Cora continued acidly.

"Not really I guess," Andrew said, keeping his eyes glued to the ground, "but I just felt so helpless."

"Not helpless enough not to get an erection, I'll bet," Cora sneered. "You've used me. I've stuck up for you all along and now I find out it's true."

"I'm sorry. You don't know how horrible I feel. I don't know if I can take anymore. I just don't have any reason to live."

As she turned in at her gate, Cora concluded, "well Andrew, I'm sorry for you, but you've lost all my respect. You're on your own from here on out."

That same pain Andrew felt in his chest the night he arrived was now back four-fold. As Andrew headed home he was in abstract emotional agony.

"How many times do I have to tell you to leave your dirty shoes in the porch?" Blanche barked as Andrew came into the kitchen. "Look at the mess you're making on the floor."

Without saying a word, Andrew took off his shoes, put them in the porch, then got a rag and cleaned up his footprints.

"You're going to have to start pulling up your socks around here," Blanche hissed as Andrew was washing the supper dishes. "Your room's a pigsty and the wood needs splitting. I told you when you came that I expected you to keep up with your share of the chores. I'm going out to visit. Besides your room and the wood, I want you to vacuum the front room and the halls. I won't be back until late, but you'd better turn in early and get rested up. Tomorrow's a school holiday. I'll be coming in to see you in the morning and I hope to hell you'll do better than you did on your last two performances. They were pretty pathetic."

Andrew sat at the kitchen table in a daze for close to an hour after Blanche left. Finally he got to his feet. He tried to clean up his room, but was feeling so down he didn't get much done.

"What have I got to live for?" he moaned as he lay on his bed. "I have no parents and now with Cora mad at me, no friends. Why are you letting this happen to me, God? Why did you allow me to be born? Why can't I ever have a break? What did I do to deserve this? I can't take it anymore. I'm hurting so much I just want to die."

As he lay there weeping, a terrifying thought crossed his mind. "Blanche will be coming to my room in the morning and I know I won't be able to manage. Worse yet, how can I go to school on Monday morning? Cora used to stick up for me, but now she'll tell all the other kids what I told her. It wouldn't do me any good to run away. They'd only bring me back here or put me in another rotten foster home. Who wants a thirteen-year-old foster kid anyway?"

He recalled saying his prayers with Lena. It had been a long time since he'd prayed. Slowly he slipped off the bed onto his knees. "Dear God, I'm hurting so much. I can't stand the pain anymore. No one wants me. No one loves me. Please forgive me God, but I've just got to end this awful pain. I want to die so badly."

Andrew found a sheet of paper and began writing a note to his Aunt Lizzie.

Dear Aunt Lizzie,

You've always treated me well. I can't take the pain anymore. The kids at school are tormenting me that I'm having sex with my foster mother. Trouble is I am. I'm so mixed up and confused. To make things worse, Blanche makes fun of me because I can't do the sex thing very good. You'll never know how much pain I'm in. Please forgive me for what I have to do. I've asked God to forgive me for taking my life. Please send a note to Anne and tell her what happened. She was always kind to me. Tell her I hope she can forgive me too.

Love, Andrew

PS
I guess I have a real Mom or Dad somewhere. If you ever find them, maybe you could tell them a bit about me, if they want to know.

Andrew addressed the letter to the orphanage and put it in his shirt pocket.

In a trance, he slowly got to his feet and headed out back to the musty old shed. It was dark inside, but he finally found the rope. A few days past, when the ribbing at school was getting impossible to bear, he remembered seeing a rope hanging from a peg in the shed. Since then he'd been fantasizing about using it to end everything.

It had turned into a beautiful early winter evening. The

snow and blustery weather had ended. There was a Chinook arch forming to the southwest. Although there was still a skiff of snow on the ground, the occasional warm puff of wind heralded a Chinook on its way. Andrew was in such emotional pain he didn't notice his surroundings. With the rope coiled up under his coat, he headed to the big gnarled black poplar tree in the Kinsman Park. Twelve feet off the ground was a large branch at right angles to the trunk. Years back, Jack taught the boys how to make the hang-man's noose. Andrew quickly fashioned the noose, then shinnied up the tree. Bracing himself with his legs, he slipped the noose over his head and tied the other end of the rope to the branch. Grasping the branch with his hands, he let himself down. As he hung there by his finger tips, his short life passed before him.

A street light illuminated the area. Just as he lost his grip, Andrew was sure he saw a tall dark figure standing close to the base of the tree. There was jolting pain as the rope snapped taut and then darkness.

****

At the small Catholic Church school on an Indian reservation many hundred miles removed, Sister Maria just finished supper. As Andrew was tying the rope to the tree branch, Maria had a sudden strong feeling that her son was in great need. She recalled having the same urge to pray in earnest for him a few months previously and then many years back when she was still in the convent. This time though, the feeling was so intense that she dropped to her knees by the kitchen table.

"Dear Lord, my boy must be going through another crisis. You know where my precious son is and what his needs are. Shield him and protect him." After retiring to her room, Maria prayed without ceasing. Several hours later, the burden lifted. She thanked God for interceding for her son, got up off her knees and crawled into bed.

****

CHAPTER ELEVEN

As the Bosler girls were coming up to the park entrance they saw Andrew hanging by his hands from the branch of the big black poplar. On second glance, they saw to their horror that the he had a rope around his neck. They clung to each other, not knowing what to do. Suddenly out of nowhere there was a tall man dressed in black standing close to the tree, blocking their view. As suddenly as the man appeared, he vanished. When they looked again they saw Andrew lying under the tree. The girls were terrified and raced for home.

In jig time the girls and their father were running back to the park. While the girls held back, Mr Bosler went over to the tree. Although Andrew was still breathing, he appeared unconscious. Bosler saw that the rope had been cut and that the noose around Andrew's neck had been slacked off. He had the girls stay with Andrew while he went home and phoned for the police and the doctor. He then rushed back to be with Andrew and his daughters. Before Doctor Dan Bell arrived, Andrew was starting to surface.

Although Andrew had some nasty lacerations on his neck, the doctor's initial examination showed no life-threatening injury. Once they got him to the hospital, the doctor x-rayed Andrew's neck.

"You're a lucky young man, Andrew," Doctor Bell began. "The x-ray shows no broken bones. We're going to have to put you out to patch up your neck. After we fix you up maybe we could talk about what happened. I understand that the police are contacting your foster mother."

Without making eye contact, Andrew reached into his shirt pocket, pulled out the crumpled letter to Aunt Lizzie and handed it to the doctor.

"Thanks, I'll read it after I get those cuts sutured up."

The doctor just finished reading and photocopying Andrew's suicide note when Blanche arrived at the hospital with a fair shine on.

"These fosser kids are all the same," she slurred. "They're so mixed up in the head that a person can't do nothin with them. What's going to happen with him now?"

Doctor Bell made no reply, so Blanche continued. "I dunno if I want him around if he's this screwed up. I tried to get him to go to Mass with me. He went a couple of times, but won't go anymore. You do your bess for these kids and look what happens."

"If I were you, I'd be very worried about my own welfare," Dr Bell sternly replied, handing Blanche Andrew's note. "I imagine you know it's a felony to have sexual relations with a minor. I've photocopied this letter and will be giving a copy to the police. They'll be here shortly. I'll be contacting the Child Welfare agency in the morning. Until I feel he's more stable, Andrew won't be allowed any visitors."

"For God's shake," Blanche wailed, after reading Andrew's note. "It's all lies. You try to help these kids out and thish is the thanks you get."

"We'll leave it up to the police and welfare officials to decide whether or not Andrew has been abused," Bell said sternly. "It's fine for you to contact the hospital to check on his condition, but as I mentioned, no visiting. Now you'll have to excuse me. I've got to see how he's doing."

The doctor was sitting beside Andrew's bed as he surfaced from the anaesthetic.

"By your letter I see you've had a pretty rough go of it," Bell began. "Would it help if we talked a bit?"

"Not really," Andrew whispered. "I really have nothing to live for. Unless you've been a foster kid with no parents you don't know what it's like. I just can't handle talking anymore about it now."

"That's alright," the doctor replied, a sad, far-away look coming into his eyes. "Maybe we can talk some in the morning. Tomorrow I'll be talking to the police and your caseworker regarding your abuse. Charges may be laid against Blanche. Before we do anything though, we'll talk to you. Once you're ready for discharge, I'm going to suggest to your caseworker that it would be wise if you didn't have to go back to school here. If you're in favour of it and your caseworker agrees, maybe you could come out to our place in the country until we find you a new home."

"Thanks a lot," Andrew replied, finally making eye contact. "I couldn't take it if I had to go back to school here. They'd never let me live it down."

After the doctor left, Andrew lay on his bed staring into the darkness. "I still don't have anything to live for," he whispered. "Why did someone have to be there to rescue me? What's going to happen to me now?"

Andrew slept fitfully. He had many convoluted dreams of being verbally and physically attacked by his classmates. His last dream was different though and he would remember it as long as he lived. A man and a lady were standing at the foot of his bed. The man was tall and dressed in black. Although Andrew couldn't clearly make out his facial features, he thought he looked like the man he caught a glimpse of in the park just as he was letting go of the branch. The lady was petite, had blonde hair and was dressed in white. Although her face was unfocused too, Andrew felt a strong attraction to her. She touched his shoulder, smiled and said, "My Andrew." Then both figures disappeared.

Andrew awoke feeling upbeat for the first time in months. "I wonder who that man and woman in my dream were?" he pondered. "I don't see how it's possible, but could they have been my parents?" He hardly dared believe that they were.

When Doctor Bell stopped in to see Andrew just before dinner, Andrew was still feeling positive.

"I've been on the phone all morning, doing a little digging on your behalf," the doctor began. "More by good luck than good management I found out some information about your biological parents that might help you. Because of Child Welfare policy, finding your biological parents can be very difficult. Perhaps someday you may be able to do so if it is your wish. Although I didn't find out who your biological folks were, I did find a bit of information that should be helpful to you. I managed to contact your first adoptive father down in the states. His last name is Perkins. Your adoptive parents got you when you were a few days old. They had you for a bit more than a year and then divorced. In the divorce, you were awarded to your mother and he lost all contact with you and her."

"The Perkins were told by the adoption agency that your biological father was in the Canadian Air Force and died in the Second World War before he and your mom could get married. Your mom wanted desperately to keep you, but it was impossible because her family was dysfunctional. The Child Welfare worker told them that your mother wanted the adoptive parents to know that she loved you dearly and would always pray for your welfare. In fact, she requested that if possible they retain the name she had given you. They honoured that request, Andrew. You are named after your father."

As Doctor Bell spoke, Andrew's heart was beating wildly. The news that his mother loved him and that he had been named after his father were words he'd so longed to hear. He tried hard to keep control, but soon there were tears in his eyes.

"I'm glad I was able to get this news for you," Bell continued, placing his hand on Andrew's shoulder. "Knowing that you were loved gives you something to live for, doesn't it?"

"Yes I guess so," Andrew whispered. "Thanks a lot."

In the afternoon, Doctor Bell, Rosanne and a child welfare psychologist, Benny Mark met with Sergeant Ray Stuart of the R.C.M.P. to discuss Andrew's case. Benny and Ray then stopped in at the hospital and got a statement from Andrew. Based on the information they had, the police officer was all for laying charges against Blanche immediately, but Benny suggested it might be wise if he talked with Andrew privately. After talking with Andrew, Benny again met with the group.

"Andrew and I discussed how legal action against Blanche would impact on him what with all the media coverage. Andrew's present stance is that he doesn't want charges to be laid. He said, 'I can't take anymore.' It's my professional view that he's endured as much emotional trauma as he can bear. He also said, 'She's a real witch, but I wouldn't feel all that good about it if she ended up in jail.' I feel very strongly that we should honour his wish. I know it would be less traumatic for him if the matter was dropped. If no legal action is taken against this woman, we must certainly blacklist her with Child Welfare and possibly Stuart should have a talk with her to impress on her the gravity of the situation."

Rosanne turned to Bell and handed him a letter. "I recognize this information may be of small comfort to us now, but this is a copy of the letter that I wrote Lillian Cathy, the Orphanage Administrator, regarding Blanche. I hand-delivered this letter to her before Andrew was placed. As you can see by the letter, I advised Lillian against placing Andrew with Blanche. She's had other foster children and this isn't the first time our department has run into problems with her."

"I sit on the orphanage board," Bell responded after reading Rosanne's letter. "With this letter, I can assure you action will be taken against both Lillian Cathy and this new hair-brained policy of hers of quick placement of kids for the sake of quick placement."

"Because of Andrew's attempted suicide, it would be best for him if he didn't have to return to school here," Doctor Bell continued. "The lad was putting up with a lot of verbal harassment by his classmates before and if he were to return now, it would only intensify. He also has some significant rope lacerations on his neck. From a professional viewpoint, he should be under close medical supervision for a few weeks. If we're all in agreement, I could take Andrew out to our acreage. My wife is a retired teacher and could help him with his school work. My wife and I could keep you posted on how the young lad is making out, Rosanne."

"When I get back to the office I'll check with my supervisor for her approval and have her contact you and your wife," Rosanne said. "From my point of view, it's an excellent idea."

After the meeting, Rosanne dropped in on Andrew. "I'm so sorry you've had such a rough time," she began as she hugged him. "I can't imagine what you've been through. Hopefully in time you'll get over it."

"Well I'm feeling a lot better now. Doctor Bell found out some stuff about my real mom and dad. That's helped me out a lot. The doctor said he's going to take me to his place out in the country for a few weeks."

"Yes we've talked about that. The best of luck to you. I'll be staying in touch. Oh, I just about forgot. I've got a letter for you."

After Rosanne left, Andrew opened the letter.

Dear Andrew,

Thank you for your letter. I'm sorry you had trouble with Aunt, Uncle and Dieter. I hope things will go better for you. Thanks again for sticking up for me. I'm at the mission school now. Mom and Dad left me here last month. I cried an awful lot for the first week. I get very lonely for them. Your letter helped a lot. I room with Susan. Her mom and dad are also missionaries close to where my mom and dad are. My little sister just turned four. I sure wish I could have been there for her birthday. Your letter helped me feel less lonely. When I feel sad, I try to remember you. I always pray for you.

Your good friend, Anne

As with the other letters from Anne, Andrew felt warm when he read it. "I'll write her later when I've got all my thinking straight," he mused.

That afternoon, Doctor Dan Bell picked Andrew up from the hospital after he finished at the medical clinic. "We won't worry for the present about starting you in a new school," Dan began as they were heading out of town. "This morning, my wife, Judith, stopped at the school and got all your schoolbooks. Judith is a retired school teacher and for now can teach you at home."

"Thanks a lot. You don't know how relieved I am that I don't have to go back to the Sunbee school."

The sun was setting as the doctor and Andrew pulled into Bell's driveway. In the twilight Andrew noticed their large white Cape Cod style house and a huge front lawn interspersed with several large spruce trees. As the doctor's wife had slipped out for a few minutes, Bell took Andrew on a tour of the grounds accompanied by Sobaka, their border collie. Behind the house the lawn gave way to a wooded area that dropped down to the river.

"Tomorrow, if you'd like, you can explore all the trails that run down to the river," Dan said, turning to Andrew. "Mom and I are getting too old to climb the steep grades. You can take Sobaka with you."

Andrew got good vibes when he met Judith. "She has a kind face just like Aunt Lizzie, and like Lizzie, she sure isn't skinny," he thought.

Judith went out of her way to make Andrew welcome. After supper they all sat around the fireplace getting acquainted.

At ten PM everyone turned in. As Andrew lay in bed he was feeling better.

The next morning, after the doctor left for the day, Judith and Andrew sat down and drew up a school work schedule.

At three o'clock, having completed his school day, Andrew and Sobaka set off exploring the riverbanks. The Chinook had blown in taking the skiff of snow with it. It was a warm afternoon and Andrew and his new four-footed friend were enjoying their adventure. Andrew found a huge spruce at the water's edge. He sat down and used its sturdy trunk for a back rest. As soon as Andrew opened the lunch Judith had packed, Sobaka came and lay by his leg. She was very grateful to Andrew for sharing his lunch with her and showed her appreciation by giving him a thorough face-licking.

After returning from their tour of the river bank, Andrew split a big pile of wood and carried it into the house. Andrew noticed a chainsaw in the shed. He had learned how to run a power saw from Jack, so after getting the wood in, he fired up the saw and cut up a couple of fire-killed spruce logs.

"Good grief, that's an awful big pile of wood you split and carried in," Dan said as they were eating supper. "Mom and I really appreciate that."

"That's alright. Lena, my first mom, used to say that doing chores helps us earn our keep. I also got the chainsaw going and cut up a couple of logs and split them."

Things were working out well between Andrew and the Bells. By the end of the first week he was starting to feel a lot better about himself.

"Let's talk about your future," Dan began Sunday night after supper. "Maybe we should talk about Judith's and my plans first. I will be retiring at Christmas. I'm sixty-eight now and it's time for some younger doctor to take over my practice. We've listed our house for sale and hope to spend the winter looking for a new home, maybe in Arizona. Judith suffers from allergies and asthma. Because of her health problems, her specialist advised her it would be best to relocate to a warmer, drier climate. Both Mom and I concur that you're a joy to have around. You're welcome to stay as long as we're here."

"Thanks for treating me so well," Andrew said disconsolately. "I don't know what will happen when you're gone. They no doubt think I'm too young to have any ideas of what I want to do. I'll probably be sent back to Miss Cathy and the orphanage. Not many people want a foster kid my age unless they want to get some use out of us, like Blanche did."

"Both Dan and I are very impressed with how well you're handling things considering all the rough breaks you've had," Judith interjected. "That's a sign you're maturing. Most important though, we observe your kindness."

"As to being sent back to Miss Cathy, you'll have no worries in that regard," Dan carried on. "I sit on the orphanage board and was instrumental in seeing that she no longer works for the government. We've cancelled her pilot project of quick placement of children without a thorough study of the homes where the kids would be sent to."

"I'm glad she's gone," Andrew replied. "She was always cold with me. It was like she didn't have a heart and couldn't get rid of me fast enough."

"Mom and I have an idea we'd like you to bounce around. It just might give you some say in your life. You don't have to make a decision right away, but kick it around in your mind."

"We have an old family friend, Edith Ogilvy, who lives up in Rocky Ridge. That's about seventy-five miles northwest of here. I was the local doctor there about twenty years ago and Edith nursed in the hospital. The Ogilvys had a general store. It was a thriving business, but Roy, Edith's husband, always had this thing about investing big sums of money in shaky ventures. Over the years he managed to get by without getting burnt too badly. Then a few years ago, just before he was going to retire, he got involved with some shyster who cleaned them right out. They lost their business plus their house in town and ended up with a small house on twenty acres half a mile out of town. Edith wanted to work as long as she could after they lost everything, but her arthritis forced her to quit. Edith and Roy were managing to scrape by on their pensions and then a year ago, Roy dropped dead of a heart attack. Edith is still holding her own with her pensions, but has little to spare. Countless times Mom and I offered to help her out, but she's proud and fiercely independent."

"Now here's where you might fit in. On her acreage there's a fifteen acre woodlot. We phoned her last week and she's trying to find someone who'd buy the wood. This would help her get by. I've observed that you're pretty handy with a chainsaw. Maybe if you're interested, this would be a chance to help Edith out and make a few dollars for yourself. As I recall it's pretty well all re-growth poplar and birch. As for Edith, both mom and I can vouch that she's a devout, honest lady."

"I kind of see where you're coming from. You're thinking for me to go stay with the old lady. She'd get help from the government for looking after me. I'd go to school and in my spare time I could cut firewood. Edith and I could make some sort of a split on the money when we sell the wood."

"That about summarizes it. It would still be important for you to keep focussed on your schooling, but if you wished, this would give you the opportunity to use some of your spare time to help you and Edith out financially. Remember, Andrew, this is just an idea. It's just something for you to think on."

"Does Edith have a chainsaw or any way to haul the wood out of the bush?"

"As near as I recall, Roy bought a new chainsaw a few weeks before he passed on. I think Edith still has a small Ford tractor and a wagon. About a month before he died, Roy started cutting firewood himself and then he had the heart attack."

"It sounds pretty interesting. I'd like to think it over some."

"If you'd like, maybe we could run up to see Edith next weekend. That will give you a chance to meet her and look the place over. Try to remember, the last thing in the world we want to do is put pressure on you."

Early Saturday morning, Dan, Judith and Andrew were on the road to Edith's place. For most of the trip the highway cut through forested land. It was a still, overcast day and the trees had pretty well lost all their leaves. Even with the windows closed, they could still smell the acrid aroma of the high-bush cranberries.

Andrew thought of Jack's and Lena's place when they pulled into the yard.

Edith Ogilvy met them at the door and gave them all a hug. Andrew liked Edith's open face. He was sure she would be kind. Like Judith, she was a bit on the plump side. Arthritis forced her to walk with a cane. Soon they were seated at the kitchen table eating a roast chicken dinner.

"So this is the young man I hear all the good reports about," Edith said, turning to Andrew. "You're certainly a strapping lad for having just turned thirteen."

Andrew turned red and Edith continued.

"Judith and Dan no doubt told you of my losses with my husband Roy's sudden death, our business loss and my arthritis. God does send us trials, but He's told us he sends trials to strengthen those he loves. Enough about my problems though. Let's talk about something positive."

After dinner, Andrew and Dan made a tour of the acreage and woodlot with the tractor. "There's sure a pile of wood out here," Dan shouted over the roar of the tractor. "If you come here, you'll certainly have your work cut out for you."

"Judith tells me you'll have to find a place to stay once they sell their house," Edith said to Andrew when he and Dan got back. "I don't know if you'd be interested in staying with a crippled old lady, but if you decide you could manage, I promise to treat you like my own son. Roy and I had a boy, but Roger was born with a weak heart and died when he was eight. Judith says you're handy with a chainsaw and I saw today that you're good on the tractor. Your schoolwork comes first, but if you decide to come, we can make any kind of a deal you want on the wood and who knows maybe we could raise a few chickens again."

"Thanks a lot for the offer. If it's alright with you I'd like to think on it a bit. I guess maybe you know I've had some rough things happen to me too."

"Yes, Judith has told me some of your troubles," Edith kindly replied. "Thank God things worked out as they did. As to my offer, take as much time as you want."

There wasn't too much conversation as Andrew, Judith and Dan drove home. All were deep in thought.

"Anytime you want to talk to Judith or me about any of this, Andrew, just let us know," Dan said once they got in the house.

"Yeah thanks. You see I really like Mrs Ogilvy, but there are a few things I sort of don't understand. I guess Rosanne will have to agree to where I go. Do you think she'll let me go to stay with someone so old? She's told me they try to put us kids in with younger parents."

"A very valid concern and you're right. Under ideal conditions, adoption agencies like to place children with parents much younger than Edith. A lot however rests on whether the caseworker is sure the prospective foster parents will provide good care for the child. You mentioned something the other day that also contributes in making these decisions. Older foster children, especially boys, are often hard to place. If you're concerned about what your caseworker will say, you can relax. I contacted her a few days back regarding the possibility of you going to stay with Edith and she was positive about it. If you decide that you'd like to stay with her, Rosanne will go see Edith. As you know, I sit on the orphanage board. I'm sure there'll be no problem in that area."

"If I go to Edith's place, when do you think I should go?"

"There's no sense rushing your thinking on this and the paper work would take a bit of time. Above all, it's going to be your decision, Andrew. As for Edith, Judith said she was quite taken with you. Although she's poor, I can say without question she'd be taking you in because she wants to help you rather than for the money that's in it for her. To be doubly safe though, Judith will phone her tomorrow just to recheck her thinking on it. If you do decide you'd like to stay with her, it might be better to do it sooner than later so you can get back in school. Do you have any other concerns?"

"I don't think so," Andrew replied, his eyes growing misty. "Thanks a lot, guys, for looking out for me. Most people don't give a damn about us foster kids."

"That's alright," Dan said softly. "You see, Andrew, I lost both parents when I was two. I was in five foster homes. Some were good and some horrible. I know some of the pain you've been through. It's an honour and privilege for Judith and me to help you out."

The next day Andrew told Judith he'd decided he wanted to go to Edith's. Once Dan learned of Andrew's decision he saw to it that Edith's application to take Andrew as her foster child was fast-tracked. In short order the paper work was nearing completion. Saturday morning all of Andrew's belongings were loaded into the trunk of Dan's car. Dan gave Andrew his chainsaw as a present. He and Judith would be heading south right after Christmas and he'd have no more use for the saw.

From the backseat, Andrew gazed out the car window, deep in thought. It had snowed throughout the week. Although there was getting to be a fair amount of snow on the ground, it was still relatively warm. There had been fog in the night and all the trees along the road were coated in heavy hoarfrost. When the sun broke through the fog, the brightness was almost too much for the eyes.

"How will I manage in a new school?" Andrew pondered. "Will Mrs Ogilvy and I get along?" Then he rested easy when

Michael Parlee

he remembered her words, 'if you should decide to come, I promise to treat you like my own son.'

CHAPTER TWELVE

Edith's house and out buildings were nestled in a large wood lot. Many years before a forest fire swept through the area. The land had never been brought under cultivation and all but the two acre yard site had reverted to second growth poplar and birch bush. Once Andrew's stuff was moved in, they all sat down for coffee.

"Dan and I would like the two of you to celebrate Christmas with us," Judith said as they were leaving. "I know that driving your car that far might be too hard for you, Edith, so we can come for you."

"Thanks for the invitation. That would be nice, but if I'm feeling up to it and the roads are good, maybe Andrew and I could drive over by ourselves."

After Dan and Judith left, Edith phoned the grade seven-eight teacher and made plans to drop by his house.

"You'll be impressed by Mr Adams," Edith said as they drove into town. "Lynn Adams is an excellent teacher. He's fair, but he doesn't abide any nonsense."

Before they met Mr Adams, Edith gave Andrew a tour of

the town. Andrew thought that Rocky Ridge was a lot like Sunbee except being a little larger.

"This used to be Roy's and my store," Edith remarked as they drove by Hanson's General Store. "A lot of memories here," she muttered more to herself than to Andrew.

Andrew was definitely impressed when he was introduced to his new teacher. Lynn was a bear of a man. He stood six foot four, had a husky build and a fiery red beard. Andrew thought he looked more like a lumberjack than a teacher. Judith had phoned Lynn to update him on Andrew's progress with his studies.

"Welcome to Rocky Ridge," Lynn boomed, shaking Andrew's hand. "I'll be your new teacher. Mrs Bell sent me your marks and they're good. That's commendable considering the number of schools you've attended in the last year. I'm sure you'll do well here."

Once they got home, Edith and Andrew spent the rest of the afternoon getting acquainted. "From what Judith tells me you've had a lot of pain in your life," Edith said as they were eating supper. "If and when you want to talk about things, I'll always be here for you. I won't be prying though. I know from experience what it's like to be in pain and have well-meaning people asking a bunch of foolish questions. Sometimes when you're hurting, the last thing you want to do is go into the details."

"Thanks a lot. I know exactly what you mean. People mean well, but at times they say some pretty stupid things."

"Judith no doubt told you I'm Catholic. I go to Mass regularly. You're welcome to come with me, but I won't be putting pressure on you."

"Changing the subject, have you heard about 'The Chronicles of Narnia?'" Edith handed Andrew a box wrapped in cellophane containing several small books.

"My teacher in Sunbee said something about them in school. Isn't there supposed to be six or seven books in the series?"

"That's right, seven. A friend told me about them. They're written for children, but she said they are for all ages. I just bought this set last week. When Roy was still alive, we'd take turns reading to each other for a half hour or so in the evenings. Would you be interested in trying that?"

"Sure thing," Andrew said enthusiastically. "I love to read. I'm not the best reader in the world when I have to read out loud, but I get by."

And so it was that the reading ritual started. Not only did it bring Edith and Andrew closer, over the years it proved both entertaining and educational.

As the snow was getting deep, Edith and Andrew decided it would be best to leave the woodcutting enterprise until the snow had gone. Sometime back a neighbour felled and hauled in a good sized pile of logs for Edith's own use. Andrew attacked the log pile with a vengeance. Working after school and on a Saturdays he had it all cut and split before the Christmas break. Edith said there was enough wood cut to last the rest of the winter and perhaps half of next winter.

Andrew was relieved that things were working out well between Edith and him. School, however, was causing him a bit of concern.

"Mr Adams is a good teacher and all, but a couple of the

kids are starting to give me a hard time," Andrew began after supper one evening.

"Let me guess," Edith interjected. "It's Ramsey and Justin."

Andrew nodded.

"Ramsey is the bully. Justin is his sidekick. All you have to do is tell Lynn about the two. He'll straighten them out. I guess I really shouldn't be too hard on Justin though. He's had a rough upbringing."

"Yeah I guess he's a foster kid too. Anyway, I think I can handle it on my own."

Monday, things came to a showdown. In Mr Adams' classes, bullying had been pretty well non-existent since he started teaching. No one dared. At the final recess, however, Ramsey and Justin threw caution to the wind. Ramsey came from a single parent home and had a large chip on his shoulder. He was big for his age and quite overweight. Up till now, although he liked to push his weight around with smaller kids in the community, he hadn't dared to bully at school. Ramsey and Justin walked up to Andrew and Ramsey began jeering, "Andrew's got no last name, Andrew's got no last name." Andrew paid no attention to Ramsey and turned to walk away. The two tormentors blocked Andrew's path and Ramsey kept jeering. "Andrew's got no last name and he's a coward too."

A couple of girls ran back to the classroom and alerted Adams to what was going on.

Mr Adams opened the school door and bellowed, "Justin, Ramsey and Andrew. I want to see you in the school on the double."

The three boys hurried into the school.

"It's just been reported that you've been calling Andrew names, Ramsey," Lynn roared. "You know the policy on bullying."

"We were just teasing a little," Ramsey muttered. "It wasn't nothin."

"What about it Andrew, were these two giving you a hard time?"

Andrew smiled at Lynn and shrugged his shoulders.

"My call is that it was bullying, pure and simple. The things you were taunting Andrew with were cruel. This will be your last chance. If it happens again, I'll be contacting the superintendent. Do I make myself clear?"

There was a trace of a smile on Andrew's face as Lynn went on. "If I were you two, I'd be keeping a low profile with Andrew. When he was in Noka, Andrew took boxing lessons from Sergeant Falk. I was talking to Falk last week. He said Andrew was an excellent boxer."

Andrew looked down and again shrugged his shoulders.

"That will be all, boys. Just remember, Justin and Ramsey. I'll be watching you."

Ramsey and Justin gave Andrew a wide berth for the rest of recess. When school was out, Justin caught up with Andrew just outside the school grounds.

"Thanks for not ratting on us. A guy doesn't want to tangle with old Adams. He's a rough bugger when he gets mad."

"I imagine he is. He's the biggest teacher I've ever seen."

"Adams says you're pretty good at boxing."

"Oh I don't know if I'm as good as he lets on," Andrew said looking away. "When I was somewhere around ten, my foster dad taught me and my foster brothers how to box some. When I came to my second last home, the police had a boxing club that I joined."

"You been to many foster homes?" Justin asked.

"Yeah, way too many. Five I guess. Some were really good and some really horrible. I had a real good home from the time I was three up till I was eleven or so, but that all came apart when Mom died and Jack, my dad, started drinking again. My foster brothers, Ralph and Ron, went to stay with some relative and I was shipped back to the orphanage. I've been trying to get a hold of my brothers for over a year now. Edith has been helping me, but they just seem to have disappeared. Sure hope I can find them someday."

"I know what you mean about being in bad homes. Why couldn't a guy just stay forever when you've found a good home? I think I've been to eight. I'll tell you one thing. This is the last one for me. I'm about ready to hit the road." After a long pause, Justin added, "I guess it's stupid to talk like that though. They'd find me and probably send me to a worse place."

"We're going back to Sunbee for Christmas and Boxing Day. When I get back, if you got nothing to do, you could drop over and I'll let you try out on my punching bag."

"Yeah thanks, I just might do that."

Andrew watched as his new friend headed down the

sidewalk to his foster home. Justin was on the scrawny side. He had red unkempt hair that had not seen a brush for some time. On his face was written the pain of his short life.

"How did things go at school today?" Edith asked when she and Andrew were eating supper. "Mr Adams phoned. I hear that Ramsey and Justin were up to their old tricks."

"Oh they tried, but it didn't amount to much. Adams talked to us, but I didn't squeal on either of them. I don't know about Ramsey, but I talked to Justin after school and I think everything will be okay between us. He might come over here in the holidays to try out my punching bag. I'll be keeping an eye out for Ramsey, but as long as he leaves me alone, I'll leave him alone."

"I'm very proud of you, Andrew, and so is Lynn. Lynn said he was sure you could have easily flattened Ramsey and Justin, but instead, you chose to befriend Justin."

After Andrew finished doing the dishes and his homework, he wrote Anne a letter.

Dear Anne,

Thanks for your letter. Hearing from you always helps me a lot. I had a very horrible thing happen to me last month. I was in a bad home. I just can't write about it now because it still hurts too much. Someday I'll tell you about it. I'm staying with Edith Ogilvy. She's a widow and is fairly old. She's very kind and I really like it here. I'm sorry you're so lonely. I know what that's like. We're going to spend Christmas with Judith and Dan Bell. Dan is a doctor. He helped me out when I had trouble. I'll explain it all to you when I can. Goodbye for now.

Your good friend, Andrew

Thursday after school, Edith and Andrew were on the road to spend Christmas with Judith and Dan. Judith, Dan and Sobaka were on the front step to greet them as they pulled into the driveway.

Over coffee, Edith gave Judith and Dan an overview of her and Andrew's comings and goings.

The Bells were overjoyed that things were working out well and relieved that Andrew was fitting in at school.

All of them enjoyed a relaxing holiday. Andrew and Sobaka spent many hours rediscovering the trails down to the river. Christmas morning, Andrew was elated with his presents. Judith and Dan's present was a pair of snowshoes. Edith got him an arctic parka.

"We have a problem knowing what to do with Sobaka," Judith began as they were eating Christmas dinner. "As you know we've sold our house and have to be out by the tenth of January. Dan and I will be leaving next week to find a place in Arizona. Sobaka's getting up in years and if we have to relocate in a retirement village, it would be no place for her. She's used to open spaces."

"Could we take her?" Andrew interjected enthusiastically. "There's lots of room at Edith's and we'd sure take good care of her."

"Sobaka would be more than welcome," Edith added. "As Andrew says, we have lots of room and she'd be good company for us."

"Well that would sure take a load off our minds," Dan said.

"We'll be coming to see you before we leave. We can bring Sobaka with us then."

On the twenty-seventh, Edith and Andrew were on the way back to Rocky Ridge. Andrew spent the next day making a pet door in the porch for Sobaka.

The following day, Justin dropped by to visit. After using the punching bag they put on the boxing gloves and sparred for a while.

"You're as good as old Adams said you were," Justin wheezed, out of breath. "If you were hitting hard, I'd be in real trouble. You move like greased lightning. How can you move so fast?"

"Practise, just practise. You can come over as often as you want. It helps a lot having a sparring partner."

"Yeah I wouldn't mind learning to box if you'd want to teach me. I brought my twenty-two along. Maybe we could do some target practise." Soon they were plinking away at tin cans out in the bush.

"I was talking to my grandma over in Sunbee," Justin said. "That's where you lived a while back, right?"

A look of dread came over Andrew's face and he gave a half-hearted nod.

"Anyway, she said there's a story going around that you tried to hang yourself." When Justin glanced over at Andrew and saw the painful look on his face, he quickly added, "You don't have to talk about it if you don't want to."

"Yeah, it's pretty rough stuff," Andrew replied despondently. "Some horrible things happened to me. My foster mother was a real witch. The story is true, I guess. Maybe some other time I'll tell you about it. I hope you don't tell anyone at school."

"I won't be telling anyone. No sir-ee, not me. When I first came to Rocky Ridge I tried to kill myself too. My foster father got drunk one night and beat me until I passed out. I just came from another bad home and figured there was no reason left for living. Unless you've been a foster kid, you don't know what it's like. I'm still pissed right off with old Emil. He still works me over when he's drunk. Someday when I'm older I'll get my chance. I'll beat him till he'll wish he was dead. I guess in a way it sort of makes me peed-off with everything."

"I know where you're coming from. At times it's hard not to get wild about how you get treated. I'm sure lucky with old Edith. She's a good one."

"Yeah it's good you got a decent one. My foster mom is alright too. She's a little strange, but she's pretty good to me. It's just that bastard old man of hers. I wouldn't cry a tear if he got run over by a big truck."

Saturday morning, Judith and Dan arrived with Sobaka. While dinner was being prepared, Andrew took Sobaka for a romp around the acreage. In no time flat she was chasing snowbirds. Once dinner was ready Andrew and his friend returned to the house. Sobaka looked very doleful when Andrew showed her to the mat in the porch, but she dutifully went over and flopped down. When Andrew opened the kitchen door, Sobaka's ears perked up and she started to whine. Andrew didn't have the heart to leave his pal in the cold porch. "Here Sobaka," he called. In a flash she was in the kitchen curled up by the stove.

"I don't know if this is a sign of things to come," Edith sighed, "but you can't blame her. She wants to be where the action is."

Dan and Judith spent the night with Edith and Andrew. The next morning they were on their way.

In the days to come, Sobaka was fitting right in and at times Edith wondered whether she or Sobaka was in charge.

Before the end of the Christmas holidays, Andrew found a part-time job working in the general store that Edith and her husband once owned.

As time passed, Andrew was doing well in school and getting along well with Justin. Ramsey's nose was out-of-joint with the friendship that had developed between Andrew and Justin. He realized that wisdom was the better part of valour though and gave Andrew a wide berth.

Soon things were settling into a predictable routine for Edith, Andrew and Sobaka. After getting home from work, Andrew brought in the wood, carried in the water and washed the dishes. Edith did the cooking. Andrew helped Edith with the housekeeping. Sobaka's main chores were chasing birds, keeping the squirrels in line, barking at the moon and following her new masters whenever they were outside. She was supposed to sleep in the porch, but most evenings would find her sleeping peacefully on an old blanket by the stove. Neither one of her masters had the heart to wake her and send her out to her cold bed in the porch. She had become an integral part of the family.

CHAPTER THIRTEEN

"We're going to be ordering school jackets and rings," Andrew said wistfully when he came home from work one day. "Trouble is they're so expensive and I know money is tight. Oh well, maybe next year."

Edith wanted desperately to get Andrew a school jacket, but she was flat broke. Before they made the trip at Christmas new tires had to be put on the car. She was only able to pay half the bill and would be paying the rest off on a monthly basis from the little she got from the government for caring for Andrew. Andrew insisted that he share his small wages with her, but that went for the extra food they needed to buy. With Edith's finances tight, she was constantly praying to find the extra funds they needed.

"Dear Lord, show me a way to buy Andrew a school jacket," she prayed one night. Suddenly she said aloud, "how about Mom's gold broach? I could use it as backing to get a small loan from Bill Hanson to buy the jacket." Instantly she was having second thoughts. "Not the broach," she moaned. "That's the only keepsake I have of Mom's."

Edith prayed and struggled with the dilemma all the next morning. At noon she finally found peace. After dinner she drove into town and stopped at the general store. Bill Hanson felt for Edith and extended credit to her whenever she'd accept it.

"I'm in a bind, Bill. I'd like to get Andrew a school jacket. They're ordering them today and as usual I'm low on funds."

"No problem," Bill interjected. "How much money do you need?"

"Not so fast, Bill. I may be poor, but I still have my pride. I need fifteen dollars and here's a broach as backing for the loan."

"You know you don't have to do this, Edith. On second thought, I guess we've been down this road before. I've learned from dealing with you that arguing doesn't do any good."

Bill took fifteen dollars from the till and handed it to Edith.

"Good gracious, this must be worth a lot," he said as he examined the broach. "It looks very old. It's eighteen caret gold and inset with a huge gemstone. Is that an emerald?"

Edith nodded.

"This must have been your mother's, right?"

Again Edith nodded.

"I imagine this means a lot to you so I'll put it in the safe. I dare say it's worth several hundred dollars. I wish you didn't make me do this. Anyway, I'll keep it for you as long as is needed."

On the way home, Edith stopped at the school and left the

money for the school jacket with the secretary. She gave her Andrew's size and advised her it was to be a surprise.

In early February the school jackets and rings came. At the last recess Mr Adams opened the large box. All those who placed orders stood around his desk. Andrew remained in the small group on the outside of the circle who had nothing coming. Like the others in his group, he was trying hard to be nonchalant. Everything was finally handed out except one jacket.

"Andrew, aren't you going to get your jacket?" Adams asked.

"But I didn't order one."

"I know that, but Edith did. Come and pick it up."

Andrew reached for his jacket, a lump in his throat. As Lynn Adams handed it to him the rugged old giant wiped his eyes with his left hand.

"Look what I got from Edith!" Andrew cried out exuberantly when he got to the store. Andrew was wearing his school jacket.

"Looks pretty sharp," Bill said. "Here's a little something for Edith and you for Valentines Day." Bill handed Andrew a small box. "Don't forget to take it home with you tonight."

Andrew ran most of the way home and burst into the house. "Thank you so much for getting me the jacket," he cried out, giving Edith a bone-crunching hug. "I can't remember when I felt so happy, but where did you get the money?"

"I knew how much you wanted the jacket so I prayed about it," Edith replied, her voice growing husky. "I used my mother's gold broach to back a small loan with Bill Hanson. He'll keep the broach in his safe till I pay him back. What's in that parcel?"

"I don't have a clue. Mr Hanson gave it to me. He said it was for both of us for Valentine's Day."

In the package was Edith's favourite, a box of chocolate truffles and a large bag of smoked almonds, Andrew's weakness.

They were well into their respective treats when Edith noticed something else in the box. "What's this?" she asked, pulling out a small package.

"Search me," Andrew replied, looking as perplexed as Edith.

With trembling fingers Edith tore it open. "My broach!" she cried out. Wrapped around the broach was a note.

Dear Edith,

The Bible says 'It is more blessed to
Give than to Receive.' Obviously you believe and practise
this. So do I, Edith. Your collateral has been redeemed
as my Valentine's gift to you. Find enclosed your Gold
Broach, free from all liens, debts and encumbrances.
Andrew is a super worker and well deserving of his
school jacket. I've enjoyed doing business with you,
Edith. I count it a privilege to be your friend.
Remember, it's ungrateful to turn down a gift.

Bill

Over the next few months Edith tried to talk Bill into

taking back some of the fifteen dollars, but he remained firm.

Andrew attended Mass regularly with Edith. She was a devout Catholic and never missed Mass on Sunday unless she was half-dead with the flu or the like.

Since Andrew came to stay with her, she'd spent countless hours anguishing over the possibility of adopting him. Finally she made an appointment with Father Bernard.

"I'm in a dilemma, Father. I need an outside opinion. Things have worked out so well between Andrew and me that I'm seriously considering trying to adopt him. I mean sure, he's not perfect and the odd thing about him irritates me, but then there are a few things about me that no doubt irritate him. By and large though, we get along so well. I know it would mean a lot to him if he didn't have to live with the stigma that I was keeping him for the money that's in it. What are your thoughts?"

"From what I know of the lad I'm quite impressed with him. Without question he's gone through some bad experiences, but seems to be overcoming them and getting on with his life. Have you talked to him about adoption?"

"In a round-about-way I have. The other day we were talking about his stay with the Smyth's. He said they wanted to adopt him and his two foster brothers, but couldn't manage financially without the government's assistance. I'll never forget the wistful look in his eyes when he said, 'every foster kid's dream is to be adopted and be part of a real family.'"

"Well we know where Andrew's coming from. Now from your point of view, I'd imagine the money thing is a real big concern for you."

"It sure is. I'm barely making ends meet. I've prayed many long hours about it. Andrew is working after school, but the little he earns is pretty well used up in the extra groceries and clothes we have to buy. As you know, all I have is my old age pension and a small nursing pension. I'm still trying to pay a bit here and there on the old bills Roy and I had. I'm trying to have faith that we can manage without the government's help, but at times I'm scared."

"As I see it, there's no easy answer. About the only help I can offer is that I'll pray along with you. You're a very courageous, wise lady. I'm sure with God's guidance and our prayers; you'll make the right decision."

That night, after many hours of prayer, Edith found peace. "Lord, with your help I'm going to adopt Andrew. I have faith that you'll provide for our financial needs."

The following day Edith phoned Child Welfare and told them of her plans.

A few days later Rosanne stopped by in the afternoon. "It always warms my heart when someone adopts a foster child, especially an older child. There are, however, a number of things we must check out. Andrew enjoys staying with you and the two of you get along well. That's a positive. You're a retired nurse. That's another positive. You are highly recommended by Doctor Bell, a former director of the orphanage board for the Red Deer area. About the only thing we have on the negative side is your financial situation. We want to be sure you can provide adequate care for Andrew without our assistance."

"I imagine then I'd have to prove to you people that Andrew and I could manage without your help."

"That's about it. We have the application you made out

when Andrew came under your care. Has your dollar situation changed any since then?"

"Not really," Edith replied, crestfallen. "Andrew worked in Hanson's General Store up till last week. Now he's cutting firewood after school and on Saturdays. He hopes to make more at that than working at the store. We're going to try to sell some wood, but realistically we can't really count too much on that."

"My supervisor suggested you could make out an application to adopt Andrew, but to be successful, you would have to show that you and Andrew could manage on your own."

"Do you have a dollar figure of what extra money the government feels I'd need?"

"Yes we have tables for that." Rosanne buried herself in her charts. "According to these tables, for a teenager, we say a parent needs one hundred to one hundred-fifteen dollars a month to provide for their care. That would be from twelve hundred to around fourteen hundred dollars a year. I'll leave you the application form and the best of luck. I'll be elated if you are successful."

"Thanks," Edith responded glumly. "I think it best we don't tell Andrew about this. There's no sense getting his hopes up if it's not going to go anywhere."

After going through the application form, they had tea and Rosanne left.

Edith was feeling very down as she drove to the church. The door was open so she went inside, dropped to her knees and started to pray. "Dear Lord, please help me. You know I'm poor. You know I still owe for my tires. You know I still owe seven hundred dollars to the lawyer. On the other hand, you know how much it would mean to Andrew to be adopted." Edith spent an hour in the church praying fervently. Finally she headed for home.

"You seem down tonight, Mom," Andrew said at the supper table. "Is something bothering you?"

"Oh it's nothing to worry about. Some days I just feel a little off. I'm sure I'll be back on top of things tomorrow."

Edith slept very poorly that night and spent several hours praying for God's will to be done.

"I have a surprise for you, Mom," Andrew beamed as they were eating breakfast. "Tomorrow is Mother's Day and there's a smorg at the hotel. I'm taking you there for brunch as my Mother's Day gift." Edith hugged Andrew and he left for the woodlot.

Edith was knitting when a car pulled into the yard. Her heart began to beat wildly when she recognised the visitor as her lawyer, Carl. "Heaven preserve us," she muttered, "he's probably come for money." Although Carl had often been blunt with Roy for getting involved in questionable ventures, he'd always treated Edith kindly.

"Morning, Edith," he said, stepping inside. "I've got a letter for you. I was going to mail it yesterday, but then I had some business to do over here so I decided to deliver it. As you'll see by the letterhead it's from the states. That old goat of a husband of yours was always dabbling here and there with your money."

"Do I have some more bad debts to pay?" Edith asked, her voice trembling.

"Not at all. The old coot had some money invested in the states that we didn't know about. Go ahead and read the letter. I just got it from the company yesterday. I've taken the liberty of asking them to sell the shares on your behalf. Unless you veto the sale, as near as I can estimate, sometime next week you'll be between thirteen and fourteen thousand dollars better off. I can have the money deposited directly into your checking account, or maybe you want to put it into a saving account?"

Edith quickly scanned the letter. "Thank you, Lord," she whispered, breaking into tears.

Edith promised Carl she'd clear up her bill as soon as the money was deposited. After a cup of tea, Carl left.

"You sure seem happy tonight," Andrew said at the supper table.

"I certainly am," Edith replied with a broad smile. "It's a surprise. I'll tell you about it tomorrow."

On Sunday, after they had returned from brunch at the hotel, Edith handed Andrew a large envelope.

"What's this?"

"It's the surprise I mentioned yesterday." Edith replied, her heart racing.

Andrew slit the envelope open with his pocket knife, took out the form and read aloud, "APPLICATION FOR ADOPTION."

"I want to adopt you," Edith whispered.

Andrew tried hard not to break down, but to no avail.

Tears started slipping down his cheeks and a few moments later he was weeping uncontrollably.

Edith went over to Andrew and put her arms around him. Andrew in turn embraced his mom-to-be.

"Thank you so much," he finally whispered, "but how will we manage without the money from the government?"

"I was wondering that too until yesterday morning. I'd been praying for a long time about adopting you, but I knew I'd never be able to do it without some help. My prayers were finally answered in the most miraculous way. Carl, my lawyer dropped by yesterday when you were out cutting wood. Roy had an investment in the states that we didn't know about. As of next week, we'll be between thirteen and fourteen thousand dollars richer."

"Nobody will ever call me a foster kid again," Andrew said, smiling. "Thanks so much."

"The pleasure is mine, Andrew. You've filled that gap I've felt in my heart since Roy and my son Roger died."

CHAPTER FOURTEEN

A month into the wood cutting venture, Andrew and Edith were having second thoughts about its viability. Although they sold a few pickup loads, they were finding that most people who used wood for heating either cut their own wood or had regular suppliers.

By the middle of June they shut down the wood cutting operation and Andrew went back working in the general store. On the last day of school, Justin walked with Andrew to the store.

"I guess this week's the last I'll have to put up with that old bastard, Emil," Justin began.

"Is that right? Going to a new home?"

"Yeah, I'm going to stay with my oldest sister. She just finished her nursing course and got a job in Calgary. She's visited me a few times over the years and knew I had a bad deal with Emil. Anyhow, I guess I'll be pulling freight on Sunday."

"Best of luck to you. I hope things work out as good for you as they did for me."

"I hope so too. If I were you, I'd be on the look out for Ramsey. He's peed-off with both of us. The other day I overheard that he's gunning for you."

"Thanks for the tip. Anytime he wants a damn good beating, that's what he'll get from me. Give me a holler before you leave."

When Andrew got home from work there was letter from Anne waiting for him.

Dear Andrew,

I shouldn't have taken so long to write. I'm sorry
you had trouble. I pray for you every night. I saw
my mom and dad and my younger sister at Easter.
She's sure growing. I asked Dad if I could go back
with them, but he said no. This made me very sad and
I'm still sad. Once school is out I'm going to
spend the holidays with them and then I guess it's
back to jail for me. I turned eleven last week, but
I don't feel any older.

Your friend, Anne

After supper Andrew wrote Anne a reply.

Dear Anne,

It was good to hear from you. I'm sorry you're feeling
lonely. I pray for you every day too. I have very good
news for you. Edith has adopted me. The legal papers
came through last week, so now I'm Andrew Ogilvy. I'm
really happy about it. School is out today and I passed.
I have a part-time job at the general store. This summer
I'll be working six hours a day. Things are going good
between my new mom and me. I go to Mass with her each

Sunday. I'm also getting along pretty well with the
priest. I told you in my last letter that something
bad happened to me. I'm still mixed up about it and
I can't write about it yet. I hope I will be able to
tell you about the whole thing sometime. Maybe you could
send me a picture of yourself. I will be fourteen in the
fall. I'll put my school picture in the letter. I got
some weights and I work out every day. Will close for
now.

Your good friend, Andrew

The summer slipped by without incident. Lynn Adams was
an avid weightlifter and set Andrew up with a weightlifting
program.

In August, the Bells spent a weekend with Edith and
Andrew. They were very pleased that Edith had adopted
Andrew and also happy that Sobaka was doing well. When
they arrived, Sobaka ran up to them, whining and wagging
her tail so hard her whole back end moved. After licking their
hands for a few minutes she went back to the more pressing
task of chasing sparrows.

The first day of school, Lynn Adams introduced two new
students who moved into the community over the summer.
Then to Andrew's surprise he added, "I'm also happy to
announce that Andrew has been adopted by Edith Ogilvy.
Let's welcome Richard, Nellie and Andrew Ogilvy." Everyone
in the class clapped except Ramsey.

In late October classes were out for the day and Andrew
was on his way to work. Hearing someone crying up ahead,
Andrew quickened his pace. "Please give me back my books,"
Linda, a grade three girl was pleading. Ramsey and Lyle, his
new sidekick, were laughing and tossing Linda's book-bag
back and forth over Linda's head.

"I'll be taking that," Andrew shouted, wrenching the book-bag out of Ramsey's hand. Andrew handed the book-bag to Linda and then turned to Ramsey. "Why don't you guys pick on someone your own size, or are you too chicken shit for that?"

"Just who the hell do you think you are?" Ramsey sneered, a foot from Andrew's face. "You must think you're pretty tough, foster boy."

"You're a low bred jerk," Andrew shot back. "I'm not a foster kid anymore. If I ever catch you creeps bugging anyone again I'll deck you both. Get the message?"

"You don't scare me," Ramsey snarled. "So how much did you have to pay old Ogilvy to adopt you? You're probably diddling her. That's why she adopted you."

Lyle's nervous titter was short-lived.

Andrew dropped low, then using the strength of his legs he shot upward with a wicked left hook to the side of Ramsey's face. The braying bully collapsed in a heap, out cold. When Andrew looked up, Lyle was already half-way down the block and running as if his life depended on it.

"Thanks for helping me," Linda said hesitantly. "Do you think Ramsey's hurt bad?"

"I hope not. Could you go get Mr Adams?"

By the time Linda was back with Adams, Ramsey was sitting up.

"I see your bullying finally paid off," Adams began, turning to Ramsey. "What have you got to say for yourself?"

"We were just having a little fun," Ramsey muttered without making eye contact. "It was nothin. We weren't hurting no one."

"Making someone cry and having fun at someone else's expense is bullying," Adams shouted. "To top things off you ripped Linda's binder. You'll be buying her a new one. You, Lyle and I will be meeting with the superintendent as soon as he's free. You just may be suspended from school. I'll be having a word with Lyle tomorrow. Linda told me what you said to Andrew. Although I don't condone fighting in most instances, I'd have to say you got what you deserved. Now come with me. I'm going to drive you to the clinic to have you checked out and then I'll take you home to let your mother know what you did."

When Andrew returned from work, Edith met him at the door. "Mr Adams phoned me about the fight and then Linda's mother called. How are you doing, Son?"

"Oh I'm alright I guess. I wouldn't have nailed him, but he said some terrible things about you. I just couldn't take it."

"I guess Ramsey pushed you a bit too far," Edith said as she hugged Andrew. "Linda's mother told me what Ramsey said to you. I imagine his comments brought back the horrors of your stay with Blanche. Thanks for sticking up for Linda and defending me."

For the next couple of weeks, Ramsey and Lyle gave Andrew a wide berth. Whether it was the threat of suspension, the flack he got from his mom, the disgrace of being knocked out cold by his rival or a combination of the three, Ramsey's behaviour improved a great deal. By the time the Christmas break came, Ramsey and Andrew were tolerating each other and even starting to be civil.........

Time passed. Edith and Andrew were doing well. The extra money Edith got from Roy's forgotten investment plus Andrew's part-time job took the pressure off their finances. Unlike her departed husband, Edith handled her finances with great care.

Soon Andrew was nearing the end of high school. Andrew and Anne stayed in touch by letter and over the years exchanged a few photographs. As they shared their joys and sorrows, the bond between them was becoming very strong. Even though they were both very attractive, neither one of them dated anyone. Andrew was becoming quite infatuated with Anne's recent photo taken on her fifteenth birthday. Anne had changed from a ten year old to a young lady with beautiful features and what Andrew thought was a knockout figure. He spent a fair amount of time holding her photo and fantasizing about them being together. Of late, the fantasies were of an intimate nature.

The evening Andrew finished writing his last grade twelve exam, the phone rang. Edith answered it. "For you," she said handing the phone to Andrew.

"Congratulations on finishing grade twelve, Andrew. I'll bet you can't guess who this is."

"I'm not positive, but you sure sound like my pen-pal Anne used to sound."

"You're right," Anne cried. "I wasn't sure you'd recognize my voice. It's been such a long time since we last talked to each other. At any rate, I'm down at the mission academy, a few miles out of Minneapolis. The academy is a sort of combination high school, Bible School and college. I'll be finishing my high school here. I arrived a week ago, but thought I'd wait to phone you until now. I wanted to congratulate you on finishing high school. I knew from your last letter you'd finish writing your last exam today."

"I can hardly believe this, Anne. I wrote that last exam this afternoon. Hopefully I've passed everything. You don't know how good it is to hear your voice again. What are your plans for the summer?"

"My folks are home on furlough right now. They helped me move to the academy. Before that we spent a week together at the mission retreat and that was nice. I have to bring my marks in French up a bit and then I'll be working right here in the academy. They're doing a bunch of renovations and I'll be helping on that until school starts. I think my folks will be heading back to the mission field in early October. Hopefully they'll stop in for another visit before they leave."

"I'll be working at the store for the summer, but somehow we've just got to get together. Do you think there's any way we could arrange that before your school starts?"

"I'd love to see you again, but we're an awful long way apart. Every dollar I make this summer will have to go for my schooling costs. My folks don't have any extra money."

"I know we're close to fifteen hundred miles apart, but still, we've just got to see each other. Mom has a sister in Duluth. She's always talking about going to see her. Maybe Mom and I could drive down in her car."

"I guess we'll have to play it by ear then. It would be wonderful though. It's been so many years since we were together. If you do make it down we'll have to remember that even though school is over for the year, they still have strict rules here. No dating is allowed and if we go out as a mixed group, a chaperone has to tag along. I think they go too far, but those are the rules. Still, we have a big lounge where we could visit, just as long as you don't mind some old spinster watching us."

"The other night I was looking at that last picture you sent me. Man, you've sure grown up. I can hardly wait to see you again. I'm pretty sure I can talk Mom into going to see her sister. We've just got to get together this summer."

"That was Anne," Andrew said to Edith when he got off the phone. "She just moved back to a mission high school in Minnesota. The school is a few miles north of Minneapolis. I'd sure love to see her again. A few days ago you were talking about how long it had been since you saw your sister, Ruby. Do you think there's a possibility we could drive down to visit her and Anne? I'm positive I could get a few days off from the store and I'd be happy to share the cost of the trip."

"That sounds interesting. I'll have to think it through. Maybe I should phone Ruby and see what we can come up with."

The next day Edith contacted her sister. Ruby was very pleased with the prospect of seeing Edith again. Ruby was working in an old folk's home and would be taking her holidays in late August. She suggested the second last week in August would be the best time for their visit.

When Edith told Andrew she'd talked to Ruby about the planned trip, he was ecstatic.

"It's good to see you so happy," Edith said, with a twinkle in her eye. "If I could though, I'd like to give you a little motherly advice. Try not to fall in love with a picture or a memory. From what you say she's a wonderful girl and I'm sure she is, but just be a little careful."

"You see, Andrew, years ago I fell for a service man at the

start of the war. We just went out a couple of times and then he was posted overseas for nearly a year. He wrote once or twice, but mostly I wrote him. I spent countless hours staring at his portrait and imagining what a wonderful life we'd be spending together after the war. When he came home on leave, I was heartbroken. I found out he was engaged. What hurt most though, was I learned he had already been engaged when we dated. At any rate, everything will probably be okay for you."

Notwithstanding Edith's words of caution, Andrew constantly fantasized about his upcoming visit with Anne.

CHAPTER FIFTEEN

The second last week in August, Edith and Andrew were on their way. Andrew was in high spirits and even though it was overcast with light rain, he thought the scenery beautiful.

With Andrew doing the driving and Edith the navigating, the trip went without incident. They pulled into Duluth late Thursday afternoon. Ruby welcomed her sister and Andrew with open arms. There was a strong resemblance between the two sisters, Ruby just being a slightly smaller and younger version of her sister. Like Edith, Ruby was a widow. She lost her husband in the war and never remarried. In the evening, Andrew phoned Anne at the academy and made plans to see her the following afternoon.

The next morning Andrew helped Ruby with some of her heavy yard work before leaving for the academy. It was a bright summer day and he marvelled how green everything still was. Back home, the leaves had started to turn yellow and harvest was underway.

After a three-hour drive, Andrew arrived at the mission school. The academy was on twenty acres in a rural setting. The complex consisted of a number of large dormitories, a chapel, kitchen, several office buildings, classrooms and an assortment of staff residences.

Andrew went straight to the large brick student lounge as Anne had directed. An officious-looking, white-haired lady at the receptionist desk glanced up from her reading as Andrew approached.

"Can I help you?" she asked cryptically, putting a bookmark in her book and closing it.

"I'm looking for Anne Prentice."

"Your name and is Miss Prentice expecting you?" she continued, putting her book aside.

"I'm Andrew Ogilvy and I made arrangements with Anne to meet her here at five-thirty."

"Well she's not here yet. Take a seat and I'll page her on the intercom."

Getting no response from Anne, the receptionist turned back to Andrew. "Family, I suppose?"

"Not really. Five or six years ago Anne stayed with her aunt and uncle for a year. Her aunt and uncle took me in as a foster kid, so we lived together for five or six months. We've been pen-pals since then."

"Hi, Andrew."

"Anne!" Andrew exclaimed, leaping to his feet. He rushed to the door, grabbed Anne and lifted her clear of the floor in a hug to end all hugs.

"Miss Prentice, that's hardly the comportment we expect from a young Christian lady," the receptionist called out sternly. "You know our policy on hugging members of the opposite sex, except family."

"I'm sorry, Miss Higgins," Anne responded, disentangling herself from Andrew. "I forgot to tell Andrew about the rules."

"Well I'd advise you to do so. We don't want to see another display like that. The two of you need to remember that even if the school year hasn't begun yet, the rules still apply."

"I just can't get over how you've changed," Andrew said as Anne led him to a table at the far side of the lounge. "Man alive, you're just so grown up, like I mean you're so pretty."

"Thanks," Anne replied turning red. "I have your last year's picture, but I didn't figure you'd be over six feet tall and so husky. It's sure good to see you again. We've got a lot of catching up to do. Where do we start?"

They had only begun comparing notes when the supper buzzer went. Anne and Andrew headed for the dining room. They sat by themselves at a table reserved for visiting guests.

"The guy with red hair at the far table," Andrew said to Anne as they were eating. "What's his story? Every time I look up he's staring at us."

"Oh that's Louie," Anne sighed. "Don't pay any attention to him. He's a student who's also working with the renovation crew. He's forever doing dumb things to try and get my attention and he's always staring at me."

"Changing the subject, tonight at our young people's meeting we have a special speaker. I think you'll enjoy him.

He's into sports of some kind and they say he's supposed to be doing a weightlifting demonstration."

"We won't be able to sit together," Anne said as she and Andrew walked to the gym for the meeting. "I'll run through some of the rules for you. As I told you on the phone, absolutely no dating is allowed for students. It's alright for us to sit together in the lounge as long as we sit across from each other at the small study tables. We can sit together in the dining room since you're classified as a guest. It's not okay to sit together in church for some unknown reason. It's okay for us to walk together to go to the dining room or to services, but we can't go for any other kind of walks on or off the academy grounds unless we have a staff chaperone with us. I imagine some of the rules must seem silly to you, but I guess it's best to go along with them."

The students who were working with Anne on the school renovation project plus the young people from a visiting church made for a good crowd. Anne found Andrew a seat across the isle from her and the meeting began. After a half hour of hymns and a short devotional talk, the guest speaker was introduced. Leroy Payne was a recent theological graduate who was trying for the United States Olympic Team in the decathlon. He was in top condition, of average height, with a wiry build. After talking for several minutes on the decathlon, he moved on to the merits of using weight-training as a tool for all types of competitive sports. He had his own weights set up on stage.

"This is a barbell with 250 pounds on it," he said. "It may not look all that heavy, but I assure you it is. Are there any of you boys who'd like to give it a try?"

Louie leapt to his feet and headed to the front.

"You would be five foot eleven?" Leroy asked.

Louie nodded as he turned back and flashed Anne a broad smile.

"You must weigh close to one hundred-ninety pounds."

"One hundred-ninety-five," Louie corrected.

"You're a couple of inches taller than I am and twenty pounds heavier. Go ahead and give the barbell a try."

Leroy showed Louie how to position himself and then stepped back. With a Herculean effort, Louie finally got the weight up to his waist.

"Good show," Leroy exclaimed. "Let's give Louie a hand."

To the applause of the group, Louie swaggered back to his seat.

"I will now demonstrate the dead lift, the clean and jerk and the military press," Leroy said.

He made the dead lift and clean and jerk with the 250 pounds without too much effort, but had to work hard at lifting 230 pounds over his head in the military press. To the applause and cheers of the students he completed the lift and brought the weight to the floor.

"Do any of you have any questions?" Leroy asked.

"I was wondering about Louie's lift," Andrew boldly interjected. "Wouldn't it have been better if you'd had him warm-up a bit and shouldn't he have lifted more with his legs?"

"Why don't you try it then," Louie muttered, looking darts at Andrew.

"You're right on both counts. I should have had Louie do some warm-up exercises. I don't believe we've met."

"I'm Andrew Ogilvy. I'm here from Canada visiting Anne."

"Welcome to the states," Leroy said, nodding. "I'm now going to put 350 pounds on the bar and give a shot at dead lifting it."

This time he had to work a little harder to stand up erect with the weight.

"Your turn now Louie," Leroy called out. "Let's see what you can do."

"I pass," Louie shot back. "Maybe Andrew should try it."

"What about it, Andrew? Is your practical as good as your theory? Maybe you could show us what you Canadians are made of."

Andrew looked uncomfortable and glanced over at Anne for guidance.

"It's all right," she whispered. "Go ahead if you want to."

All eyes were on Andrew as he walked up to the front. He peeled off his suit jacket and handed it to Leroy. Dropping to the floor, he did a few warm-up exercises.

"I think I'm in trouble," Payne interjected with a chuckle. "Just a glance at this fellow with his suit coat off and I'd have to say he's been weightlifting quite awhile."

Andrew smiled, rolled up his sleeves, hitched up his pants and walked over to the 350 pound barbell. Without any show of effort, Andrew lifted the weight to his waist in the dead lift and then did another four quick repetitions for good measure. Leroy and everyone except Louie cheered.

After a short pause, Andrew approached the barbell again. "This 'clean and jerk' lift is for my friend, Anne."

Andrew bent over, locked his hands on the bar and concentrated for a few moments. Letting out an ear-shattering roar, Andrew hoisted the weight off the floor and in one clean motion brought it up high between waist and shoulder. Without pausing and in another fluid motion, he bent his knees, slipped under the weight and stood up straight bringing the barbell to shoulder height. Andrew rested a moment or two. Letting out another roar he dropped down again in a partial squat, then using the strength of his legs he shot up. At the end of the lunge he pushed the weight overhead to arms' length, completing the lift. Again, everyone except Louie cheered.

"That was tremendous," Leroy said giving Andrew a slap on the back. "You are one strong Canadian. I dare say you've been lifting for a while."

"Oh, for a few years," Andrew replied with a smile. "Quite a few years I guess."

"That was just marvellous," Anne said to Andrew as they walked with the rest of the young people back to the dining room for lunch. "I knew from your letters that you were strong, but I had no idea you were that strong. I'm so proud of you! Thanks for dedicating that last lift to me."

After lunch, Anne and Andrew spent an hour in the student lounge and visited until it was curfew time.

"I talked to the dean of women this morning," Anne said as they were leaving the lounge. "She told me they have a guest room for you in the boys' dormitory. She seemed pretty tense about your visit though, so no goodnight hug."

On Saturday the renovation crew worked a half day. Andrew volunteered to help with the building project. Andrew, Louie and three other young fellows were assigned to paint the inside of one of the office buildings.

"It's sort of none of my business, but are you Anne's boyfriend or something?" Louie asked Andrew during the morning coffee break.

"Not really the kind of boyfriend you're thinking of," Andrew answered, chuckling. "We just know each other from years ago. We've been pen-pals for five or six years. My mom is visiting her sister in Duluth so I decided to drop by for a visit."

"I see," Louie replied, sounding most relieved. "I'd sure never have tried those weights last night if I'd known you were so good at lifting. You must have been doing it forever."

"What's the chance we could get a bit of privacy?" Andrew asked Anne as they were eating dinner. "I'd like to tell you about some of the horrible things in my past, but I feel uncomfortable with big ears around."

"I'm sorry, but it's pretty well the study tables in the student lounge. On second thought, I guess we could go over to the little park in front of the administration building. There's an old picnic table and a couple of rickety old chairs that hardly anyone uses. Still, if we did that I guess we'd be breaking the stupid rules."

"Well we've sure covered a lot of ground," Andrew said as the supper buzzer sounded. "I'm still hung up on talking to you about my stay at Blanche's place though, unless we have privacy."

"I'm trying to think of a spot where we'd be more to ourselves," Anne continued as they walked to the dining room. "Off the top of my head though, I can't come up with another place. It doesn't help that the staff are pretty suspicious of boys and girls getting paired up. It seems they're doubly suspicious of you and me. Have you noticed how they're always glancing our way?"

"I sure don't want to get you in trouble. Maybe after supper we'll have to make do with a spot over in the corner of the lounge."

After eating, they selected a table in the far corner and sat down across from each other.

"Okay now what about this woman, Blanche, I believe," Anne said. "Let's hear your story. I know you went back to the orphanage after your fight with Dieter and that you were feeling down for some time. After that what happened?"

"It's pretty rough stuff, but here goes. You see, Blanche was a harsh one. She was always going on about how she hated men. I was feeling pretty down for the first few days I was there. By the time I'd been there ten days though, I was starting to get along not too bad at school and was managing better with her. On Friday evening she even had a cake for my thirteenth birthday. Then the next morning......." Andrew stopped and covered his face with both hands. Finally he gained his composure again. "You see, she started this sex thing with me," he whispered. "She came into my room, took off her nightgown and climbed into bed with me. I was so shocked. Afterwards, I felt so dead and mixed up that I just wanted to run away. There was no hugging, kissing or any show of emotion and as I said, I'd just turned thirteen the day before."

Fighting for control, Andrew blurted out the whole story of the trauma of staying with Blanche, the torment he endured at school and then his attempted suicide. Trying to maintain his composure he silently rubbed his finger along the old scar that the rope had left on his neck.

"It's much better now, but I still think about it quite a lot," he finally added. "When I do, it's like I get mixed up all over again. I sometimes wonder if God really did forgive me for trying to kill myself. Man, if I could just somehow take it all out of my memory. Other than the Bells and Edith, you're the only one I've told. It helps a lot to be able to talk to someone about it."

"I feel your pain," Anne whispered as she reached over and lightly touched the scar on Andrew's neck. "You were there when Dieter did that awful thing to me and now I'm here for you. I'm honoured to share your hurt. You know, Andrew, God was there looking after you. I just know that. Another thing I know is that God has forgiven you. He promises to forgive us if we ask him to."

Andrew reached for Anne's hand. "Yes, that's what Edith says. She said that God has an important plan for my life and that's why he saved me. I'd like to think that. Somehow, I'd like to help out. I'd like especially to help kids that are having a rough time. I don't know what kind of work that would be, but I'm thinking on it a lot. What about you? Do you have any plans?"

"Not really," Anne replied, taking her hand away. "For sure I'll finish high school. My folks think I should go on to Bible School after that and become a missionary. I guess I'll have plenty of time in the next few years to decide on what to do."

"I don't know," Andrew said, turning red. "I'm not sure how to say this, but have you ever thought about us somehow being together in the future?"

"More than you'll ever know," Anne whispered wistfully, reaching over and squeezing Andrew's hand. "When I think hard about it though, I feel sad because it seems so impossible. We're so many miles apart, but the biggest thing is I'm Protestant and you're Catholic. My dad would never go for that. He tries to convert Catholics into Protestants."

Staff Higgins was suspicious of Andrew and noticed him and Anne doing some handholding. She was going to go over and talk to them, but decided instead to bring it to the attention of the dean of women.

The rest of the evening slipped by all too fast for Andrew and Anne. Then it was curfew time.

Sunday morning they went to church together. After dinner it was time for Andrew to leave. In the afternoon, Anne walked Andrew back to Edith's car.

"I'm always imagining us together," Andrew said as they walked along. "I just hope and pray there's some way it will all work out. In the meantime, I guess we can write and visit the odd time. Why does life have to be so hard for us?"

"I hope no one's been spying on us," Anne said as they got to the car. "Despite all the strict rules, I've had a wonderful weekend. We'd better not hug in case someone is watching."

Andrew held Anne's hand for a brief moment and looked deep into her eyes. "I'll write you next week," he said from the open car window. "I care for you so much."

"I wonder if we'll ever be together," Anne whispered as she stood watching the car pull away.................

The dean of women and the academy principal were in his office standing at the window, watching Anne walk Andrew to his car. Dean Brenda was a severe, tall, very slight lady who kept her hair in a tight bun.

"I think I made a big mistake allowing Anne Prentice to have her male guest here this weekend," she said. "Staff Higgins witnessed this young man hugging Anne in what she described as much more than a 'family hug'. They've been inseparable since he arrived. Last night Staff Higgins reported that she saw them holding hands in the lounge."

"That's him just getting into his car?" the principal asked.

Dean Brenda nodded.

"Oh yes, I recognize him now. He's the young fellow who showed Payne up on Friday night with that weightlifting demonstration. I hope he's family."

"He really isn't and I take full responsibility for the situation we're in. It was one of those grey areas. About five or six years ago Anne lived with Andrew when she was spending a year in Canada with her aunt and uncle. Andrew was a foster boy they took in. This morning I got some more information on him from Anne. The young man lives with his adoptive mother in Alberta, Canada. He just finished grade twelve and here's the frightening part, he's Catholic."

"I see your point," the principal continued gravely. "I think we have to be very vigilant with this sort of thing. I can see it easily getting out of control. We at the academy have an awesome responsibility. Our missionary families have entrusted their children in our keep. In October, Anne's folks will be stopping to see Anne before they head back to Nigeria. I know Anne's dad, Burt, personally. I'll brief him on this young fellow. I'm sure he won't be all that happy knowing his young daughter is interested in a Catholic. I'll get his approval for nipping this thing in the bud. In the meantime, I think we'll have to tighten up our rules for student visitation."

"I couldn't agree more," Dean Brenda added. "This has been a wake-up call for us. With your permission, I'll draw up some new visitation rules."

Unbeknownst to Anne and Andrew, the new rules would stymie their plans for future visits.

CHAPTER SIXTEEN

As Andrew headed back to his Aunt Ruby's place he was on cloud nine. He couldn't get Anne out of his mind, not that he wanted to.

"Have a good visit?" Edith called out as Andrew stepped inside.

"The best! It would have been even better if it wasn't for all the dumb rules they have there. Anne and I hit it off like the old days. Anne's a very beautiful girl as you'll see when I show you her most recent photo. It's a shame we live so far apart. I don't know how it will all work out. She says her dad is suspicious of Catholics and as I just said, they have very strict stupid rules at the academy. I guess I'll just have to be patient."

Andrew was in top spirits on their trip home and talked almost non-stop about Anne. Edith wondered if there would be disappointments ahead for him, but felt it wise not to dampen his enthusiasm by telling him to be cautious..................

Back at the academy, things were getting sticky for Anne. Monday after work, the dean of women called Anne to her office.

"I've talked to the principal at length regarding your weekend visitor. I'm not blaming you for having your friend come since I gave my approval. I can understand how you would be attracted to him. He's a very handsome, extremely athletic young man and from what I've observed, has a pleasing manner about him. Having said that, our mandate here is to educate our young people in a disciplined, Christian atmosphere and not provide a dating service. We are quite concerned that your friend is Catholic. The Bible instructs us not to be unequally yoked. After prayerfully evaluating the situation, the principal and I have decided we must be more specific in our rules for visitors. In the future, any visitor who is of the opposite sex to the student being visited will be restricted to immediate family. That would include brothers, sisters, fathers, mothers, grandparents and aunts or uncles."

"Does this mean Andrew won't be able to visit again?" Anne asked with concern.

"I'm afraid so," Dean Brenda replied with no show of emotion. "Please believe we're only thinking of your best interests in making this decision."

Anne left the dean's office with a heavy heart. "I've been lonely all my life and so has Andrew. Just when it looks like we could get to know each other better, they have to make a stupid new rule."

When Anne wrote Andrew about the new student visiting guidelines he was disappointed. "I guess we'll have to stay in touch by writing," he wrote back. "Maybe we can get together over the Christmas break or next summer once school is out."

A month after Andrew got back from visiting Anne he got a phone call from Father Sebastian in Stohler. Jack Smyth, his old foster father had passed away.

"It's rather a sad situation," Father Sebastian said. "The heavy drinking was finally his undoing. There's only so much alcohol a person's liver can take. He hasn't much for family so I'm handling the funeral arrangements. I was wondering if you could be a pallbearer. I located your foster brothers Ralph and Ron and they'll be pallbearers too. The funeral will be here next Saturday at two PM."

"It's a shock to hear that Jack's gone. I guess he never did get over Lena's death. Sure, I'll do that. I might add it's also a shock that you located Ralph and Ron. From the time I was thirteen till last year I've tried to find them. Finally I gave up. At any rate, tomorrow I'll make arrangements at the place I work to get the day off."

"Man, you're as big as a horse," Ralph exclaimed when Andrew picked up him and Ron at the airport the day of the funeral. "It must have been six or seven years since they split us up."

"Something like that. What are you guys up to?"

"Ralph and I are both working for Northern Airways at The Pas, Manitoba," Ron added. "Our uncle got us on with them. He's been a pilot for them for years. We started something close to a year ago. What are you doing?"

"I'm working at a store in Rocky Ridge for the summer. I finished grade twelve in June. I still haven't figured out what I'll do with myself."

After the funeral, Ron, Ralph and Andrew spent a few hours getting caught up on what had happened since they last saw each other. Then Andrew drove his brothers to the airport.

"It's been so good to see you guys again," Andrew said as they shook hands goodbye. Andrew watched them heading down the tarmac to their small company plane. "Neither of them are big men," Andrew thought. "Handsome buggers though. Wonder when we'll meet up again?".................

Ely Morgan, a middle-aged, single missionary, came to the academy in early September. Ely was a timid little lady. Although her features were plain, the bigness of her heart made up for what she lacked in good looks. She took a one year sabbatical from the mission field to teach a course on child evangelism. Ely knew Anne's folks from her work in Nigeria and soon a friendship developed between Anne and her.

"I had a very lonely life at the mission school," Anne said one evening when Ely dropped by for a visit. "No one knows how I missed my folks. Right now it's almost like they're strangers to me. They were here last week for a few hours, but then they had to go to some church to raise money for their mission work. I probably won't see them again for another three or four years."

"I can appreciate the pain you're going through. I taught at Worsley School a number of years before you started there. I'm still haunted by the sound of the missionary kids sobbing at night in the dorms. The poor kids were desperately lonely for their moms and dads. My views are not popular with the mission board, but if you're a married missionary, I feel you should either remain childless or be prepared to raise your own children. I've seen all too many of these children leave the school warped."

"It's just not fair. I hardly know my sister and now she's already at the Worsley Mission School."

"The Bible tells us 'whatever your lot in life, therewith to be content,' Anne. We all have some pain in our lives. I've sacrificed married life and a family to pursue God's work. Regardless of all I may have passed up, I'm perfectly content knowing I'm in the centre of God's will."

The next weeks proved very trying for Anne. Part of her wanted to reach out to Andrew so their relationship could grow. Part of her wanted to look for God's leading for her life.

"I'm in a real dilemma as to what I should do in the future," Anne began when Ely was visiting her one evening. "Part of me feels I should become a missionary and the other part of me, well...." Anne handed Ely Andrew's picture.

"My, he's certainly a handsome young man. You've told me your young friend is Catholic though."

Anne nodded.

"The way I see it, if you stay focussed on him, the missionary part of the equation will be totally out of the picture. I'm not going to go any further than that. I assure you I'll be praying that God's will for your life be made very clear to you."

Anne had trouble getting to sleep that night. She knew that sooner or later, she'd have to make a choice.

On the first weekend in November the academy held a conference on child evangelism. Ely was the keynote speaker. Since mentioning her dilemma to Ely, Anne spent many hours praying and anguishing over making the right choice for her life. The impact of the messages she heard at the conference tipped the balance for her. At the end of the Sunday evening service, Ely asked all those wishing to dedicate their lives for mission work to come forward. Anne was one of the first to head for the front.

"I've never felt this happy in all my life," Anne said to Ely after the service. "What a relief. It feels like a huge weight has been lifted off my shoulders."

"Being in the centre of God's will is a very satisfying place to be. Now I don't want to use scare tactics, but you should be aware that the devil is going to be working overtime trying to persuade you that the decision you made tonight was the wrong one. I speak from experience. I was about your age when I dedicated my life for missionary work and the devil did his best to convince me I should find a fellow, marry and settle down."

The next morning the principal stopped Ely on the way to her class. "Wasn't Anne Prentice one of the students who dedicated her life to missions last night?"

"She was indeed and it would be hard to find a happier girl."

The next evening Anne wrote Andrew a letter.

Dear Andrew,

Writing this letter is the hardest thing I've ever
done. I hope and pray you won't be too upset. It's
just over three months since your visit. A lot has
changed since then. What I'm trying to say is that my
thinking has changed a lot since then. I don't know
if you could tell that by my last letter or not. Anyway,
here goes. After talking with Ely for many hours over
the last two months, doing a lot of praying and
finally, attending a conference on child evangelism
this weekend, I now feel very strongly that God is
leading me to become a missionary. I probably will
never marry. You already know how I feel about married

missionaries putting their kids in mission schools.

So that's it. Part of me is happy with my decision and part of me is sad. I'm looking at your picture right now and there are tears in my eyes. I hope we can still be friends. I'll stay in touch, but won't write as often.

My plans are to take two years of college here at the seminary once I finish high school, then two or three years of Bible School. The funny thing is my head is telling me that I've made the right decision, but my heart is saying, 'I love you Andrew and why can't we be together?' I guess in the long run its best we don't get too close. That would just make for more heartache. Thank you for always being there for me. Thank you for your kind offer of buying a bus ticket for me so I could spend Christmas with you. The school principal and the dean of women would never go for that and as I just mentioned, it's probably best we don't get too close.

Your dear friend, Anne

Andrew read Anne's letter with a heavy heart. Since their visit in the summer, he'd spent much of his spare time fantasizing about Anne and was so looking forward to them spending the Christmas holidays together.

With a lump in his throat, Andrew handed the letter to Edith.

"My heart aches for you," Edith whispered after reading Anne's letter. "Would you like to talk about it?"

"What's to talk about?" Andrew muttered. "It's just a continuation of what's happened all my life. Just when things start to look up for me, the rug's pulled out from under my feet and I'm knocked down again. I should have known it was too good to be true. What have I got to live for now?"

* *

Some five hundred miles to the northeast, Sister Maria just finished doing the supper dishes. As Andrew lay in his bed, tears of disappointment in his eyes, God miraculously communicated his pain to Maria.

Maria spent several hours on her knees in prayer. This time she felt the need to pray for another person involved with Andrew. Although Maria had no idea who that person was, she prayed for them both and would continue to do so at the end of each day. Andrew and Anne of course knew nothing of it, but a very godly lady was praying daily for their welfare.

* *

Over the next few days Edith did her utmost to help Andrew out of his depressed state, but her efforts didn't seem to be helping. Finally she persuaded him to talk with Father Bernard.

"The 'Dear John' letters are hard to handle," Father Bernard responded after Andrew told of his plight. "It was many years ago when I was about your age that I got my 'see you around' message from my girlfriend. Like you, I was planning on us being together for the rest of our days. World War II was only a few months old when she told me she was joining the army. When I asked her 'what about us,' I'll never forget the puzzled look that came over her face. I had made the age old mistake of thinking her commitment to me was as strong as my commitment to her. I suffered for quite some time with her rejection, just as you're doing now. In retrospect though, God was looking out for my best interest. Molly did join up. She spent two years in the service, but drinking forced her out of the army. She did marry, but that ended in divorce. Over the years she's been in and out of detox centres a number of times. God saw what would be ahead for me if we got together.

I know it's hard to understand, but we must believe that God knows best and that he is guiding us. On the positive side, Anne is dedicating her life to help others and that's a noble calling."

"Why can't I have a bit of happiness? Is that too much to expect from life?"

"Happiness comes from within, not from others. You're very let-down now and at times like these it's hard to remember we have much to be happy for. I have faith in you, Andrew. You're sound. Time will lessen the sting. I'll be praying that you'll be able to work your way through this. I have a good friend who's a professional counsellor. If you'd like, I could arrange an appointment for you with him."

The next few weeks were heavy for both Andrew and Edith. Andrew was very down and spent all his spare time in his room feeling genuinely sorry for himself and re-reading Anne's letter. Edith tried in vain to get him to go for walks in the woodlot with Sobaka.

Finally he followed Father Bernard's and Edith's advice. He began praying about the situation and started seeing the counsellor. After a few sessions with the counsellor and many more hours of soul-searching and prayer, he found peace.

"You're sure upbeat tonight," Edith commented to Andrew as they were finishing supper. "Has anything happened that you'd feel comfortable in sharing with me?"

"I guess it's about time I got hold of myself again. I've been sort of dragging my butt for the last five weeks or so. I know my attitude has made it hard for you too. Talking with Father Bernard and the counsellor got me over my sulk, but up until last night I still wasn't sure what to do with my life. The dream I had was so powerful. You remember me telling you about the dream I had the night after I tried to end it all?"

"Yes I remember."

"Well last night's dream was every bit as powerful. I dreamt about this lady in white. It was so strange. Her face was still a bit unfocused and she didn't say a word. She took me by the hand and led me down this path through the bush. We came to this opening. As we continued walking, I saw a man walking towards us. Then I really did a double-take. The man was me, dressed in priest's clothes. I stared for a moment and then looked back to the lady, but she was gone. Then I awoke."

"You see, Mom, for the last while I've been thinking hard about becoming a priest. Father Bernard supports me, as long as I'm doing it for the right reasons. I want to do something where I can help young people. I talked about that with Anne when I visited her. Although it makes me sad we'll probably never get together, the neat thing is that we both want to go into work to help kids. This dream tells me I'm on the right track."

Later that evening Andrew wrote Anne a letter.

Dear Anne,

Sorry I took so long to write, but your letter kind
of sent me into a tailspin. Seeing both of us have had
such lonely lives, it seemed to me that it was God's
doing that we'd be spending our lives together someday.
I was really down and feeling powerfully sorry for myself
for quite a spell. Finally, with the help of my priest,
a counsellor, Edith and a whole lot of praying, I got
back on track. Like you, I've prayed a lot about you
and me. Even though I still love you, I can see where

you've got to do what you feel is God's will for your
life and so do I. I've been thinking a lot about what
to do and have decided to go to seminary and study to
become a priest. The neat thing is that although we're
in very different religions, we both will be trying to
help young people. Father Bernard will be helping me find
a seminary. I'm happy for both of us. Still, when I look
at your picture, I'm wishing I could be with you. Our
hearts still pine for each other, but I guess that's not
what God wants in our lives. Will stay in touch.

Love, Andrew

When Anne opened Andrew's letter, her feeling of
apprehension turned to relief when she read that he was
able to accept her decision to become a missionary. Still, the
mention of them pining for each other brought tears to her
eyes.

"It's funny," she mused. "Even though I feel relief, my
heart is crying for what could have been."...........

As the days slipped by, Anne did her best to concentrate
on her studies and relegate her feelings for Andrew to the
back burner.

In late spring, she signed up for an academy-sponsored
program amongst the slum children of Mexico City. A week
after Anne signed up, Ely dropped by her room for a visit.

"I'm happy to see you've volunteered for our summer
program in Mexico City. It will give you valuable insight
into what mission work entails. How are you feeling about
committing your life to missionary work?"

"For the most part I'm feeling pretty good about it, but it's
hard at times to get Andrew out of my mind. Once in a while

I have doubts whether I'm making the right decision. Like last night for example. I was thinking about Andrew before I went to sleep and I had this very vivid dream about us being together in bed. I can't tell you about the details because it's too embarrassing. At any rate, when I woke up, I'd have sworn I could smell Andrew's cologne. What are your thoughts?"

"It's normal to occasionally have doubts, Anne, but be aware that the devil will use every trick in the book to get you to change your mind. I have a suggestion that might seem heartless, but give it some prayerful thought. I see you still have Andrew's picture on your desk. I can't imagine anyone asking you to end your friendship with him, but as long as his picture is in prominence like that you won't be able to focus on your studies or your calling to dedicate your life to the Lord's work. The dream is a good example of how low Satan will stoop. He used sexual debauchery to try to sway you. My suggestion is that you put his picture away or at least in a place where you're not constantly staring at it."

"Changing the subject, I've just accepted a position here at the academy. I'll be going on permanent staff continuing to teach child evangelism. Sometime back, the principal told me he felt there was a real need to teach this course on an on-going basis.

After Ely left, Anne debated long and hard about putting Andrew's picture away. She couldn't bear the thought of putting it in her desk drawer. Finally, she compromised by putting it on top of her dresser. Moving Andrew's picture did help some and although Anne still thought of him, with the passage of time, the strong longing she had to be with him was starting to wane.

Anne thoroughly enjoyed her work in Mexico City working with young families in the slums. Holding little new-born babies, however, made her long to have her own children.

Like Anne, Andrew made a concerted effort to put his feelings for the one he loved on the back burner and concentrate on his career choice. With Father Bernard's help he enrolled in Morning Star seminary in northeast Alberta. Unbeknownst to Andrew, the seminary was located less than a hundred miles from the convent where his mother took her training....................

Time passed and soon Anne finished her grade twelve. Andrew and she exchanged letters four or five times a year. Andrew was doing well in seminary and like Anne, was working the holidays in church outreach with children.

With the passage of time, Anne and Andrew continued to feel in the centre of God's will. Although the love they had for each other was now muted, it was still there, waiting for fate to fan it into full flame again.

CHAPTER SEVENTEEN

Shortly after the semester break in Anne's second year in the mission college, a tragedy occurred that shook her faith to its foundation. At the start of the school year, she worked on a class project with Adam Foot, a first year student and they became good friends. Adam was also a missionary kid so they had lots in common. Adam excelled in sports, was on the academy football team and planned on becoming a phys-ed teacher. The two had many long talks in the student lounge. Although Anne thought a lot of Adam, she made sure their relationship stayed strictly on a platonic level. At the Christmas break, Adam left to spend the holidays with family. A few days later Anne got a letter from him.

Dear Anne,

I hope you won't hate me when you read this letter. It's bad enough that I hate myself. I'm sorry I didn't have the courage to talk to you in person. At any rate, here goes. I'm sure my roommate Marvin and I are homosexuals. God alone knows how many hours we've pleaded with the Lord to deliver us from this horrible sin. Right now the devil seems to be getting the upper hand. Both Marvin and I feel terribly guilty about it and we're trying to figure out what to do. After the Christmas break we're going to try to get different roommates.

Hopefully that will help. I trust God forgives me, but if I don't get deliverance, the thought of destroying myself keeps cropping up. I know that's not the answer though. I know you'll keep this in confidence. Please pray for Marvin and me.

Your friend, Adam

Anne was sick with worry after reading the letter and spent many hours praying for the two boys. She thought of talking to Ely about the situation, but because of Adam's request for confidentiality she knew she couldn't. Anne was aware of the strident fundamentalist views the school held and was fearful of what the staff's reaction would be if they discovered what was going on.

A week after the Christmas break and after many hours of prayer, Adam and Marvin felt compelled to confess their homosexual behaviour to the dean of men. They met with him, told him of their homosexual relationship and requested that one of them be moved to a different room.

Rather than granting them their wish, the dean of men contacted the principal. The next day, Adam and Marvin were summoned to appear before a meeting of the staff. They were given a merciless interrogation.

"Marvin and Adam, under normal circumstances this type of sinful conduct would have resulted in your immediate expulsion," the principal read from a prepared statement. "The only reason we're not expelling you is that you came to the dean of men on your own volition. All of us have spent many hours in prayer over this matter. At our staff meeting this afternoon we decided to grant you another chance. For the rest of the year you will be billeted in separate rooms and are to have no contact except under supervision by a staff member. We staff members are sworn to secrecy and for the good of the school and yourselves, we think it best that this be kept from the rest of the student body. Finally, Adam and Marvin, may God grant you forgiveness for this horrible sin you've committed. May he give you the strength never to engage in this immoral act again."

The two boys left the meeting completely shell-shocked. That same evening, Adam and Marvin were moved into their own separate rooms. The dean of men thought it wise for the immediate to isolate them from other roommates. Unfortunately for the boys, some member of the staff was not as sworn to secrecy as the principal said they would be. Tongues began to wag and before long the whole student body knew what happened.

Marvin couldn't take the pressure and quit school the next weekend, dejected, humiliated and heartbroken.

A few days later, Adam didn't appear for breakfast or morning classes. The dean of men found him dead in his room from a massive overdose of sleeping pills.

Anne was devastated with the news of Adam's death. She'd talked with him two nights before and he told her of the awful night of interrogation Marvin and he were forced to endure. He was very down and said with everyone at school knowing about it, he didn't know how much longer he could hold on. His folks were home on furlough and when he talked with them at Christmas, they had been very unsympathetic towards him. He confided to Anne that he really didn't have much to live for.

A couple of weeks later, Anne was still very distraught over Adam's death. Finally she asked the dean of women if she could meet with her, the principal, the dean of men and Ely to talk about the concerns she had.

As they were walking to the meeting, Ely advised Anne that although she was there to support her, she wouldn't engage in the discussion as she hadn't been at the meeting with Adam and Marvin.

"I wonder if all of us didn't fail Adam and Marvin," Anne began. "I feel guilty because Adam confided in me. He told me how he hated what Marvin and he did and how they prayed for deliverance. He also mentioned that suicide was an option for him and that it was becoming impossible for him to manage with all the student body finding out about it. Couldn't we have done more? Couldn't they have been given counselling?"

"Recognizing that you and Adam were friends, let the two deans, Ely and I offer you our heart-felt sympathy," the principal replied. "I can assure you that I advised our staff to treat this issue in the strictest of confidence. I don't know who leaked the contents of the meeting we had with the boys and we're certainly not happy about it. Not only do we regret that confidential information at the meeting was leaked, we are most devastated with Adam's death. Without question, it's the worst thing that has ever occurred at this academy. Having said that, we still maintain that God views homosexuality as a horrible sin. We felt that this sin had to be dealt with by separating the boys. Dean Forman, many of the other staff and I spent many hours agonizing and praying about this terrible incident before we met with the boys. We have re-evaluated the meeting we had with the two young men and all agree that we did what the scripture required us to do."

"But couldn't you have talked with them one on one, or got an independent counsellor to speak with them? Adam confided in me he told you at your meeting that he was thinking suicidal thoughts. Wasn't that a cry for help? I feel so horrible. I'm constantly asking myself if there was more I could have done."

"Both boys knew how repulsed I am with homosexual behaviour," Dean Forman interrupted. "Nonetheless, I offered Adam counselling after the news got out and Marvin had left. He had wanted to talk with me the night he took his life, but I had other commitments. Tentatively, we were to have met the next night. I recognize that all of us have pangs about this tragedy. Like you Anne, all of us wonder if there wasn't more we could have done. That's the pain of dealing with a suicide. There never is a clear answer. That's why we're here talking with you tonight. In the end though, we all have to accept that it was his own decision to end his life, not ours."

"Please bear in mind, Anne, we did what we thought was right, based on scripture and after much prayer," Dean Brenda interjected. "I'm sorry if you think that our efforts were insufficient. As Dean Forman and you just said, suicide always leaves one with the haunting question of what could have been done differently. May I reiterate, based on scripture, we did what we thought was right. You'll have to excuse us now. Our staff prayer meeting starts in five minutes. Thank you for voicing your concerns, Anne. We will be remembering you and Adam's folks in prayer this evening."

"Right now, other than you, I'm totally disillusioned with the whole staff here at the academy," Anne said to Ely once the meeting was over and they were by themselves. "I can see them being upset with Adam and Marvin for what they were doing, but I thought Christianity was about love and compassion. It seems to me they're saying that if they pray long and hard enough about something, then the resolution to that problem is God-given. What if their solution is a stupid one? Does that mean that God is stupid?"

"I would have to agree with you. I wasn't at the meeting with the boys, but the way I see it, the dean of men and the principal are too fixated on the legalistic side of their

Christianity. More compassion could have been used. Try to remember though, Anne, part of the process of maturing as a Christian is in accepting different points of view. God has instructed us to accept and obey those in authority over us. Whether we like it or not, that means being submissive to the staff here at the academy."

Over the next few months Anne was haunted by Adam's death. The callous attitude of the principal and deans weighed heavy on her.

The Easter break brought an even more stressful time for Anne. A few days before school was out, Anne received a telegram from the mission board her folks worked under. The telegram advised Anne that her mother had been admitted to a hospital in London, suffering from severe depression. She had requested to see her daughter. The board provided Anne with a return air ticket and on Easter Friday, she took a flight to London.

Uppermost in Anne's mind were the wherefores and whys of her mom's depression. When she phoned the mission board they had been quite nebulous. She asked them to have her father phone her, but up to the day of her departure, she had not received a call from him.

With apprehension, Anne walked into her mom's room. Jessie was sitting on the edge of her bed, looking most disconsolate. Anne was shocked at how much her mom had aged. Her once beautiful auburn hair was now nearly all white. She seemed so much smaller now and her face was lined. Jessie slowly got to her feet, embraced Anne and started to sob uncontrollably.

"I'm so happy you came," she finally blurted out. Jessie motioned Anne to a chair and then sat down on her bed again. She cupped her head in her hands and wept. Finally regaining her composure, she reached over and took Anne's hand.

"I'm so glad to see my little girl again, but I have such a sad story to tell you. Please bear with me if I break down as I piece it together for you."

"Go ahead, Mom. Take as much time as you need. I'll understand if you have to stop. Remember, you don't have to tell me anything you're not comfortable sharing."

"Thank you," Jessie responded after a long pause. "Being on the mission field has been difficult for me. I've never told you this before, but without question, the hardest part was being separated from you for all these years and now it's repeating itself with your sister. Our marriage started out good, even though your dad was a bit on the controlling side. The first few years after you were born were alright. Then I had to drop my seven-year-old girl off at the mission school." Jessie again broke down. Anne moved her chair closer and put her arm around her mom.

"I cried myself to sleep for over a month. I got little comfort from your father. His favourite saying was, 'the Lord's work must take first place in our lives.' He said it a thousand times if he said it once. I got so I could have killed him every time I heard him say it."

"I know where you're coming from, Mom. Every time you brought me back to the mission school after a holiday, I'd cry myself to sleep for weeks too, but look, Mom, despite it all, I made it through."

"Yes you did and I thank the Lord every day for that. If being lonely for my kids was the only problem I had, I guess I could have managed." Jessie tried hard to continue, but again her face crumbled. Finally she gained control. "You're an adult now, Anne, and if you can manage it, I need to talk to you about your dad's and my personal life."

"I'm here for you, Mom. Let it all out."

Jessie nodded. "This is embarrassing for me, but it's important for you to know. You see, your dad's and my bedroom life was never that great, but I accepted it. Some time ago your dad became impotent, or so he claimed. I tried to get him to get medical help, but he declined. The hardest part for me was that he cut off all intimacies. There was no more hugging, kissing or touching. At the time, I thought it was because he felt so uptight about his condition."

"Your father was working with a young indigenous lady on translating some of the New Testament into the local dialect. Her name was Rosey. His little office was on the other side of the village. Your dad often worked after sundown at his office as it was cooler then. We'd have supper once he got home. Around seven one evening, I got this strange almost eerie compulsion to go to his office. I got my bicycle out and a few minutes later I was nearing the compound."

"It had been a blistering hot day and by the time I got there I had worked up quite a sweat. A couple of hundred feet from the office I dismounted and parked my bike. I was ambling along, trying to cool down. I heard a noise coming from the small storage shed behind the office. Again, I had this strange urge to check it out. It was horrible. I looked in the back window of the shed. In the twilight I saw your dad and the young lady helper lying on a blanket on the floor. They were having sex. I didn't say a word. I took his jeep and drove to the police station. They were the only ones in the village with a phone."

"I contacted the regional head of the mission and told him

what happened. It was an awful ordeal to go through, almost like a circus."

"The regional head for the mission came out. Guess what he did first? He fired your dad's young helper. Your dad asked for my forgiveness and although I felt under pressure, I forgave him. All this of course was done in front of the mission head. Your dad vowed before God that the relationship had only been going on for a month and promised never to stray again. I wondered about his one month figure as he had been impotent, or claimed to have been so for about six months."

"It came to a head again three weeks ago. After your dad and I made our peace, things were not too bad for awhile. Although he was still impotent, he would hug and kiss me the odd time. One day I was going through our closets and found the box we kept the condoms in. I recalled there had been about thirty of them left the last time we used one. Anyway, now there was only one left."

"I decided to look into things on my own. I found out that Rosey returned to her home village some seventy-five miles to the north. After I drove your dad to work, I took the jeep, drove to her village and found her at her married sister's place. At first she was afraid to confide in me, but after sympathizing with her for losing her job, I won her over. According to Rosey, the affair had been going on for around six months. She said it started shortly after she began working on the project. Her sister interrupted Rosey and told me that some five months ago she had warned her sister that even though they used condoms, there was still the possibility she could get pregnant."

"When I confronted your dad with Rosie's version of the length of the affair, he became quite irate that I'd take her word over his. I told him about all those missing condoms and what Rosie's sister said. He grudgingly admitted he may have underestimated the length of the affair. Then he said the most hurtful words I've ever been told in my life." Fighting for control she whispered, "He said because I had gained weight, I was no longer physically attractive to him and that I was to blame for his impotency. Although he didn't come right out and say it, he implied that I was responsible for him finding another woman. I haven't spoken to him since."

Again Anne put her arms around her mom and comforted her.

"What are your plans, Mom?" she finally asked.

"I wish I knew. The mission board has your dad in the regional office for the time being. They're hoping our differences can be resolved. I'm having an awful time. I've never felt this down in my life. Strangely enough, despite how he's hurt me, I'm pretty sure I still love him."

"I phoned the mission board several times and asked them to get Dad to phone me. I can see now why he didn't return my calls. It's hard not to despise him for what he did to you, but I guess that's not the Christian way."

Anne stayed with her mom for five days, giving her all the support she could. She had wanted to contact her dad and straighten him out, but Jessie implored her not to do so.

On the last day of Anne's visit, her mom seemed a bit more cheerful. "Thank you so much for coming to look in on me. It's helped me immeasurably." After a long pause she continued, "I've been doing a lot of thinking and praying over the situation with your dad and I've finally come to peace with myself. I've had to swallow a lot, but I'm thinking that in another week or so I'll go back to your father. Really, what other choices do I have? Besides, the Bible tells us to forgive seventy times seven and despite his inadequacies, I think I still care for him."

"I know it's been a difficult decision, Mom. I'll support you in whatever choice you make. Remember, regardless of what happens between you and Dad, I'll always be here for you."

The flight back to the states was a time of sober reflection for Anne. As she gazed down at the ocean some thirty thousand feet below, she was deep in thought. "What an awful six months it's been. First there was Adam's death and now Dad's infidelity. How will Mom make out? What's next?"

Adam's death and her folks' marital problems continued to burden Anne after she returned to her studies. She talked with the student counsellor, but that was a dead-end. He was male and viewed the action the principal took with Adam and Marvin to be both scriptural and appropriate. In regard to her father's unfaithfulness, he stated unequivocally that marriage was sacred. From his perspective, despite the grave sin her dad had committed, her mom had no choice but to forgive her husband and return to him.

Finally, when the pressure was getting too much for her, she wrote Andrew. She told him about Adam's death, her dad's unfaithfulness and how she was struggling to come to grips with all of it.

I'm also beginning to have some doubts about my career choice. I got to thinking that I was still a young teenager when I decided to become a missionary and never marry. Was that God's leading, or was I just an impressionable young girl swayed by some missionary sales pitch? When I started working with young toddlers, I realized how much I longed for my own babies. I'm really wrestling with all of this now. What with the way the staff handled the Adam and Marvin thing, Adam's death

and then Dad's behaviour, I've not seen too much real
Christian love or compassion of late. There, I
feel better now after venting to you. I hope you're
doing alright with your studies. As for me, I'm going
to have to think long and hard about what I'll do
once university is out. Please write me as soon as you
can. I respect your views and I need all the ideas I can
get.

Love, Anne

As Andrew read Anne's letter, his heart was racing. "How
can this be? How can this be?" he kept repeating. He had a
term paper to write, but that would have to wait.

Dear Anne,

I just finished reading your letter. My heart goes
out to you over the loss of your friend and your
dad two-timing your mom. I'll be praying for your
mom. I wouldn't mind giving your dad a bit of a thrashing.
He sure deserves it. I could hardly believe my eyes
when I read that you're having exactly the same feelings
of uncertainty about your chosen career as I am. I have
one more year of seminary before I take my vows of chastity.
I guess we all have our own personnel demons that we fight.
As I've told you, during my summer breaks, I have also
been working with young kids. I too yearn for children
of my own. Then I must confess I'm still infatuated with
you. That's part of the problem. I've tried hard to think
of you in a platonic way, but it doesn't work. You're just
too pretty and I'm too hot-blooded for my own good. I know
if I told you of the fantasies I have of you, you'd run a
cold shower for me. Getting more serious, it looks like
we both have to be sure our choices of vocations are well
thought out. Before I start on my last year of seminary

I'm going to talk with Father Bernard and maybe someone higher up in the church. I know it's been a heavy time for you, but it's so nice to touch base again. I'll be praying that both of us get clarity on the choices we must make.

Love, Andrew

With only six weeks left until the summer break, Andrew had to concentrate on his studies. Nonetheless, he still spent many long hours working and reworking his choice of a career. It wasn't helping the process any that he was again wondering if fate was bringing Anne and him back together. Andrew took time out from his studying to write letters to Edith and Father Bernard regarding the uncertainty he felt.

Once the last exam was written, Andrew headed back home to spend some time with his mom. It was over five months since Andrew had been home and they were overjoyed to see each other.

"As I wrote you, I'm beginning to have qualms about going into the priesthood," Andrew said as he helped his mom prepare supper. "I've spent a lot of time thinking about it and the more I ponder it, the more uncertain I'm becoming."

"It would do you a world of good to talk it over with Father Bernard. He's a good head and discussing it with him will give you another perspective. I have complete faith that you'll make the right decision. It's far wiser to have second thoughts now than after you've taken your vows of chastity. Just remember, even if you choose not to become a priest, all your training will put you in good stead for many other lines of work."

The next morning Andrew phoned Father Bernard and in the afternoon drove into town to see him.

"To doubt is human," Father Bernard replied, after hearing about Andrew's misgivings. "I don't know if this will be of any comfort, but I and probably every other student studying to become a priest have had periods of uncertainty. The tricky part is in evaluating these doubts to see if they are major or minor."

"God alone knows how much I've prayed about this. You see, Father, my biggest problem is my strong sex drive. It's embarrassing to have to talk about it. So far the only one I was ever intimate with was Blanche. I'm afraid of what would happen once I'm a priest, though, if I can't control it."

"Studies have shown that as a rule, sexual abuse before a person is fully mature can cause problems with the individual's sexuality later in their lives," Father Bernard continued. "Without question, it affects them emotionally. It may well be that your experience with Blanche is still impacting on you. I would suggest we make an appointment for you to see Father Black. I know him personally and he's a fine Christian. He was a practising psychologist before he joined the church. He has helped several priests and nuns with all sorts of problems. Some have stayed with the church and some have left. His territory covers all of Western Canada. Unfortunately, it's going to be a long jaunt for you to go see him as his office is in Regina. He was in this area just a month ago and probably won't be making his rounds again for another four or five months. I'm sure he'll be of great help to you. Without question, your mother was right when she advised that it's better to make your decision now rather than after you're a priest."

Towards the end of the school year, Anne too had her day of counselling. She met with the new dean of women to discuss her future plans.

"You are wise to think long and hard about choosing a vocation based on a decision you made when you were a young teenager," Dean Sarah began after listening to Anne. "I've known quite a few people who, like you, made a career choice at a young age only to find they had no aptitude whatsoever for the calling they thought the Lord had led them into. That choice you made when you were that age could well have been God's leading, but it's also possible you were swept off your feet by the romance of the moment. I feel strongly that for a Christian, finding the right career is a combination of seeking God's will and looking into vocations they have the aptitude for. Unfortunately, I can't give you an easy answer. The only thing I might add is you're on the right track in prayerfully and objectively thinking your choices through."

Over the next weeks, Anne spent many hours in pragmatic thinking and prayer. Finally she had her answer. "I'll teach for one year. This will give me a chance to see if I'm cut out to be a teacher and what's going to happen with my relationship with Andrew. Next year, I'll be in a better position to make a decision on whether or not I should return to Bible School and study to become a missionary."

Anne's Uncle Arthur was now teaching in Red Deer. On a whim, Anne phoned him to see if he knew of any teaching positions open at the school division he worked in.

"There are no positions in our school that I'm aware of. You'll have to check with our superintendent and the superintendents in the surrounding school divisions for openings in the area. I imagine they may well be needing teachers in the other city schools, or for that matter in the communities around Red Deer."

"Why not come up for a visit?" Dorothy interjected on their phone extension. "We haven't seen you in a long time and it would also give you the opportunity to check on work first hand."

"That sounds great. I finished my second year of university a few days ago and have nothing planned for the next while. I should contact the bus depot for schedules. Would it work out for you and Uncle if I came right away?"

"That would be fine for us," Dorothy replied. "We're not going on holidays till the third week in July. It will be so good to see you again."

When Anne contacted the bus depot for schedules, she discovered there would be a twelve hour wait-over in Winnipeg. She finally decided to take the bus to Winnipeg, fly to Calgary and then take the bus to Red Deer. Once Anne had finalized her travel plans, she phoned Andrew. He was ecstatic with the news. She would arrive in Calgary at two in the afternoon. The only inconvenience would be a three hour wait in Calgary to catch the bus to Red Deer.

At six the next afternoon, Anne boarded the bus for the long trip to Winnipeg. She was very excited with the thought of seeing Andrew again. Unfortunately, Anne found herself seated by an older lady who was intent on telling her all the trials and tribulations life had brought her way. Finally the old lady wound down and went to sleep. As the bus droned on and on, Anne was deep in thought.

"Would things have changed or would they be the same as they were on Andrew's last visit? Is God bringing us together for a reason?"

"Dear Lord, if it's your will, let it be forever," she prayed.

CHAPTER EIGHTEEN

Anne slept intermittently throughout the night and at six AM, the bus pulled into Winnipeg. After breakfast in the bus depot, she took a taxi to the airport. In early afternoon her airplane touched down in Calgary. She was waiting for her luggage when someone behind her tapped her on the shoulder. Anne whirled around and let out a cry of glee. There stood Andrew, a wide grin on his face.

"You've become even more beautiful," he blurted out as he hugged her and kissed her full on the lips.

Anne reached up with both hands, cupped Andrew's head and pulled him even closer.

"I've wanted to do this for many, many, years," Andrew whispered in Anne's ear. "I knew our first kiss would be good, but not this good. WOW!"

"It's been a long wait. I prayed most of last night while I was on the bus. I asked God to work things out between us. As for you, Andrew, in my unbiased view, you're the handsomest guy I've ever seen."

Andrew put Anne's luggage in his car and after grabbing a bite to eat, they were on their way.

"What kind of a reception do you think I'll get from Arthur and Dieter?" Andrew asked once they were on the road. "We certainly didn't part on the best of terms. Dorothy was there to say goodbye when I left, but they weren't."

"I think you'll be pleasantly surprised with Arthur. As for Dieter, there's no worry there. He's gone to Europe for the summer. Uncle and Aunt visited me three years ago. Arthur used to be, well...."

"A pompous ass," Andrew interjected.

"Yes, that about says it, but he's changed a lot for the better. I think it had to do with problems they had with Dieter. He got into some serious trouble. There's nothing to worry about though. I'm an adult now and they have no more control over me."

Anne was tired so curled up on the front seat, laid her head on Andrew's lap and was soon asleep. As Andrew glanced down at his sleeping beauty, he'd occasionally run his fingers lightly over her hair. "I wonder if we'll be spending the rest of our lives together," he thought wistfully.

Andrew woke Anne up when they got to a service station on the outskirts of Red Deer.

"I haven't told you much about my talk with Father Bernard," Andrew said once they were in the car again. "He gave me his full support and referred me to Father Black in Regina. Father Black was a psychologist before he became a priest. Now he just works with the clergy of the church doing counselling. I've an appointment to see him in three days. I don't know. If you'd asked me last night what my plans for the future were, I'd have said I was leaning toward not taking my last year of seminary. Now, unless the counsellor is very convincing, I'm pretty sure I won't. Want to know what swayed me?"

"I'm not sure," Anne said with an impish grin. "If I had to guess though, I'd say it's got something to do with us."

"Yes you're right. It was the way you kissed me. Up until then I didn't know how strongly you felt for me. As you were sleeping with your head on my lap, I was trying to imagine how exciting it would be to make love to you. Then I thought, if I become a priest, I'll never know what that would be like."

"We'll have to do an awful lot of soul-searching about what both of us want for our vocations. For the present, I'm keeping my fingers crossed that relations will be a bit more amicable between Arthur and me."

Both Arthur and Dorothy were on the front step to greet Anne and Andrew. "Welcome to our home again," Arthur said, extending his hand to Andrew. "I owe you an apology for the way I treated you when you stayed with us and in particular how badly I handled that set-to you and Dieter had. I should have looked you up sooner. I shouldn't make excuses for myself, but when Dieter got into trouble a few years later, I was so ashamed of what he did that I couldn't seem to handle it. Will you forgive me?"

"Of course I will," Andrew replied. "Every family has their problems. I'm sure when I find my biological parents there will be lots of skeletons I'll have to deal with."

Over a cup of tea, Arthur carried on. "Our biggest problem, no, I've got to be honest, my biggest problem was I was trying too hard to make a perfect son out of Dieter. I made the mistake of gloating with him over his good points and overlooking his bad ones. That's a convoluted way of saying we spoiled him rotten. When he sexually attacked you, Anne, instead of facing it, I minimized what he did. It was unfair to Andrew, but by trivializing his attack on you, it taught Dieter that we considered his assault of no great consequence."

"The year before you two came to our house, Dieter was involved in another incident," Dorothy interjected. "He exposed himself to a small boy on the way home from school. We should have done something then, but we didn't. When he assaulted you, Anne, we should have seen the handwriting on the wall."

"It was my fault," Arthur interrupted. "I was selfishly trying to save face and unwilling to admit my model son had a real problem. It all came to a head when Dieter was fifteen. He volunteered to help a mentally challenged twelve-year-old boy after school till the boy's mother got home from work. The mother was divorced and he was an only child. It was just horrible." Arthur covered his face with his hands.

"The mother got suspicious of what was going on between her son and Dieter and had someone set up a surveillance camera," Dorothy carried on. "The film showed Dieter sexually assaulting the boy. The police called in Dieter for questioning. Although he admitted to it, he insisted it was the first time it happened. The mother had evidence that showed it had been going on for a couple of months. Dieter was still legally underage and they couldn't use the witness of the boy. It was so upsetting for us, especially for Arthur, seeing he was a school teacher. Dieter had to attend a reform school for a year. While he went to that school he was allowed to stay at home with us. It was a lengthy commute for me to drive him each day."

"It's a sad story," Arthur interjected. "I learned my lesson the hard way. I was so wrapped up in the legalistic side of religion that I missed the core concept that compassion and love are really what being a Christian is all about. We felt we owed it to both of you to tell it all. After things got sorted out with Dieter, he took four years of university. He now teaches in Toronto. He doesn't share much of his personal life with us, but tells us he's doing alright."

Anne went to her aunt and uncle and gave them a hug.

"I guess every family goes through some painful experiences," Anne continued. "I imagine you knew about the problems Mom and Dad had earlier this year?"

"The last contact we had with them was at Christmas when they sent us a card," Dorothy replied, looking perplexed.

With tears in her eyes, Anne shared the horrors of her dad's infidelity and her mom's depression.

"I feel so sad that my brother brought so much pain to your mom, your sister and you," Dorothy said. "When we're forced to go through these trials, it's hard to have faith that God will help us to the other side. He always does though."

"From experience, I've learned that even though we proclaim that we're God's emissaries, we're only human and can slip," Arthur added. "Let's talk about something a bit more positive now. We know that you're looking for a teaching position, Anne. Now what about you Andrew? Are you still in seminary?"

"There's one more year before I'll be able to take my vows of chastity and become a priest. Of late though, I'm having second thoughts about taking my final year, what with the way Anne and I now feel for each other."

"Andrew and I have spent countless hours anguishing and praying over making the right career choices in our lives,"

Anne said. "Originally, I'd planned on staying single and becoming a missionary working with kids. Andrew's plan was to become a priest and minister to young people. The strange thing was we both worked in church outreach helping with children during our summer breaks. After working with youngsters, both of us came to realize how much we wanted children of our own. Andrew is going to Regina in a couple of days to talk his situation over with a church counsellor. Tomorrow, we'll both be looking at what the job market looks like around here."

After an enjoyable visit, Dorothy showed Anne and Andrew to their bedrooms in the newly renovated basement. As soon as Dorothy went back upstairs, Anne hugged Andrew tight and gave him a very warm goodnight kiss.

"What a day it's been," she whispered. "There's been so much emotional stuff I feel like I'm on overload. Remember, Andrew, no sneaking into my bedroom in the middle of the night."

"Let's make a deal. I'll go for that as long as I get one more kiss."

"What's a girl to do?" Anne sighed, wrapping her arms around Andrew again.

The next morning at breakfast, Arthur gave Anne the names, addresses and phone numbers of the school superintendents for the school districts in the central part of the province. After finishing breakfast, Anne and Andrew were on their way.

"I haven't seen the church counsellor yet, but I think I should check the job prospects with the Child Welfare Department," Andrew said as they backed out the driveway.

Their first stop was for Andrew at the Child Welfare Regional office. Andrew met with the personnel supervisor, gave him his résumé and told him of his feelings of uncertainty in becoming a priest.

"I'm quite impressed," the supervisor stated after reading the résumé. "We'd classify your training in the seminary as a minimum of a Bachelor of Arts degree. I don't know if you recognize this, but having been a foster child gives you, shall I say, an inside track. For better or worse, you know how the system works. Of greater importance, we have found that workers who were brought up in the system tend to have more compassion for the disadvantaged child. We are reviewing our personnel needs next week. I'm very interested in your résumé, Andrew and I'll go over it with my supervisor. After meeting with your counsellor, if you decide not to continue your studies to become a priest, get back in touch with me. We have a couple of staff taking maternity leave. Should you decide you wish to work for us, I feel fairly confident we'll have a position for you."

"If I decide not to take my last year of seminary, this lead looks promising," Andrew said to Anne when he got back to the car. "The personnel officer wants me to drop back in a few days. He said he was impressed with my résumé. Now let's see what luck is in store for you."

After several phone calls they drove out to Innsburg, a town some twenty miles from Red Deer. Anne met with the superintendent of schools.

"I've just got word that the grade three teacher in the elementary school in town is retiring," the superintendent said after reviewing Anne's résumé. "Her position will come open this September. There are also a number of positions I'm trying to fill in the smaller centres that surround Innsburg. I like your résumé as a whole. It's a bonus you worked two summers in Mexico with a youth program. I think you'd do well in our division. The only problem I see is that it would be mandatory for you to take a six- week teacher training course, seeing you attended university in the states. There's one being taught at the college in Red Deer starting in mid-July. Call me again next Monday and I'm sure we'll have something for you."

"Well, it looks pretty promising for both of us," Andrew commented as they were driving back to Arthur's and Dorothy's place. "Nothing written in stone yet, but I bet we'll both have firm offers within a week or so."

By ten the next morning, Andrew was on the road to Regina to see the church counsellor. He was so deep in thought that he hardly noticed the passing scenery. At nine in the evening, Andrew stopped at a roadside motel for the night. Although he was bone-tired after his long drive, sleep wouldn't come. He spent several hours lying in bed, working and reworking his state of affairs, trying to anticipate what the counsellor would say and what his responses should be.

At seven, after breakfast, Andrew was on the road for the half hour drive to the church compound. Andrew arrived at the administration building fifteen minutes early. After parking his car, he spent a few more minutes again rehearsing what he would say. Finally he went inside, found the right office and knocked on the door.

"Come on in," a male voice called out. Andrew opened the door and stepped inside. Framed in the doorway of his inner office stood the church counsellor. He was a big man, at least six foot two. He was dark complexioned with a bushy head of hair that was starting to turn white. His keen blue eyes seemed to see right through you. Andrew had expected that he'd be older and smaller.

"You must be Andrew Ogilvy," he continued, striding over and shaking Andrew's hand.

"That's right, Father," Andrew replied. "I hope I haven't kept you waiting."

"You're right on time," he said, smiling. "The secretary isn't in today so I have to be counsellor, receptionist and steno."

The counsellor ushered Andrew into his small Spartan office, closed the door and showed him to a chair.

"I've been going over your file since eight this morning. You're certainly sound academically. I've just finished reading Father Bernard's recent letter on your behalf. I see you've had some rough breaks in the past. I'm going to do a lot of listening this morning so the floor is yours."

Over the next hour Andrew poured out his soul. He told of the good homes he'd been in and the bad ones, his friendship with Anne and his misgivings of continuing his studies to become a priest. The only time the Father interrupted was to get clarification on some point.

"Let's deal with your concern that you may have chosen a career of becoming a priest on the rebound," the counsellor stated when Andrew was finished. "This was when Anne told you she planned on becoming a missionary and would remain single. I would rate this concern of secondary importance. There are very few priests or nuns who at some time in their career didn't question whether they'd chosen the right vocation for the right reasons. As you were talking what I was focussing on was the strong longing you've had since you were a youngster to help kids."

"Now, about the other reason you gave; your concern over

your strong sexual drive. In First Corinthians chapter seven the Apostle Paul lays out the guidelines our church follows in priests and nuns staying celibate. Paul carefully states that they are his suggestions and although he indicates that in his view, one can serve the church better if they remain unmarried, he also says that those who can not remain celibate should marry. Unfortunately, there are some of our clergy who should have taken his advice in that area. You and you alone know how strong your sexual nature is and if it would be a stumbling block to you if you should become a priest. Tragically, you were sexually abused when you were still a young boy. From case histories we know that sexual abuse of this nature at an immature age can contribute to future problems."

"God alone knows how I've prayed over this, Father. Pardon me for being frank. We're told that masturbation is not the way to go, but being single, I feel the alternative could be much worse."

"I would have to concur with you on that. We all know of clergy in the Catholic Church, in Protestant Churches and for that matter in all religions, whose uncontrolled sexual passions have caused terrible damage. Far better you recognize the strength of your sexual drive now. Sadly, too many of our own have disregarded their sexual natures and brought reproach to the church and themselves. Of far greater concern is the irreparable damage they have caused to the individuals they've abused."

"Another thing you should recognize, Andrew. Although becoming a priest is a noble calling, you don't have to be one in order to help people. There are numerous lines of work where you'd be helping others. There are the vocations of teachers, social workers, nurses and doctors to mention a few. In the final analysis, you will have to make your own decision. From what I've heard, it appears that you're both compassionate and intelligent. I have faith you'll do the right thing."

"I can't tell you how much our talk has meant to me," Andrew said getting to his feet. "I'm able to see the whole picture much clearer now."

"Let's evoke some wisdom from above," the Father said as he too stood up.

Placing his hand on Andrew's shoulder, he asked God to assist him in making the right decision.

They said their goodbyes and Andrew headed to his car.

"There's something strange going on here," Andrew mused, as he pulled out of the parking lot. "Why does my shoulder still feel hot and why was Father Black's presence so powerful? It's odd, but there's something so familiar about his face. I feel like I've just been through the most spiritual time of my life."

The miles slipped by and Andrew continued to ponder the power of the Father's presence.

As he was driving along in western Saskatchewan, he was trying to envisage Anne and him together as husband and wife. "Lord, give me a sign that Anne and I will be together," he prayed. A few minutes later the car motor sputtered and stopped. Andrew shifted into neutral, coasted up to a gravel road that intersected the highway and braked to a stop. When he engaged the starter again, the car immediately started.

"Strange," he said aloud, "very strange. Is God trying to tell me something?" Andrew decided to stretch his legs. He had just started walking down the country road when he saw something glistening in the sunlight on the roadbed up ahead.

The closer he got, the brighter it gleamed. He reached down in the gravel and picked up a beautiful agate the size of a golf ball. He held the gem up to the sun. It was translucent, the colour of liquid honey and had streaks of crimson running through it.

"Thank you Lord for this sign," he whispered as he headed back to his car.

Back on the road, the more he thought on it, the stronger he felt that he should not show Anne the agate until after they were married.

Several hours later, a weary Andrew pulled into Arthur's and Dorothy's driveway.

"How did it go?" Anne asked, greeting Andrew at the door with a hug.

"My visit with Father Black went well. I've never experienced anything like this before. I find it hard to talk about it. I guess I'd have to say it was the most spiritual feeling I've ever had. It was awesome, just awesome!"

"It will only take me a few minutes to warm up our supper. I waited for you so we could eat together. Aunt and Uncle left after they ate and probably won't be back till eleven-thirty or so. Come to the kitchen with me and tell me about your talk with Father Black."

"Well, he helped me a lot. I mean, when I talked with him it was like he knew more about me than I did. When we said goodbye, he put his hand on my shoulder and prayed with me. My shoulder felt hot for at least a half hour afterwards. Father Black didn't tell me what to do, but the talk helped me realize I was on the right track. I've now made up my mind.

I'm not going to become a priest. You can't imagine how much relief I feel."

"You seem so at peace with yourself," Anne said, coming over and hugging Andrew. "All morning I was praying that God would let us stay together."

"You must be pooped right out after that long drive," Anne said when they finished eating. "I'll do the dishes. You'd better lie down and rest."

"Alright, but after you're finished, come to my room. We've got a lot of talking to do."

Anne quietly eased Andrew's door open and stepped into his room. Andrew was asleep. She carefully moved a chair over beside the bed and sat down. "I love you Andrew," she whispered, lightly rubbing the back of his hand.

"I love you too," Andrew whispered back. "What wonderful words to wake up to. Come lay beside me. I promise I won't get out of control."

"I won't lay down with you, but if you'll move over a bit I'll sit beside you," Anne replied with a smile. "You'll have to be content with that. Your intentions may be honourable, but I've noticed that your hands have a tendency to wander a little."

As it was warm in the bedroom, Andrew was lying on top of the bed with just his jeans on.

"I can't believe how developed you are," Anne said, running her hand over Andrew's chest. "You've become much more massive since you lifted that weight for me back at the academy."

"A little, I guess. I'd have to say your chest has developed more too," he added, grinning. "You're rubbing my chest. It's only fair you let me rub yours. I'll even help you take off your blouse and whatever."

"I don't think so," Anne said wryly. "It's different with women. We can control our basic instincts. Men can't. For someone who was studying to become a priest, you're certainly not comporting yourself in a priestly manner."

"I guess I promised you I'd be good, so I'd better behave myself."

"I phoned Child Welfare in Red Deer and told the personnel manager of my decision not to become a priest. He said to drop in on Monday."

"I'll contact the superintendent then too," Anne interjected. "By Monday he should know something definite about that position for grade three in Innsburg."

"Tomorrow morning maybe we should head over to Rocky Ridge to see Mom. She's dying to see you and I'd like to show you off to her and the rest of the people in town."

"Seeing we've made our plans, let's get down to the more interesting stuff," Andrew continued. He reaching up and pulled Anne down, then half rolled on top of her.

During their long intense kiss, Andrew's hands were gravitating to the areas Anne had put off limits.

"Please stop," she implored. "Remember, you promised. You're getting me all flushed. Even though it feels wonderful, we can't get carried away."

"We're sure going to have to do something with those

hands of yours," Anne smirked as she got to her feet. "Maybe we'll have to tie them behind your back."

"We could give it a try," Andrew replied with a devilish grin. "Then you could ravish me to your heart's content."

"Go to sleep, you wicked man." Anne bent over and kissed Andrew again and whispered, "I can see I've got a lot of work to do on you."

CHAPTER NINETEEN

Early the next morning Andrew and Anne were on the road to see Andrew's mom.

"I should stop and see Father Bernard," Andrew said when they reached the outskirts of Rocky Ridge. "He'll want to know how I made out with Father Black. I'll just be a few minutes."

"Nice to see you again," Father Bernard said, greeting Andrew at the door. "Sorry about the mix-up with Father Black. His secretary phoned me about his sudden illness a couple of days before your appointment. I phoned around trying to contact you, but had no luck. Your mom thought you were somewhere in the Red Deer area, but didn't have a phone number for you. I hope it wasn't a total wild goose chase for you."

"I don't understand," Andrew replied, looking quite confused. "I saw Father Black at his office. We talked for over an hour and it was most helpful."

"I'm so relieved to hear that. He must have recovered enough to make it. He's quite the fellow, that Black. Did he make any jokes about his bald head? He's forever making light of his baldness."

"You say Father Black is bald?" Andrew said, looking still more confused.

"As bald as a billiard ball."

"There must be some mix-up here. The priest I saw had thick black hair that was starting to get a tinge of white to it and I'm sure he must have been well over six feet. He had a very distinctive birthmark the size of a quarter on his forehead, over his left eye."

"I have no idea who you saw, but it certainly wasn't Father Black," Father Bernard said, looking quite astonished. "Black is in his mid-fifties and not a speck over five feet six. A kind way of putting it would be to say that he's rotund and he certainly doesn't have a birthmark over his eye. Did he not introduce himself?"

"Now that you mention it, he really didn't. When we met he said, 'Good morning, you must be Andrew Ogilvy' and I replied, 'Good morning, Father.'"

"I'm totally confused," Andrew continued after a long pause. "If he wasn't Father Black, who on earth was he? Whoever the man was, his counselling was most helpful. Just talking with him was the most spiritual experience I've ever had. He put his hand on my shoulder and prayed that God would give me guidance. His hand was so hot my shoulder felt warm for at least a half hour."

"We may never know who your counsellor was. I know most of the staff at Regina and no one there fits the description of the man you saw. Now you may think this is outlandish, but I wonder if there's a possibility you talked with an angel. God sometimes works in mysterious ways."

"From first-hand experience I'd have to agree," Andrew said, shaking his head in wonderment. "Thanks so much for your support. My counselling session may always be a mystery, but it's good to know that miracles still happen. Some evening while Anne and I are still here we'll have you out for supper. I'd like to introduce you to her and tell you about our plans."

Still shaking his head, Andrew headed down the path to his car. On the way to the acreage, Andrew told Anne about his remarkable talk with Father Bernard.

"Without question, what you experienced in Regina was divine intervention," Anne said. "In all likelihood, you'll never know who the counsellor was, or if like Father Bernard speculates it was a spirit. Spirit or mortal, God's hand was in it."

"So this is the girl I've heard so much about," Edith said when she met Anne. "Andrew was certainly right about you being beautiful. Come on in. Supper is just about ready."

"Your interview with the priest makes a person marvel at how God works," Edith commented after hearing Andrew's remarkable story. "I have my own strange story too. Up till now only my sister, Ruby, knows about it. About three months after my husband Roy passed away I went to the cemetery to put flowers on his grave. I was terribly lonely and crying as I walked back to my car. 'Edith,' someone called from behind me. I whirled around. There, no more than twenty feet from me, stood Roy in his old hunting coat with a wide grin on his face. I rubbed my eyes and he was gone. I'm sure God sent Roy to comfort me."

After supper Andrew took Anne for a walk around the acreage. As they were passing the end of the garden, Andrew stopped.

"Remember me talking about our dog, Sobaka?"

"Yes, you wrote me about her."

"Well here's her grave."

They walked over to a mound beside a big poplar tree. Nailed to the tree was a small sign.

"Something I wrote for our old dog," Andrew said quietly.

Anne stooped down and read aloud.

Ode to Sobaka

Here lies Sobaka the joy of our lives.
Although gone in body, her spirit still flies
Chasing birds in the fields and in the tree tops
Circling around us when we're out on our walks.

As we stand by her graveside, we hope and we pray
When our life here is over we'll meet her some day.
Then we'll call, "Here Sobaka," and she'll come oh so fast
And flop down beside us, together at last.

"That's so beautiful, Anne whispered, tears in her eyes. "It's right from the heart."

Andrew, Anne and Edith talked till well past midnight. The next morning Edith phoned Father Bernard and invited him for supper.

After breakfast Andrew took Anne on a tour of the town and introduced her to a few of his old friends. In the afternoon while Edith went to the ladies' meeting, Andrew and Anne began cleaning out the garage. They had worked for less than an hour sorting junk into piles when Andrew announced it was time for a break. He lead Anne back to the house, filled two glasses with ice water, put a half dozen cookies on a plate and headed for the couch in the front room.

"Come sit in here with me. It's comfortable here on the couch and well, I just want to sit close to you again."

"I'd have never guessed," Anne replied, grinning. "I'm starting to realize that when we're together you have only one thing on your mind."

"So what's on my mind right now?" Andrew countered with a chuckle.

"I don't know exactly what it is, but I'll lay odds it has something to do with sex and me."

"Wrong, wrong, wrong," Andrew shot back. "I was thinking of something that's very innocent. I was just trying to imagine what a glorious sight it would be to see you without your clothes on. From the shoulders down, I imagine there's nothing but beautiful skin, some nice curves and a few feathers."

"You're a vile, vile man," Anne replied, catching Andrew in a headlock. "If you don't start to act better, I just might have to send you to bed without supper."

"That's okay with me," Andrew said, lifting Anne clear of the floor with one arm and putting her down on the couch. "I'll go to bed without a whimper just as long as you lay down beside me to keep the boogie man from getting me."

In no time flat the two were into some heavy necking. As it was a hot day, Anne was not wearing a bra and just one of Andrew's old shirts. Anne was trying to hold Andrew back, but finally relinquished. Andrew slid his hand under her loose-fitting shirt and began fondling her breasts.

"We shouldn't be doing this," she whispered, breathing heavily. "We'd better stop while we still have some control."

Anne wiggled out from under Andrew and stood up.

"Didn't I just say you only had one thing on your mind?" she said as she tucked in her shirt. "What do you have to say for yourself, bad boy?"

"I guess you're right," Andrew responded, looking sheepish. "It's good one of us has some control. I'm not telling you this to pressure you, but once in a while I panic that I might not be able to handle making love to you. I have no trouble managing on my own, if you know what I mean, but you see, on my last couple of encounters with Blanche, I was........ well, impotent."

"I'm positive you'll have nothing to worry about," Anne said, sitting down by Andrew and putting her arm around him. "You must remember you had just turned thirteen then and were under a lot of emotional stress. You're a wonderful, handsome, strong man. I love you and I know we'll make out just fine. Want to know something more? You really turn me on. You have such sensuous fingers."

Edith returned from the ladies' meeting and soon she and Anne were busy in the kitchen preparing Father Bernard's favourite dishes, Southern Fried Chicken and mashed turnips. Dessert was Edith's weakness, strawberry rhubarb pie. Supper was on the table when Father Bernard pulled into the driveway.

After supper, Andrew, Anne, Father Bernard and Edith

spent an enjoyable evening discussing the young couple's plans.

"Thanks for having me over, Edith," Father Bernard said as he got up to leave. "The meal was wonderful. Without question, I've overindulged. Andrew and Anne, I'm honoured that you'd share your dreams and aspirations with me. I'll be praying for both of you."

"Mom, I've noticed it's getting a bit more difficult for you to move about," Andrew said after Father Bernard left. "Is your arthritis flaring up again?"

"I'm afraid so. I didn't want to throw a damper on our visit by whining about my health problems, but my doctor has told me that fairly soon, I'll either have to have someone living in, giving me a hand, or I'll have to go to an old folks' home. It's not too bad when it's warm, but I seize right up when it gets cold."

"Have you made any decisions as to what you'll do and is there anything Anne and I can do to help out?"

"I suppose I have the option of looking for someone who is in better health to live in with me. I've thought a lot about that. Seeing I'm a pretty independent old girl by nature and accustomed to living by myself, that probably isn't the answer. I really like it here in Rocky Ridge so I'm planning on holding out on the acreage for as long as possible and then moving into the old folks' home here in town. As to what I need from the two of you, about all I can think of is for you to stay in touch and visit me when you can."

In mid-afternoon the next day, Andrew and Anne bid Edith goodbye and were on their way back to Arthur's and Dorothy's in Red Deer.

"Tomorrow's Sunday," Anne said. "Have you thought how we're going to resolve this church thing? I wonder how healthy it will be for our relationship if each of us goes to our own church."

"Now this may sound like a radical solution, but what about going together to early Mass and after that, going to Arthur's and Dorothy's morning service at the Protestant church?"

"You're right about it sounding radical," Anne added.

"From my perspective, we go to church to worship God," Andrew interjected. "I don't think any church has a monopoly on that. What do you think?"

"I'm with you. The more I think about it, the more I like it. I'm willing to give it a try."

Sunday morning Andrew and Anne attended early Mass at the Catholic Church in Red Deer and then went with Dorothy and Arthur to their eleven o-clock service.

On Monday morning Andrew and Anne drove to Innsburg. When Anne met with the superintendent, he had good news for her. The grade three teaching position in Innsburg would be open to her. It was contingent on Anne completing the six week teacher training course in Red Deer. Her classes were to start in early July.

Andrew also had good news. Although there were no permanent openings in the Red Deer area, one of the caseworkers would be retiring and the position would come open at Christmas. In the interim, one of the staff was taking a six month maternity leave starting in July. Andrew would spend the first week of July in orientation and then take over her position.

Andrew found an apartment in Red Deer, while Anne decided to stay with Dorothy and Arthur for her teacher-training course. The next few weeks were heavy for Anne. She wasn't able to spend much time with Andrew as her studies occupied most of her spare time. Andrew was having his own struggles getting oriented to his new job and for the first two weeks was feeling a bit down.

At the completion of her course, Anne found a small apartment within walking distance of the Innsburg Elementary School.

Friday evening of Anne's first week of teaching, she and Andrew were busy making supper when the phone rang. "For you," Andrew said, handing Anne the phone. "It's Dorothy, I believe."

"I just got off the phone with your mom, Anne. Your folks have landed in Boston. They knew you had been staying here with us and are flying into Calgary tomorrow. Jessie said she wanted to spend the first few days of their furlough with you. Arthur and I will be picking them up at the airport. Did you not tell them about Andrew?"

"No I didn't," Anne replied testily. "I'd have no problem in telling Mom, but as for Dad, until he comes clean to me on what he did to Mom, I have no time for him. When Mom was in the hospital in London, I left countless messages for him to contact me about her condition. He never returned my calls. I had to fly to London and get the sordid tale from Mom. It's been over four months now and even though he knows that I know about the mess he got himself into, not one word from him about it. It's like this, if he'd come clean, I'd forgive him and things could sort of get back to normal."

"Thanks for that information, Anne. He's my brother,

but when we pick them up I'll try to give him the message straight. When I talked to them I mentioned that you had a boyfriend, but not much more."

"That's alright. I'll talk to them when they get here. Thanks for looking out for me."

"You're more than welcome. We're picking them up at the airport late tomorrow. If it isn't too late I'll give you a call when we get back."

"With Dieter, we learned how wrong it was keeping things covered up," Arthur said after Dorothy got off the phone. "I think we should be a little cautious in what we say to Burt, though. It's alright to give your brother Anne's message, but it probably would be wisest to let Anne take him to task rather than you taking a strip off him."

"There's certainly the temptation to tear into Burt, but on second thought, I think you're right. His relations with us have never been the best, so maybe I should be a little careful."

Nothing contentious was mentioned by Dorothy and Arthur when they picked up Jessie and Burt at the airport. Everyone was on their best behaviour and the conversation was light.

"Have you folks made contact with Anne?" Burt asked as they were pulling out of the airport. "We've phoned her a couple of times, but she's never been in. Jessie and I had some heavy sledding earlier this year. Since then, Anne has been pretty frosty towards me."

"Anne has a real problem with you," Dorothy replied, turning to her brother. "You're right. It's got to do with your infidelity to Jessie. We found out about your problems from Anne a few weeks ago."

After an agonizing silence, Jessie quietly responded. "If you'll remember, Dorothy, some time back I wrote you that Burt and I had gone through some rough times. I guess I should have been more open with you."

"Anne told us about the whole terrible incident. I think it best that you phone her, Jessie, once you get to our place. I don't think it would do any good for Burt to phone her. To put it mildly, she's not kindly disposed to her father right now."

"I was hoping that my failure as a husband and a Christian was all in the past," Burt said disconsolately. "Although I confessed my sin to my wife and my fellow workers at the mission board, I failed in not confessing it to you two and Anne."

There was a dearth of conversation the rest of the way to Red Deer.

"We've got to resolve this tonight," Burt said as they pulled into Red Deer. "It would help if I knew what Anne said, Dorothy."

"I can't give it to you verbatim, Burt, but Anne is very distressed with you for not contacting her by phone after Jessie was hospitalized. She said she left several messages with the mission board for you to call her, but never heard a word from you. Of course, Anne's other beef was that since then you never talked to her about the cruel thing you did to her mother. That's about it and if you don't mind, I think it best if you leave Arthur and me out of this and resolve it with Anne directly."

"Oh my God, what have I brought on this family?" Burt

blurted out. In the silence that ensued, he covered his face with his hands and wept. "I did sin against God and my wife, but my pride got in the way of confessing my sin to the rest of you. Instead of coming clean about my sinful conduct, here I am letting Jessie tell you about it. I should have been asking for your forgiveness. I won't make any excuses because they'd be hollow."

"I'm going to phone Anne right away," Jessie interrupted, as they were pulling into Arthur's and Dorothy's driveway. "We've got to get to the bottom of this or we may lose our daughter. I knew Anne was cool towards her dad, but had no idea how hurt she was."

"Hi everyone. I decided to smarten up and come to see you."

Jessie looked up to see Anne running down the sidewalk to meet them.

"So nice to see my little girl again," Jessie cried out as she embraced Anne.

"Hi, Dad," Anne said quietly.

"Before I hug you, Anne, I have a confession to make," Burt replied, fighting hard for composure. "If I'd been more of a man, yes and more of a Christian, I'd have come clean with you, Dorothy and Arthur when it happened. I committed the horrible sin of adultery against your mother. I sinned against God, against Jessie and against all of you. Will you forgive me?"

"Of course I will," Anne cried out. She ran to her dad. They held each other close and wept.

"I'm so happy we can start rebuilding our family again," Anne finally added.

"It seemed that your dad and I had to hit the bottom in our marriage before it could become whole," Jessie said. "I should have told you that we renewed our relationship, but it was such a sensitive area for both of us. Now it's out in the open like it should have been. Thanks so much for making it happen, Anne."

Anne and Andrew spent many enjoyable hours visiting Anne's folks. "It's unreal," Anne said to Andrew when they were alone. "Not one negative comment from Dad about you being Catholic, or for that matter about me not becoming a missionary. It's almost like Dad and Arthur both had to have a calamity in their lives to make them change from phoney Christians into real ones."

CHAPTER TWENTY

Once Anne's folks left, it was back to the regular routine for Anne and Andrew. On Sundays, Andrew would come to Anne's place for breakfast before early Mass. Following Mass at the Innsburg Catholic Church and after a cup of tea they'd be off to Anne's Evangelical Assembly Church for the morning service. Being a small town, it didn't take the Innsburg parishioners long to discover that Andrew and Anne were attending both churches. Most of them thought it quite alright, but not so the clergy. When Father Porter realized what was happening, he went out of his way to welcome Anne, but began to gently lobby Andrew that they should exclusively attend the Catholic Church. Likewise, youth pastor Fritz tried to convince Anne that she and Andrew should exclusively attend the Evangelical Assembly Church. Despite the lobbying from the men of the cloth, Andrew and Anne continued to attend both churches together.

By late fall, Anne and Andrew were fitting in well at their respective jobs. As they were less than twenty miles apart, they'd see each other a couple of times in the week and always spend weekends together.

On a trip to Calgary in early November, Anne and Andrew shopped for an engagement ring. Anne picked out a design she liked and the size of a diamond Andrew could afford.

Andrew put a deposit on the ring and would pick it up in December in time for Christmas.

On the first Friday in December, Andrew and his co-workers drove to Calgary for their regional monthly meeting. Andrew had been scrounging every cent he could with the hope of being able to pick up Anne's ring before his next payday. He was still seventy- five dollars short. It would be Andrew's lucky day. At the lunch-hour break, he won the Christmas raffle of one hundred dollars. After the meeting, he picked up Anne's ring, then stopped at a chocolate speciality store and bought her a big box of chocolates. Carefully opening the box, he removed one of the centre chocolates, put Anne's ring in the pocket and as inconspicuously as possible wedged a Kleenex in around it.

Anne was at her apartment when Andrew got back and had supper just about ready.

After a hug, Andrew handed Anne the chocolates. "Thanks dear," she said, putting them in the centre of the table. "Let's not get into them till after we eat."

Andrew did his best to look nonchalant while they were eating. After they finished dessert, Andrew handed Anne the box of chocolates again.

"You first," he said, as he lifted the lid off.

"Let's see," Anne replied, glancing at the selection. "Why do I always have such a hard time making up my mind?"

"Andrew, you trickster!" Anne exclaimed, plucking out the ring. "I should have known you'd be up to something like this!"

Anne slipped the ring on. "I'm engaged! I'm engaged!"

she shouted, skipping around the room like a five-year-old. Finally, she threw herself into Andrew's arms and started kissing him as if there was no tomorrow.

"I'm glad you like it," Andrew said, scooping Anne up and carrying her over to the bed.

"You're going to be a good boy now, aren't you?" Anne whispered, pulling Andrew down beside her.

"I promise to be pretty good," Andrew chuckled, rolling Anne over on her back.

After kissing passionately for a few minutes, Andrew unbuttoned Anne's blouse, unhooked her bra, and began fondling her breasts.

"We mustn't go all the way," Anne said, breathing heavily.

"I promise," Andrew said.

With their lips pressed together, Andrew slipped his hand down Anne's flat belly.

"Remember, you promised." Anne whispered.

"I know," Andrew replied huskily.

"Oh, Dear Lord!" Anne cried out, pushing Andrew away and leaping to her feet. "How could I forget our staff party? We've got less than fifteen minutes to get ready and drive over to the school."

"Why does it happen that just when things get interesting, something comes along to put a kybosh on it?" Andrew muttered wistfully. "Any chance we can finish off a bit more after the party?"

"Well maybe just a wee bit more of a visit," Anne replied, grinning impishly. "You'll have to be a much better boy though, if that's humanly possible. Right now we've got to get a move on."

Both hurried and they were only a few minutes late. It was a happy evening for them. Anne had the time of her life showing off her ring to everyone.

"This has got to be the happiest day of my life," Anne whispered to Andrew as she snuggled close to him on the way home from the party. "Ever had a moment you wish would never end?"

"I can think of one in particular. It came to an abrupt end when a certain young lady exclaimed, 'how could I have forgotten the staff party?' Maybe we can salvage that moment again when we get back to your place."

"Who knows," Anne sighed, snuggling even closer to Andrew. "Maybe we can."

"You promised we wouldn't go all the way," Anne murmured as Andrew lay beside her on the bed.

"Yes I promised," Andrew whispered, "but I'm sure we can still get quite friendly."

"Just as long as we're not too friendly," Anne sighed, unbuttoning Andrew's shirt and massaging his chest.

Soon they were undressing each other and into some heavy petting. Finally, fully relaxed, they lay in each other's arms, relishing their new-found closeness.

"Isn't it truly marvellous how God has worked in our lives," Anne said, breaking the spell. "He brought us together years ago at Aunt Dorothy's and then He separated us when I was in Nigeria. Next, it looked like things might work out for us when you visited me at the academy. Then, with me getting all bound up about becoming a missionary and you a priest, we were apart again. Finally, God said, 'that's it. They've waited long enough.' Then He brought us back together for the last time."

"I couldn't have put it any better. Let's see if there's anything to eat in this place. I'm hungry as a bear."

On December twenty-second, Andrew and Anne headed out to Rocky Ridge to spend Christmas with Edith.

Edith came out on the porch step when Andrew's car pulled into the yard. With the help of her cane she hobbled down the path to greet them. Edith had the kettle on the stove and soon Anne was pouring the tea.

"Mom, I'd better take your car down for servicing," Andrew said after they'd visited for a spell. "It's been quite some time since you had it looked at."

With Andrew looking after Edith's car, Edith and Anne started on supper. While everything was cooking, they stopped for another cup of tea.

"I just don't know how long I can stay out here on the acreage," Edith said. "My arthritis is much worse than it was in the summer. I'm thinking seriously about making out my application to get into the old folks' home later this winter."

"Turning to something more cheerful, I'm so pleased that things have worked out so well for you and Andrew and that you'll soon be my daughter-in-law. Years back, when Andrew got the letter about your plans to become a missionary and then started taking training to become a priest, I pretty well gave up on ever being a mother-in-law or grandmother."

"Yes I remember," Anne replied. "It didn't look good for Andrew and me getting together. Sometimes God leads us through the wilderness for a long time before he brings us to the Promised Land."

"That's quite true. Life is never clear sailing. I don't know if I should mention this, but has Andrew told you about his down times?"

"Yes he has and I've experienced a bit of his depression first hand myself. He's told me there have been times over the years when he's been pretty depressed. Considering some of the horrible experiences he's been through, it's not surprising. I know for the first month at his new job he felt pretty rough. He's told me it's something that's been with him as long as he can remember. On the positive side, he always seems to be able to manage to get back on his feet."

"Yes he does. Sometimes it takes him a bit of time, but then he's back on top of things. Years ago I took him to a psychologist when he was feeling low. I think it was his memory of the abuse from Blanche and his attempted suicide that was haunting him that time. Anyway, the psychologist felt that as long as he could manage these bouts without using medications, he'd be better off. I'm glad he's talked to you about them. He's been a wonderful son and despite this problem, I'm sure he'll make a very good husband."

"Yes I know he will. I guess all of us have some personal burdens we must bear. We just have to love and support each other. The way I see it; that's all that counts."

"So if all goes as planned, I will probably be spending next Christmas in the lodge," Edith noted sadly to Andrew and Anne on Boxing Day. "If I were living in town I might hold on a bit longer, but it's getting kind of scary for a crippled old girl living out here in the country."

"If you're in the lodge, Anne and I will just bring Christmas to you," Andrew replied.

Soon it was time for Andrew and Anne to bid Edith goodbye and head for home.

"It's hard to see Mom getting so frail," Andrew commented to Anne as they were driving back to Innsburg. "We'll have to make a concerted effort to keep in closer contact with her."

"Yes we will. You don't know how much it's meant to me to be with you and your mom for Christmas."

Over the holidays, the clergy in Anne's and Andrew's respective churches heard of their engagement. After Sunday early Mass, Father Porter took Andrew aside.

"Congratulations on your engagement. Anne is a fine girl. Have you decided on a wedding date yet?"

"Not as yet. In all likelihood it will be sometime in the early summer."

"I would like to think you'll be getting married here in the Catholic Church," Father Porter said expectantly.

"That's just about the same message Anne got from the pastor in her church," Andrew replied with a grin. "Anne and I will have to give it some thought. Maybe we should flip a coin."

For the rest of the winter and spring, Andrew and Anne were kept busy at their respective jobs. Every second or third weekend they drove out to Rocky Ridge to check on Edith. Finally on the May long weekend, Edith was ready to make the move. Andrew borrowed a pickup and Anne and he moved his mom into the old folks' home in town.

"It's kind of sad to say goodbye to the old place," Edith said wistfully as they pulled out of her driveway for the last time. "Lots of memories. Lots of memories. A few pretty sad ones, but mostly good ones."

"Yes it must be hard for you, Mom." Andrew replied. "I feel the tug myself. What are your plans for the house? Are you thinking of renting it? Maybe it would be better to sell it."

"That will be entirely up to you, Son. I won't need it anymore so last week I went down to the lawyer's office and made arrangements to have the title transferred into your name. All you'll have to do is sign the papers and it will be yours."

"Thanks, Mom, but as long as you're alive that won't be happening. It would be best if we put it in both our names, but whether it's rented out or sold, all the revenue will be yours as long as you're alive. Anne and I are making good money and it wouldn't hurt for you to have a few extra dollars to supplement your pensions."

Andrew contacted the lawyer regarding his mom's house and had the title made out in both his mom's and his name. Andrew was pleasantly surprised when he dropped in on Les Gathercole, the realtor.

"I could have sold your mom's acreage three times over in the last few months," Les said. "The markets are up right now and acreages are in demand."

Andrew and Les stopped in to see Edith and listed the property. In two days the acreage was sold. Les had known Edith and Roy for over thirty years and refused to take any commission from the sale. Through an investment firm, the proceeds from the sale were invested jointly in Edith's and Andrew's names. All interest earned by the investments would go to Edith on a monthly basis until her death.

After the property was sold, Andrew and Les again stopped in at the lodge to see Edith.

"Thank you both so much," Edith said as Andrew and Les were leaving. "Although it's sad in a way to see the old acreage go, now the money will be working for us and be there when Andrew and Anne want to buy or build a house."

CHAPTER TWENTY-ONE

As spring turned to early summer, they still hadn't resolved the issue of who would marry them and in which church the wedding would take place. Andrew's suggestion to Father Porter that both clergy take part in a joint marriage ceremony was met with stony silence. Anne's pastor was not enthralled with the idea either.

It was the retired Father Bernard who finally came up with the answer. "Why not see if the United Church Minister, John Hemstock, would marry you in the United Church? The United Church is less fundamentalist in their views than those in Anne's church and possibly a bit more liberal than those in the Catholic Church, so it would be a compromise. I've known Hemstock for years and he's blessed with a good sense of humour. I'm sure he'd love nothing better than to solve the problem for you, especially seeing the other two clergy are so petrified in their thinking."

"I'd be happy to help you out," Pastor Hemstock replied after listening to Andrew's and Anne's plight. "We'll make sure we have nothing else booked for the fifth of July. We can arrange the details later. Why don't you ask Father Porter and Pastor Fritz to be ushers?" he added with a twinkle in his eye. "Then it really would be an ecumenical wedding."

By June, Anne and Andrew were busy making wedding preparations. Anne so wanted her folks there and once they started on the wedding guest list, she phoned her mom and dad.

"I'm really sorry, but we won't be able to make it unless a miracle happens," Jessie said. "Dad, Rachel and I would love to be there, but the price of tickets is out of our reach. The mission board has a plan where they'll cover half the cost of a flight to a wedding in one's immediate family, but that still leaves close to fifteen hundred to come up with if Dad, Rachel and I were to come. Right now all we have is a couple of hundred dollars in savings."

"What a bummer," Anne muttered to Andrew when she got off the phone. "It seems we've been apart all my life. I guess I was expecting a little too much. Still......."

Andrew made no reply, but a plan was starting to form in his mind. On Monday evening while Anne was at the school doing parent-teacher interviews, he phoned his mom and filled her in on Anne's conversation with her mom.

"I feel awkward in bringing this up, Mom, but I was wondering if I could borrow fifteen hundred dollars from the investments for the cost of plane fare for Anne's family? It would make Anne so happy to have her folks here. Anne and I could have the money paid back in a year's time."

"You don't know how happy your call makes me feel. Of course you can use the money. Remember, it's in your name too. After all, helping out needy people is what money is for. The last thing in the world you need to do is pay it back. It's all going to be yours and Anne's anyway when I pass on."

"Here's a little something for your folks and sister," Andrew said when he dropped in at Anne's place the next afternoon.

He handed Anne a money order for fifteen hundred dollars made out to Burt and Jessie Prentice.

"Thank you so much," Anne cried out, giving Andrew a hug, "but how in the world did you manage it?"

"I just tapped into Mom's and my investments a bit. Mom was tickled pink with the idea. I said we'd pay it back, but she vetoed that suggestion. The fifteen hundred is only a small percentage of the principal. Mom says she never spends all the monthly investment cheques, so this won't impact her any."

"Such a gift of love," Anne whispered. "Very few men would be big enough to do this. I know God will reward both you and your mom for being so big-hearted. I can hardly wait to phone Mom."

When Anne contacted her mom with the news, Mother and daughter had quite a crying spell. Jessie and Burt were so impressed that the trip was a gift from their future son-in-law. That evening, Jessie phoned Rachel to tell her that they all would be going to the wedding and that Anne wanted her as a bridesmaid.

Anne's maid-of-honour would be Sarah Frum, Anne's roommate when she was at the academy in the states.

Andrew phoned his foster brother Ralph in northern Manitoba.

"You're getting married!" Ralph exclaimed. "To the girl you had the hots for the last time we talked at Jack's funeral?"

"That's the one. The wedding is less than six weeks away."

"Yeah, if I remember right, you were thinking on giving up on becoming a priest and your girlfriend on being a missionary the last time you phoned me. Well holy mackerel, good for you."

"We're getting married on the fifth of July. That's a Saturday. Anyway, I was wondering if you and Ron would stand up for me."

"Man, I'd love to and I'm sure Ron would too. We'll sure give it a try. I'll have to check with Ron and then with our boss. I'm flying into the Arctic now. We're going pretty steady in the winter, but things slack off in the summer. We'd sure be honoured if we could. My girlfriend and I will be getting married one of these days. We're pretty happy. She just found out last week that's she's pregnant."

"Sounds like you're doing your homework," Andrew said with a chuckle. "Congratulations!"

"I'll check with Ron next week. He's gone on a course for a few days. We both work for the same company. He doesn't fly though. He wanted to, but his eyes are too poor. He's a mechanic and works on the planes. The odd thing is his girlfriend and mine are sisters, but they're not twins. That would be too strange."

"Just give me your phone number. I'll check with the boss right away and with Ron when he gets back. I should be able to get back to you in a few days. Maybe we could make a deal. We'll stand up for you. You and Ron can stand up for me."

"Sure, I'll go for that."

A week later, Ron called back. He and Ralph had talked to their boss. Not only did he give them extra days off, he gave them the use of one of his planes.

Saturday evening in late June, Anne and Andrew were returning from Red Deer after Anne's final fitting for her wedding dress. It suddenly occurred to Anne that Andrew was not very chatty.

"Is something bothering you? You haven't said much in the last while."

"Yes, I guess so. Just a little of my past haunting me again."

"If it would help you any, go ahead and talk about it."

"I thought I was doing pretty well until last night and then I had this stupid dream. It started out with Blanche making fun of my sexual performance. I was in bed with her and she was right. I wasn't able to perform. The horrible part of it was that when I looked over at Blanche, she'd turned into you. I woke up in a dead sweat. Over the last few months I've tried to tell myself that I manage okay by myself and with you helping me. Still, my dream reinforced those old fears. Now I'm terrified that when I try to do the real thing with you, I'll flake out like I did with Blanche."

"I've told you countless times I'm sure you have nothing to worry about as far as being able to perform," Anne said, snuggling close. "On second thought, I guess it's easy for me to say that seeing I'm not in your head, but then what more can I say or do?"

Conversation was sparse the rest of the way to Anne's apartment. Andrew had just placed the last grocery bag on the kitchen counter when Anne came up from behind and put her arms around him.

"I've been trying to figure out how best to help you

overcome your fears that you won't perform well. Because I love you, if it would really help, we could go all the way tonight, but I think it best we don't sleep together."

"Would it put too much pressure on you if we did? As much as I'm crazy about the thought of making love to you, I couldn't live with myself if you felt forced."

"I wouldn't have offered if I felt forced," Anne whispered, undoing Andrew's belt and sliding her hand down his bare stomach. "It's the safe time of the month for me. Let's go into my bedroom."

Afterwards as they lay naked on the bed, Anne sighed. "Well Big Boy, does that prove I was right?"

"It does and you'll never know how much pressure that takes off me. Are you as relaxed as I am?"

"If I were any more relaxed I'd be asleep. That was just so beautiful."

"If that's the way you feel about it, maybe after a cup of tea we should try for an encore," Andrew said with a twinkle in his eye.

"No way," Anne replied, grinning. "We agreed that for now once was enough. After we're married though, I imagine I'll be spending a lot of time praying for strength."

The week before the wedding was hectic. Jessie, Burt and Rachel flew in on the first, Sarah on the second. Soon all the ladies were hard at it with the countless wedding details. Andrew, Burt and Arthur were there when needed.

"I've got some exciting news," Rachel began one afternoon when she and Anne were by themselves. "Dad just got word last night that they'll be moving back to the mission head office in the states in September. Dad's been having trouble with high blood pressure and the mission board decided it would be better if he left Nigeria and worked in the head office."

"So you'll be able to stay with Mom and Dad then?"

"Yes and I'm so excited. I always hated being left alone at the mission school. Are you okay with Dad now? Mom told me that you had been upset with him cheating on her."

"Yes I've forgiven him and we've made up. It's too bad things couldn't have been straightened out when it happened, but I guess that's life."

"I didn't know about it until a few months ago myself and I was really shocked. According to Mom, Dad has really smartened up after she was depressed and in the hospital. She told me they're getting along much better and really love each other now. Dad should have told you and me about it when it happened. Anyway, I'm glad you're not mad at him anymore."

The day before the wedding, Father Porter, on Pastor Hemstock's urging, agreed to take part in the wedding ceremony. Pastor Bob Layman of the Evangelical Assembly was away on holidays, but when Pastor Hemstock invited youth pastor Fritz to help out in the wedding, he declined. Andrew asked his old teacher, Lynn Adams, to be master of ceremonies at the reception. Lynn enthusiastically accepted.

At ten o'clock the morning of the wedding, everyone was on pins and needles as Ralph, Ron and their girlfriends still hadn't arrived. Finally, at eleven their bush plane set down.

Shortly after two PM a nervous, but beautiful Anne walked

down the church aisle to her waiting husband-to-be. Her dad was holding Anne's right arm, her mom, her left.

With Father Porter leading in the scripture reading and prayer, the wedding began.

"We are marrying a very ecumenical couple this afternoon," Pastor Hemstock stated before the exchange of vows. "You see, Andrew is Catholic while Anne is Protestant. Anne and Andrew are attending both the Catholic and the Evangelical Assembly Church."

Following the exchange of vows and the picture taking, the wedding party returned to the church hall.

"I've known Andrew for about ten years and Anne for a year or so," Lynn began at the reception. "This morning I was talking to Andrew's mom, Edith, as we drove out from Rocky Ridge. We both agreed that Andrew's and Anne's relationship is kind of a fairy tale story. They had been pen-pals for years, but when Anne started her training to become a missionary and Andrew his training to become a priest, it looked pretty bleak for them getting together. The Almighty, in His wisdom often redirects us though, so here we are this afternoon celebrating their marriage. I'd like to call on Andrew's brother, Ralph, to propose a toast to the groom."

"I'm not having much luck of late," Ralph began with a grin. "Ron and I flipped a coin last night to see who would be best man and who'd do the toast to the groom. I lost both flips. Anyway, I guess pretty well all of you know that Ron, Andrew and I are foster brothers. We were together from the time we were three or four. Man, we got along so good. Ron and I are natives and sometimes other kids used to pick on us. Andrew was always pretty husky and never let that happen when he was around." Turning to Andrew he asked. "Remember the fight you had with old Lenny, the morning he pushed me and told me to go back to the reserve?"

Andrew smiled, nodded his head and looked down.

"So then when we were eleven or twelve our foster mom died and Jack, our dad, started drinking heavy. Us three guys knew we'd have to go to a new home and really wanted to stay together because we were brothers. Anyhow, it didn't work out that way. Andrew had to go back to the orphanage. Ron and I went to stay with my aunt and then we moved to New Brunswick. We never saw each other again until a few years ago at Jack's funeral. If I remember correctly, Andrew had finished high school and just got back from visiting Anne down in the states, but enough of the past."

"I wish you and Anne a good life together. Never forget Anne, Andrew's one hell of a good man. To my brother then," he said, raising his glass.

Rachel proposed the toast to the bride and then thanked Edith and Andrew for making her folks and her trip possible.

Out of deference to Anne's folks, Dorothy, Arthur, Ron and Ralph, no alcohol was served at the reception.

After the reception, Andrew and Anne drove Ron, Ralph and their girlfriends to the airport.

"Well, sometime soon it'll be Andrew who is the best man," Ralph said as they were saying their goodbyes. "Our girlfriends were talking last night and now it sounds like we're going to have a double wedding."

"That would be great," Andrew replied. "Give us a shout when you've got your wedding date picked out."

Once the plane lifted off, Andrew and Anne picked up their luggage and left on their honeymoon down the Oregon coast.

At nine PM they stopped at a motel in Lethbridge for the night.

"If you can't control those hands of yours, I'll have to get a set of hand cuffs," Anne whispered, caressing Andrew's cheek. "What am I going to do with you? It's two in the morning. You've made love to me twice and by the feel of things, you want to make it three in a row."

"You can't blame me for trying," Andrew quipped. "It's just that I'm so relieved that everything works. I promise to behave now, until morning anyway."

"Good morning, Mrs Ogilvy," Andrew whispered into Anne's ear. "It's daylight in the swamp. Should we get up and have breakfast, or should we play some?"

"Breakfast sounds good," Anne retorted with a grin. "I'd have thought you had enough playing last night to last you for a week or two."

"I have a small present for you," Andrew continued, placing something in Anne's palm. "This is my morning-after gift to the most beautiful, sexy girl in the world. You must not look at it until you're in full sunlight."

Anne kept her eyes closed while Andrew led her to the window.

"It's okay to open your eyes now," Andrew said, pulling the curtains aside. In Anne's hand lay the huge, honey-coloured agate Andrew found in Saskatchewan.

"Hold it up and look through it at the sun," Andrew instructed.

"Oh it's so beautiful," Anne cried. "The light shines right through it. Look, it's interlaced with crimson streaks. It looks like it's on fire. Thank you so much my darling! I'll treasure it for the rest of my life."

"There's quite a story to it. I've never told you about this, but you remember the trip I took to Regina to see Father Black, or whoever he was?"

"Yes, go on," Anne replied, still holding the agate up to the sun.

"After seeing the counsellor, I hit the road. I was still somewhere in Saskatchewan. As I was thinking about wanting to spend the rest of my life with you, I said out loud, 'Lord, give me a sign.' You won't believe this, but within a few minutes, the old car engine sputtered and quit. I took it out of gear and coasted up to an intersection. I cranked the starter over and the old goat fired right up. 'That's eerie,' I said. I was a bit stiff so decided to stretch my legs. There was a gravel road that ran to the south, so I started walking. I'll never forget it. It had showered and the sun was shining again. I had only walked a couple of hundred yards when I saw something on the road up ahead of me gleaming in the sunlight. I ran up to it and there, lying in the gravel was this agate. I said, 'Thank you Lord.' I was going to tell you about it when I got home, but something inside of me said 'now's not the time to tell her.' A couple of nights later I had this dream that I gave you the agate the morning after our wedding and that's just what I've done."

Andrew stroked the small of Anne's back while she kept looking through the agate at the sun.

"The only difference is that in my dream you had a few clothes on," he added.

"Oh good grief!" Anne cried out, reaching up and closing the curtains. "Here I am, standing in front of an open window, stark naked."

CHAPTER TWENTY-TWO

After breakfast, Anne carefully wrapped the agate in a piece of tissue paper, stashed it in her purse and they struck out. At King's Gate they crossed into Idaho. From there they angled for the Oregon coast.

Anne and Andrew took the coast highway from Seattle down southwest Washington, through Oregon and into northwest California. If it wasn't raining, they'd pitch their tent on the beach. They spent hours curled up close to each other in Andrew's big sleeping bag, listening to the ceaseless pounding of the surf. During the day they hiked through the majestic old forest groves of gigantic Redwoods. One evening, just as the sun was setting, they trekked up a hill just off the highway a few hundred yards from the shoreline. Topping the hill they could see the endless beach going north and south till it blended with the horizon. A few hundred feet back of them was a grove of huge Redwoods.

"Let's just forget about going home," Anne wheezed, out of breath. "We could build a little house here and let the rest of the world go on its merry way."

"It's tempting," Andrew replied. "Realistically though, this would be a wonderful place to live when we retire."

Their two week honeymoon came to an end all too soon and it was back to the rat race for Andrew and Anne.

In August, Anne took some courses at the college in Red Deer so they stayed in Andrew's apartment. Once Anne's courses were finished, Andrew gave his notice to his landlord and they got a bigger apartment in Innsburg, close to Anne's school.

In mid-October, Andrew received a letter from Ralph.

Dear Andrew,

This is kind of a hard letter to write, but two weeks ago, Bev, my girlfriend had a miscarriage. That was horrible enough, but now we've broke up. It's a long messy story. If you'll remember last time we talked, Ron and I told you we never touched alcohol seeing we were messed up as kids with our folks drinking and then with Jack being a booze-hound. Anyway, when Ron and I started going out with Bev and Jane we had no idea they had trouble with the bottle. Once in a while they would take off for a weekend. Later, we found out they would be partying it up. Ron and I were kind of dumb that way or maybe we just didn't want to know. So two weeks ago the girls took off on Friday night. At about two in the morning I get a call from the hospital that Bev had lost the baby. It turned out she was drunk at a party and fell down the basement stairs. There was a big fight when Ron and I found out the girls had drinking problems and of course everything came apart. So that's it. The wedding for Ron and me is off and no baby. If you could, Ron and I would like it if you and Anne could pray for us. We're kind of hurting pretty bad.

Your brother, Ralph

Andrew and Anne read Ralph's letter with heavy hearts. When they prayed together each evening, they always remembered to pray for Ron's and Ralph's welfare................

Time moved on. Both Andrew and Anne were working hard at their respective jobs. They continued to attend both churches and both men of the cloth continued to lobby them to attend their church exclusively. Every second weekend, Andrew and Anne tried to visit Edith at the lodge in Rocky Ridge.

At times, Anne worried over Andrew's commitment to his work. In her eyes he seemed incapable or unwilling to turn his job off at the end of the day. Sometimes he'd visit a client on Saturday and he often brought his paperwork home. Notwithstanding Andrew being a bit too wrapped up in his work, things were going well between Anne and him and they were very much in love.

Sixteen months into their marriage, Fritz, the youth pastor in Anne's church phoned her one evening.

"I have a big request to make of you, Anne. Mary, our Sunday School teacher for grades one and two is moving in a couple of weeks. Would you consider taking over her class?"

"I just don't know. I'll have to talk it over with Andrew. We get back from early Mass around a quarter after nine. Would there be a time conflict there?"

"Well Sunday School starts at nine-thirty. It would be a bit tight, but you could manage I think. Anyway, give it your prayerful consideration. I'll get back to you sometime next week. You're well qualified and I know you'd do a super job."

"Who was that?" Andrew asked, looking up from his papers.

"Fritz at the church and of all things he wants me to teach a Sunday School class. We get home from Mass at about nine-fifteen and Sunday School starts at nine-thirty. I just don't know. What do you think?"

"It's entirely your call. If you'd like to do it and figure you can handle it, well, go for it."

"I'm going to think on it for a while and get back to Fritz next week."

A week later, after talking Fritz's offer over in depth with Andrew, Anne accepted the Sunday School teaching position. While Anne taught her class, Andrew sat in on the adult class which Fritz led.

It wasn't long before things came to a head for Andrew in the adult class. One morning they were discussing different religions. The consensus of the group was that those adhering to a religion that did not strictly follow the guidelines for salvation that their church laid down, were all lost and bound for hell.

"After this morning's class, I feel awkward worshipping with this Sunday School group," Andrew said to Anne when they got home from church. "Their narrow view on condemning to hell all those not following their belief in salvation is quite repugnant. I kept quiet and that was hard to do. The way I see it, there's no percentage in causing dissension. I think maybe it's best I don't attend anymore. I'll drop you off at nine-thirty and come back for the eleven o-clock service."

"I'm sorry you have to do that, but I sure won't be placing pressure on you. It's a shame some people have to be so dogmatic in their beliefs. As for me, I'm really enjoying my class."

For the next six months, Andrew and Anne continued to attend both churches.

It was now the Catholic Church's turn to thicken the plot. A number of Father Porter's parishioners began lobbying him to start the early Mass at a later time. As a result, early Mass was moved from eight to eight-thirty.

"This is really going to put us in a bind," Andrew said to Anne when they heard the news. "Mass won't be over till fifteen minutes after Sunday School starts. I guess the only way we can manage is either for you to quit your Sunday School class, or for me to go to Mass by myself and then come for the eleven o-clock service."

"Well I sure don't want to quit my class," Anne replied adamantly. "Both pastors have told me I'm doing an excellent job. There are young lives that I'm influencing for the good and I feel very strongly that I'm doing God's will."

"I guess I'll have to go to Mass by myself then. It would probably be best if we took our own cars."

A month into the new arrangement, Andrew didn't show up for the eleven o-clock service.

"You didn't make it to church," Anne said when she got back home after service. "Is there anything wrong?"

"Yes. You see I'm having a bit of a problem. I've been thinking a lot on this of late. Fair was fair when we went to both our churches, but now, when you aren't coming to my church anymore and when I get insulted when I attend yours, it makes me wonder why I'm doing it."

"Who insulted you and when?" Anne asked.

"Fritz, your youth pastor did last Sunday. If you'll remember, he was filling in for Bob. He mentioned that only God could forgive sin and made light of the religions where the clergy held confessionals."

"I hadn't noticed," Anne said, running her hand through Andrew's hair. "So what are we going to do now? I don't like how things are moving. I feel very strongly that I should keep teaching my class and you're upset with something the minister said."

"I guess there's only one solution," Andrew said sadly, looking off into space. "You go to your church and I'll go to mine."

Anne shrugged her shoulders. Neither one said anymore. Anne went into the kitchen and started making dinner while Andrew went back to his paperwork.

Although not being able to attend church together was putting some strain on their relationship, by and large Andrew's and Anne's marriage was still very strong.

It was now into the third year of their marriage. Knowing that Andrew had studied to become a priest, Father Porter asked him to help in the catechism classes and Andrew agreed. Without fail, when classes were over, Father Porter would lobby Andrew that their children, when they had them, should be baptized in the Catholic Church and attend it exclusively.

Because Anne would be helping with Daily Vacation Bible School at the church, she and Andrew only had time for one week of holidays.

Late in the fall, Andrew booked off the catechism classes as he was getting behind with his work. Anne, on the other hand, agreed to help with the church young peoples. As Anne and Andrew were now busier than ever, their social life was pretty well non-existent and they were spending less and less time with each other. Andrew was spending the odd evening and Saturdays seeing clients. Most evenings during the week he would spend an hour or two on paperwork.

"I'll be going back to seminary in January for a number of months," Fritz announced at the December Sunday School teachers' meeting. "Becky Simmons, a graduate of our Bible School college will be filling in during my absence. She's had four years of Bible School training and is making plans to go into fulltime church work. I understand she'll be moving here right after Christmas. Becky comes highly recommended from our college. Let's see. She's single and what else? Yes, she'll be working part-time as a nurse here in the hospital."

Even though Anne thought Becky a bit on the forthright side, she was favourably impressed by her. Becky was a large woman, but in good physical shape. She had long red hair, striking features and dressed somewhat on the severe side. Becky, unlike Fritz, was a very hands-on type and asked to individually meet with all the Sunday School and youth group leaders. In mid-January, Anne invited her over for supper. Andrew had to meet a client so left shortly after they finished eating.

"I noticed your husband was very quiet tonight," Becky said when she and Anne were alone. "Is he always that way?"

"Not when you get to know him he isn't. He's been under a lot of pressure of late with a couple of kids he's responsible for. The parents are going through a messy divorce and are fighting over custody. Unfortunately, Andrew can't separate himself from his work at five."

"I can relate with that. My dad was a workaholic. He was a foreman for a big machinery company. He'd be lucky to get home from work by ten. Dad was a control freak. He had to control everything from what we kids wore to school, to who our friends were. Even though Mom was a very competent housekeeper, he'd always be critiquing her efforts with his sick sarcasm. She never dared make a decision on her own. Using the old vernacular, one day he just up and died. I had left home by then. Mom had an awful time as she knew nothing about their business affairs."

"Anyway, I shouldn't go on about my dad like that. Let's talk about your Sunday School class. I'd like to know how things are going for you. Are you enjoying your class? Do you have any problems and is there anything our church could do to help you out?"

"I'm really enjoying my class and I can't think of any problems I'm having with my kids. This doesn't involve you, but the only real concern I have is that Andrew and I don't attend church together anymore. For over two years we attended both the Catholic and our church."

"Fritz told me about Andrew having training to become a priest and your church-going arrangement. I take my hat off to you for going the extra mile for him. It's one of those sad facts of life that often men's egos create a lot of problems, but like talking about my dad, I should cease and desist. My intent this evening is not to bash men."

"Andrew is a good man and I love him dearly, but some of the comments made in the adult Sunday School class were not all that edifying to say the least and quite offensive to him. Andrew thought it wisest not to get involved in the discussion so opted not to go to the adult class anymore. We still attended morning service together, but unfortunately, Fritz made light of some of the Catholic beliefs in a sermon and now Andrew feels uncomfortable attending the morning service."

"Of course I was not there when these incidents occurred so it wouldn't be proper for me to comment on them," Becky quickly interjected. "Changing the subject, I should tell you a bit about myself, even if some of it is painful."

"I was raised in southern Ontario and as you may have surmised; my upbringing was not a Christian one. After high school I went into nurses training. It was there I met Rod, my future husband. Once we were married, I nursed for a year while he finished University. Our marriage lasted three years, but then it came apart, so I'm divorced. I wanted to clear that up because there were rumours about that I was a widow. I became a Christian shortly after we separated and then went on to Bible College. I'm hoping to eventually get into full-time ministry."

Becky and Anne clicked. Becky was the combination of big sister and mother that Anne never had. Although Becky had a bias against men in general, at first she was careful not to come down hard on Andrew when she talked with Anne. Before long, Becky had Anne helping out in two more church clubs.

As the months passed by, Andrew was becoming more and more involved in his work. One day in March, his supervisor called him into his office.

"Your dedication to your caseload is most commendable. In all the years I've been here, I've yet to see one of the staff as hard-working as you. That's both a blessing and a curse though. I'm really concerned for you, Andrew. Unless you cut yourself a bit of slack, I'm afraid you're on your way to burnout. For your own good, I think you shouldn't be seeing clients after hours. Can you live with that?"

"Yes I guess I could," Andrew replied after a long pause. "You're right. I've been hitting it pretty hard. Part of it is that I went through so much as I was growing up. If I'm honest though, another big part has to do with Anne and me. We still get along well, but she's so committed to her church that we hardly have any time for ourselves. I guess I'm sort of reacting to Anne's new commitment by burying myself in my work. Thanks for being straight with me. I'll try to back off a bit."

Although Anne was happy that Andrew had cut back seeing clients after hours, it didn't mean she was spending any more time with him. What with teaching full-time, preparing school lessons, marking assignments, attending her church club meetings, teaching Sunday School and trying to keep house, she didn't have much spare time for her husband.

"I have some wonderful news," Anne said excitedly one evening over supper. "Becky is organizing a trip to the Holy Land for our church at Easter."

"Let me guess," Andrew countered. "Becky wants you to go with the group to help out."

"Well yes she does," Anne replied defensively. "It sounds like you aren't all that up-beat about it."

"They won't be giving the tickets away, I'll bet. What will it cost?"

"The cost will be about one thousand dollars apiece for double occupancy. Becky says that they charge more during the Easter season, but she believes being at the scene of

Christ's crucifixion and resurrection at Easter is well worth the extra cost."

"Whatever," Andrew said dryly. "Exactly where are we going to get two thousand dollars? We have less than eight hundred in our account."

"Well, would you really want to go too?" Anne asked hesitantly. "I assumed you would feel uncomfortable going with the group. In all likelihood they'll be some of the same people you had an issue with in the adult Sunday School class."

"It sounds like you'd just as soon I didn't go along," Andrew said sarcastically.

"I didn't say that," Anne countered, raising her voice. "If you really want to go, what would be wrong in taking a bit out of our savings? All you seem to want to do is keep that money stashed away."

"Hold the horses," Andrew shouted. "That so-called savings you refer to is the money from Mom's house. Even though it's legally in both Mom's and my names, from my point-of-view it's still her money as long as she's alive. We took a little out to help your folks get here for the wedding, but we won't be doing it again."

"So, it's alright to look out for my folks, but it's not okay to use a bit of it for us," Anne shot back.

"I just can't handle this," Andrew said as he headed for the door. "You used to be so considerate of others. Ever since you started dealing with Becky, all you can think of is what's good for the church and to hell with anything or anybody else's feelings. The last two times I've visited Mom, you've been too caught up in your church thing to come with me. I'll be back in an hour or so when I cool down."

"I'm sorry I've hurt you," Anne blurted out later as Andrew walked in the door. "I've been doing a lot of thinking while you were gone. You were right. I should have been with you when you went to visit your mom. I'd love to see the Holy Land, but visiting it now is not important enough to me to sacrifice our relationship over."

"I'd like to apologize too. I shouldn't have been so hot-headed. I can see that the Holy Land trip means a lot for you. We'll each have a pay check before you leave, so with them, plus what we have in our account there'll be a thousand plus for you. Our finances will be a little tight for a while, but we'll manage."

"What about you, Dear? Couldn't you come along too?"

"I'm sorry, but as I said before, we just don't have enough money for the two of us to go. It wouldn't be right for me to tap into Mom's investments again so I could go on a holiday. I couldn't live with myself if I did that."

"I've been doing a lot of thinking of late," Anne said a couple of days later. "Considering that you gave fifteen hundred dollars so my folks could come for our wedding, I just wouldn't feel right about taking the trip and leaving you behind. I'm going to talk to Becky. Maybe she can find someone else to take my place."

"Don't get all tied up about it. You wanted to go and I'm backing you. Go for it."

Despite having Andrew's blessing, Anne continued to feel uneasy about going on the trip.

"Is there any way you could get someone else to help you out on the trip?" she asked Becky when they next met.

"Let me guess," Becky said cryptically. "Andrew's kicking up a fuss and doesn't want you to go."

"No, not at all. He supports me going on the trip, but we're kind of strapped right now and don't have enough money for both of us to go."

"It does rather put pressure on the success of the whole trip if I can't find someone to replace you. You and I are the only young ones going. The rest are all seniors. As you know, there are three or four old ladies going who will need assistance. I'll be conducting the tour and would be hard pressed to care for them by myself and lead the tour. I'll see what I can do, though."

When Anne told Andrew of her conversation with Becky, he insisted she phone Becky back and confirm that she'd go on the trip with her. That evening she did so.

In the weeks up to the trip, relations between Andrew and Anne were much smoother. They talked at length about the need for Andrew to rethink how much energy he was investing in his clients and for Anne to cut back on some of her church involvement.

CHAPTER TWENTY-THREE

The first week of April, Becky, Anne and the church group took the church bus to Calgary and then boarded the plane for their flight to Israel. Becky sat with Anne and briefed her on their itinerary. Becky and Anne would be sharing a room throughout the trip. Anne knew the tour would be a most spiritual experience and was so excited she didn't sleep much the first night. They followed the steps of Jesus from his birthplace, throughout his ministry, then on to the place of his crucifixion and the tomb where he was raised from the dead. Notwithstanding it being spiritually uplifting, caring for three old ladies, two with walkers and one confined to a wheelchair, was heavy work. At the end of each day Becky and Anne were exhausted.

Most evenings, Becky had a short inspirational time where they reviewed the day's spiritual journey and made plans for the next day.

"You had a failed marriage," Anne began one evening when Becky and she were alone. "If it doesn't make you too uncomfortable, could you tell me a bit about it?"

"Why I got married in the first place, I'll never know. I liked Rod, but when I think back, I really wasn't in love with him. I had pressure from friends and family and that probably had something to do with it. During our short courtship, he was a gentleman. You know, the typical male, always trying for sex, but I guess that's normal. Like many newly married couples, our first few intimate encounters were pretty awful. It was really disappointing for me and it pretty much stayed that way throughout our marriage. I guess the best way to put it is that we just drifted apart. He turned out being a sloth and felt that it wasn't a man's responsibility to help with the housework. At any rate, the little flame that once was there sort of flickered and died. When I found out he was having an affair, even though it hurt, in some convoluted way I was relieved that the charade was over. I still think he's a total scum-bag, but maybe most men are that way if given a chance. Anyway, he moved out and a few months later we were divorced."

"That's sad," Anne said quietly. "It's always rough to hear of marriages that didn't work out. Andrew and I have our differences, but by and large our marriage is good. I do worry some about how he slips into depression every so often. Even though he's hard to live with then, it's short-lived and he always manages to get back up on his own power. Ever think of getting married again?"

"Not a chance, not a chance. For starters I don't believe it's scriptural for a divorced person to remarry. Secondly, after my troubled marriage, I don't really find the other sex all that interesting. As I've said before, for me, this sex thing is way overrated. I'm trying to follow the Apostle Paul's suggestion. I'm sure I'll be much more able to serve the Lord as a single person."

All too soon for Anne's likening, the group was at the airport boarding the flight back to Canada. Anne's flight would arrive back in Calgary at eleven AM.

At five that morning, Andrew got a phone call from the

Lodge. His mom had suffered a heart attack and was in the hospital in Rocky Ridge. By the time Andrew got to the hospital, Edith's condition had stabilized and they were about ready to move her out of I.C.U. back to the ward. Andrew phoned Anne's pastor from the hospital and asked him to relay the word of his mom's heart attack to Anne.

"Well I guess the Lord wasn't quite ready to take me home yet," Edith said, reaching over and taking Andrew's hand. "Thank goodness one of the staff heard me calling for help."

"It's so good to see you're still perking," Andrew said, rubbing the back of his mom's hand. "I was only hitting the high spots on the road coming in."

"I'm glad you're here. Where's Anne? Oh what's the matter with me anyway? She's with that group visiting the Holy Land."

"That's right. Her flight's getting in at eleven this morning. I've left a message for her. Probably she won't be out until sometime this afternoon."

"Correct me if I'm wrong, Son," Edith said after a long pause. "My motherly instinct tells me things might not be quite as smooth between Anne and you as they could be. Over the years, when I get that feeling, most times it proves to be close to the mark."

"I guess you're right again," Andrew said looking down. "I think things are going somewhat better now than they were a couple of weeks ago. I don't know, hope so anyway. It's just that Anne's so wrapped up with her church that there's no time left for us. I'm to blame too because the more she got caught up with her church things, the more I turned to my work. A month or so ago my supervisor got me to slack right off. Unfortunately Anne is still tied up three days a week with church clubs plus her Sunday School class on Sunday. Before she left on the tour, we had a long talk about all her church commitments. She promised she'd slack off soon."

"I always pray for you and Anne. Now I'll be able to pray with more insight."

Anne arrived at the hospital at four PM in good spirits. "I'd have been here a lot sooner, but we had trouble with the old church bus," she chirped. "The church is just going to have to invest in a new one."

Over the next hour and a half, Anne talked non-stop, filling Andrew and Edith in on all the comings and goings of the tour.

"I hate to have to pull out, but its five-thirty," she said getting to her feet. "At seven, we're having a church informal hour. Those of us who were on the tour will be sharing the blessings we got from visiting the Holy Land."

"Just a parting thought for both you and Andrew," Edith said as Anne bent over and kissed her goodbye. "You've heard the old saying 'you can't see the forest for the trees?'"

"Yes," Anne said, a perplexed look coming over her face.

"A word of advice from an old lady who's seen a lot of life. When it comes to your work, your friends, your church or whatever, don't get so wrapped up in always looking out for others that you and your loved ones suffer."

Anne nodded and with a shocked look on her face, headed out the door.

After his mom had her supper, Andrew was preparing to leave. "Thanks for your words about the forest and the trees.

I know your words were for both of us. Hopefully we'll soon be able to apply it to our lives."

Andrew got home fifteen minutes before Anne returned from her church meeting. After they had eaten a late supper, they sat together in the living room, holding hands and sipping tea. Anne again talked non-stop about the tour.

"I'm so glad you insisted that I go. The tour will always be a highlight of my life."

"Changing the subject, when we visited Mom, I got this feeling the two of you were talking about us."

"Yes, a little. It was she who brought it up. She said she noticed things had been getting a bit strained between us. I just told her about being so bound up in my work and you in the church stuff. I told her I'd cut way back in my commitment to my work."

"Well did Mom say anything more?" Anne asked with apprehension.

"I just said you were still going full-bore at the church, but would soon slack back some. She said she'd pray for our relationship. That was it. Because of her condition, I'd have never mentioned a word if she hadn't asked. Let's call it a night and hit the sack."

"Those hands of yours, groping, always groping," Anne sighed as they lay in bed.

"Remember, it's been close to two weeks," Andrew said.

"I know, but it's that time of the month for me."

"Maybe we'll have to go back to the old way we did things before we were married," Andrew said, pulling Anne close.

"Do we have to?" Anne asked, holding onto Andrew's hand. "I'm so tired from the trip and then there's your mom's heart-attack. Couldn't we just take a rain-check tonight?"

"Yeah, I guess so," Andrew muttered moving over to his side of the bed.

"Have you given any thought about slacking off a bit on some of your church stuff?" Andrew said after a long pause.

"Yes I have, but couldn't we talk about it tomorrow? I'm just so beat."

"Last night you asked me about whether I was prepared to cut back some in my church commitment," Anne said after they finished supper the next evening. "I've thought a lot about it over the last two weeks. The way I look at it, there are so many little lives out there badly needing to be moulded. I have this strong feeling that the work I do with these children is of God's leading."

"Strange how much a week or two with Becky can warp your mind," Andrew sneered. "I'll lay big odds that you discussed this with her. We had a deal. I cut out my after hours work and you said you'd cut back a bit on your church thing. I lived up to my end of the bargain and now you're backing out on your end."

"I'm just trying to serve the Lord," Anne replied on the verge of tears.

"Baloney, you're trying to serve the Lord. You're trying to serve Becky. She could give a rat's rump about our marriage. You've said before she's pretty negative about men. I'll lay it to you straight. If you don't back off some with your church stuff, I'm going to start tutoring Latin in the evenings. The high school principal found out I have four years of it. Ever since I stopped working after hours, I've sat around, twiddling my thumbs, waiting for you to come home from entertaining kids. I'll tell you right now, I've had it. Besides, in all truth, I'm just enlarging on what Mom said."

"Please," Anne cried. "I get so frightened when we fight. Please don't start the tutoring right away. I can sort it all out in a day or two."

Over the next two days Anne spent all her spare time grappling with the dilemma she faced. She did not talk with either Andrew or Becky. Finally, having made up her mind, she dropped in at the church to see Becky.

"I'm sort of between a rock and a hard spot. Before I went on the tour, Andrew and I made a deal seeing our marriage was being stressed out by his working after hours and all of my church involvement. He stopped working in the evenings and on Saturdays and my part of the deal was for me to give up on the church clubs I was helping with. We both agreed that my Sunday School class would be exempt."

"It's obvious you're being pressured," Becky replied, her face turning red. "It's the man-thing of control without question and it puts me in a hard spot too. I have no one to fill in for you in either young peoples or the other two clubs. I guess I'll have to phone around to the mothers and see if I can drum up some help. I mean, couldn't your husband compromise a little? It's not as if you're going to the bar in the evenings. Can't he occupy himself with something else?"

"Not only can he, but he will," Anne replied, her voice strained. "He took four years of Latin at seminary. The high school principal is pressuring him to tutor Latin for two hours a night several nights a week at the school."

"Well, let him go then."

"But if I did, we'd have no time together in the evenings at all," Anne pleaded.

"And that's why I'm not married," Becky sighed, putting her arm around Anne. "You're a fine Christian girl and I know you did your best. Now I'll have to do my best to find some replacements for you."

On Saturday morning, Becky phoned Anne. She'd been able to get replacements for Anne's mid-week clubs, but was not able to find anyone to take over the Friday night young peoples. Anne agreed to carry on with the young peoples until the school summer break.

Andrew and Anne visited Edith twice a week while she was in hospital. By the end of April, the old lady was back in the lodge and doing well.

"Doctor McFee said he was very pleased with my recovery," Edith announced to Andrew and Anne one afternoon when they dropped in to visit. "He said I have angina now and will have to live with it for the rest of my life. I still experience some chest pain if I exert myself too much. The doctor prescribed nitro spray and it sure helps. All in all, I'm very grateful that God spared me. I don't know how much time I have left, but I thank the Lord for every day he gives me."

CHAPTER TWENTY-FOUR

The first week of July a horrific incident occurred that sent Andrew into a tailspin. Although it wasn't required of the social workers, Andrew tried to be a big brother or dad to a number of his younger clients. Occasionally he'd pick up his young friends right after school or after supper and try to do something special with them for a couple of hours.

Friday after supper he picked up Katrina, a seven-year-old client from her foster home and took her to a Walt Disney show at the local theatre. Andrew was unaware that the young girl had recently become very allergic to nuts in general and peanuts in particular. Andrew got two chocolate bars laced with peanuts and gave one to Katrina. The show just began when she started to cry.

"I can't breathe," she wheezed.

Recognizing that something very serious was happening, Andrew grabbed her, rushed her to his car and sped to the hospital. By the time he got there, Katrina's face was turning blue and she had lost consciousness. After dropping Katrina off, Andrew picked up the foster mom and rushed back to the hospital with her. They met the doctor as he was coming out of emergency.

"We've done all we can for the little girl," the doctor said, looking most grave. "We've given her adrenalin and pumped her stomach. That's about all we can do here. Sometimes these allergic reactions to peanuts can be immediate and very severe. By the time you got her into emergency, Andrew, her breathing had stopped. Now she's breathing on her own again, but remains unconscious. We have no idea if any damage has been done to her brain from lack of oxygen. We'll be sending her by ambulance to Red Deer right away."

Saturday afternoon Andrew and Anne went in to see Katrina, but she was still unresponsive. By Saturday evening, Andrew was not doing well. Although he had been unaware of Katrina's allergies, he took full responsibility for her allergic reaction. Sunday morning, he again drove to the Red Deer hospital to see Katrina. When the nurses told him Katrina was still not responding, he became so wrought up he had to leave without visiting her.

Monday morning he forced himself to go to work, but looked like death warmed-over. Andrew's supervisor was aware of the incident. He told Andrew to go on sick leave and suggested he contact his doctor.

The doctor was familiar with Andrew's occasional bouts of depression. After talking the situation over with him, the doctor said, "Let's start you on some medications."

"I don't think so," Andrew replied without making eye contact. "I'll just go home and let it play itself out like I always do."

Anne reached out to help Andrew through his downtime, but he rebuffed her attempt as he had always done in the past.

"Please don't take it personally," he said disconsolately.

"You know from before that when I'm down like this, I just have to work it out on my own. It makes it worse if someone tries to hover over me. Know I'm raw inside and hurting bad. Just leave me alone. In a few days I'll get a handle on it. I always have."

That evening, Becky phoned in a panic. "I'm in a real bind. I made arrangements with a Bible School graduate to help me with the Daily Vacation Bible School. It's starting tomorrow. She just phoned an hour ago. A family emergency has forced her to cancel. I know you were trying for less involvement, but everyone else is on holidays or tied up. Is there any earthly way you can help me out for four or five days?"

"Oh dear Lord, I'm in a bind myself. One of Andrew's clients is in grave condition in the hospital. I shouldn't go into it any deeper than that, but Andrew, for some reason is blaming himself. He's on a real downer. Just a minute Becky, I think Andrew's calling from the bedroom. I'll get right back to you."

"That's not the hospital in Red Deer calling is it?" Andrew asked, very distraught. "They said they'd contact me if Katrina's condition changed."

"No that was Becky. She's having trouble. The other teacher can't make it for Daily Vacation Bible School tomorrow. She asked me if I could fill in, but I told her I was going to stay with you because you weren't feeling well."

"You might as well go. I'll do better if I can be left alone anyway."

Fighting back tears, Anne got Becky on the phone and told her she'd fill in for her.

After supper Anne met Becky at the church to go over the lesson plans for the next few days.

"Correct me if I'm wrong, Anne, but you seem a bit down tonight," Becky said after they finished their planning session.

"You're right. I'm under a lot of pressure with Andrew. It's so hard to deal with him when he's depressed. I shouldn't be burdening you with my troubles, but I just have to talk to someone."

"That's what friends are for," Becky responded, sitting down by Anne and putting her arm around her. "Let the pain out, Dear."

"Well it's like this," Anne continued, trying hard to pull herself together. "When Andrew's feeling up, things are alright. I mean, he's totally independent and very self-reliant. I can accept those character traits though because I know he had some pretty rough times as he was growing up. You know, at times I get the feeling that he doesn't need me. No, let me re-word that. It's as if he could manage without me at times. I can handle that when he's up, but when he's down, in mental anguish and suffering, I'd so love to be able to comfort him and even talk to him. He builds this big wall around himself and won't let me in. It just hurts so much. He's considerate of my needs to a fault, but won't allow me to look out for him when he so needs help. When you phoned, if you remember, I told you I had to stay with Andrew because he needed me. When I mentioned your problem to him, he told me to go ahead and help you out. He said he'd do better if I left him alone. That really hurt."

"I feel your pain," Becky responded, "but I can't give you an easy answer. If I was able to figure men out, I'd probably still be married. Please don't think I'm bashing Andrew, but could I give you a word of caution? When I was married, I made the mistake of trusting my husband implicitly. Before we split up, he too had a real down-time. Remember me telling you about Rod having an affair? Well when Rod and I started talking about a divorce, he confided in me that being involved with another woman while still married to me caused his depression."

"In his work, Andrew deals with a lot of foster moms and single moms, but I don't worry about that. I guess if I'm honest, I should say that I don't worry very much. No question, Andrew has this sex drive that far exceeds mine. I guess I wonder sometimes, but I think every wife does that occasionally. Mark is one of the young boys he's working with right now. His mom's single. June something is her name. From what I gather she's quite a flirt. She's pretty plain, but sure has a good figure. Still, Andrew has never given me the slightest hint of being untrue."

"I'll be remembering you in prayer," Becky said as they got up to leave.

The next afternoon Anne left the church with a heavy heart. The classes had gone well, but now she'd have to try to reach out to a suffering man who didn't want help. "He'll either be pacing the floor blaming himself for Katrina's condition or lying in bed weeping. On the other hand, he could be skipping off the ceiling if there's good news from the hospital."

She opened the door and there her man stood, all six feet two of him, with the widest smile on his face.

"You're the most beautiful girl in the world," he said, reaching out for her.

Anne stood there in disbelief. "Thank you so much, Lord,"

she finally whispered. "I'm just so relieved that you're doing better. What broke the spell?"

"It's unbelievable, just unbelievable, a real miracle," Andrew said, leading Anne over to the couch.

"I hardly slept a wink last night. Then when you left for your Daily Vacation Bible School, I fell into a deep sleep. Now just listen to this. I dreamt that Katrina had regained consciousness and that she was standing at the nursing station. I could see the nurse dialling a number on the phone. I awoke to the phone ringing, scrambled out of bed and ran in here to answer it. Guess who it was?"

"The hospital?" Anne cried.

"It was," Andrew continued; his voice breaking. "The nurse said 'there's a little girl here who wants to talk to you.'"

Anne was in Andrew's arms and they both wept. Finally, Andrew gained control.

"It was Katrina. The hospital had already phoned Katrina's foster mom, but she was looking after three young ones and couldn't come. I jumped into my car and headed to the hospital. The doctor who checked her out said that other than having some strange dreams, Katrina was okay. All her vital signs were normal. She had regained consciousness early in the morning. The hospital gave her a medic alert bracelet."

"And get this. As we were driving along, she kept saying, 'He was so bright.' Finally, I asked 'who was so bright?' 'The big man in a nightie,' she said. 'I saw him when I was going to the hospital in Innsburg. It was like looking at the sun. He was so nice. He hugged me and said I had to go back.'"

"I got her an ice-cream cone, but made sure there were

no nuts in it. Her foster mom was so relieved to see her. She's going to phone all of Katrina's friends and tell them about her allergies. When I got home I phoned my supervisor and told him what happened."

"I'm so glad that Katrina's alright and that you're back on top of things," Anne whispered, holding Andrew tight. "Now, let's make something to eat."

"Seeing you are going to be tied up till Sunday, I was thinking of taking young Mark out for a couple of days," Andrew said as they were eating supper. "The poor kid's never been to Calgary or even to the Badlands. His mom's having a lot of grief with him. As for next week, I'll be working and I guess you'll be at your church camp. I've got Mark registered in your camp so I'll run him out Monday morning."

"It sounds like we're still up to our necks in our commitments," Anne sighed, "but it's kind of you. As you say, I'll be tied up with both DVBS and camp. After that though, I trust there'll be no more commitments for the rest of the summer for the both of us."

"I hear you. As you know, my supervisor felt I should slack off in my after hours involvement with my clients and I did that before Easter. Trouble is, at the Christmas break I promised Mark that the two of us would spend a few days together as soon as school was out. I feel strongly that I should live up to my end of the deal."

When Anne returned from DVBS the next afternoon, Andrew was gone. He left a note saying if all went as planned, he and Mark would be back Friday afternoon.

It was a hot day, so after having a bite to eat, Anne drove to the ice cream parlour for some ice cream. On her way back home, on a whim, she drove by June's place. There she was, sitting out on the deck in front of her apartment, clad in a skimpy two-piece swimming suit that left very little to the imagination.

"That's hardly a display for a lady," Anne muttered. "That thong bottom of hers is nothing short of scandalous. On a beach that would even be questionable, but on your deck, in the middle of town, that's gross. I sure hope she's not trying to shine up to Andrew."

All that evening June was on Anne's mind. She gave herself stern lectures that there was nothing to worry about. When all the lectures were over though, she still could see June sitting there in her skimpy bikini.

Mark was having a great time with his big chum. Visiting the Calgary Zoo and the Drumheller Badlands were the highlights of the trip for him. On Friday afternoon they spent too much time hiking through the Badlands and it was five PM before they got back to the car. Andrew stopped at a service station and phoned June and Anne that they would be late.

After a bite to eat, they were on the road, but luck was not with them. Twenty miles out of Drumheller they got a flat tire. To further add to their trials, the spare tire was also flat. Andrew got a passing driver to take them to a service station. Once the tire was repaired, one of the service station employees drove them back to the car. By the time they got mobile again, it was crowding ten. All the hiking tired Mark right out and he was soon asleep.

At a service station fifteen miles out of Innsburg, Andrew phoned Anne about their misfortune of having a flat tire and asked her to phone June. "I'll drop the young fellow off first and should be home in forty-five minutes or so."

"I just made a carrot cake. We'll have it and some tea when you get back."

Once at June's place, Andrew carried Mark into the house, laid him on his bed and then went back out to get Mark's suitcase.

"You got time for a quick iced tea?" June asked.

"I should be getting home. Anne will be waiting for me, but I guess I've got time for a quick one."

"One quick one coming right up," June retorted with a seductive grin.

Although June was wearing a pair of decent shorts, she was wearing the same flimsy bikini top Anne saw her in. She swung her large breasts like pendulums as she came in with the tea on a tray. Andrew was sitting on the couch. As she bent over to put the tray on the coffee table, Andrew was wondering if the material could retain the load, or if gravity would overcome the strength of the cloth, resulting in major fall-out.

Andrew was nervous. Every time June talked to him, he tried to force himself to make and retain eye contact. It was a losing battle though. Invariably, his eyes would glance down to where they shouldn't be looking.

"Got to get going," he said, putting his glass down.

Suddenly, June was all over Andrew, kissing him, pushing him down and half-lying on top of him.

"I know just what you need," she said in a throaty voice. "Anne can wait a few minutes. I've been waiting a long time for this."

"This isn't going to work," Andrew said sternly, untangling himself from June and getting to his feet. "I'm flattered by the offer and if I weren't married, we'd already be in your bedroom. I hope we can keep this to ourselves. I'll drop by Sunday afternoon to take Mark to camp."

"Sissy," June said suggestively, walking Andrew to the door.

"Whew, that was a close one," Andrew muttered as he pulled away from June's place. "I see now that my supervisor knows what he's talking about. Best not breathe a word of this to Anne. Maybe later, but now is not the time."

"Oh, your kiss tastes like iced tea," Anne said as she greeted Andrew at the door.

"Yeah I had a glass at June's," Andrew replied nervously. "Can we get into that carrot cake now? I've been hungry for it for the last hour."

"Was she wearing something decent?"

"Was who wearing something decent? Oh, I suppose you mean June. Yes, pretty decent."

"I drove by her place the other day and you should have seen what she had on or to put it a better way, what she had off. In the middle of town it just looked most vulgar."

"Yeah the poor dumb broad doesn't have a clue, doesn't have a clue."

Sunday, Andrew went to early Mass as usual and then went to Anne's church for the afternoon performance by the DVBS kids. In mid-afternoon, Andrew picked Mark up. To save Andrew a trip, Anne took Mark out to the camp with her.

As she lay in bed in her little cabin that evening, Anne's mind again focused on June. "Andrew had tea with her. Is something going on? No, it can't be. Andrew has always been true to me. Still, what if?"

CHAPTER TWENTY-FIVE

Anne stood on the white sandy beach of Sylvan Lake, supervising the children as they splashed and squealed in the shallows. It was a perfect summer afternoon, the gentle breeze making the water dance. Despite the beauty of the surroundings, Anne was feeling most uneasy. Thoughts of June were again on her mind as she wiggling her toes in the hot sand. Over the last few days she had told herself countless times that her fears were ill-founded and that Andrew was trustworthy. Despite constantly reassuring herself, she still had an uneasy feeling about Andrew's fidelity.

"I wonder if I should have vented to Becky about Andrew the night we were preparing for Daily Vacation Bible School?" Anne pondered. "Since then, every chance she gets, she wants to talk to me about our marriage. No question, I probably said more than I should have. Quite likely I shouldn't have mentioned anything. If I talked to anyone it should have been Pastor Bob instead of Becky. Bob's older and he's married. Becky isn't. Still, I'd feel uncomfortable talking to another man about my marriage. Maybe I should have talked to Bob and his wife or even Fritz and his wife. I sure hope it doesn't blow up in my face. I've got to be careful not to say anything more to her about our marriage."

Anne looked up with apprehension. Becky was walking towards her.

"I feel strongly led of the Lord to talk to you again about your marriage," Becky began, placing her hand on Anne's shoulder.

"Here it comes again," Anne thought, her face growing hot. "Why did I blab to her? Why, oh why did I spill the beans?"

"I think it would be best if we talk later," Anne countered, gently taking Becky's hand off her shoulder. "There's liable to be big ears out here. Drop by my room after supper."

"That's a good idea," Becky said and headed back to her side of the beach.

Anne was tense for the rest of the afternoon and only picked at her supper. She just finished taking a sponge bath in her little cabin when Becky stopped by.

"We'll have privacy here," Anne began. "My roommate Cora is usually busy in the kitchen till about nine."

"That's good. As I mentioned on the beach, I feel very strongly that the Lord is leading me to talk to you about your marriage again." Becky sat down beside Anne and took her hand. "You see, in the Bible we Christians are instructed by God not to be unequally yoked with unbelievers and there's a good reason for that. It's hard enough for us Christians not to sin, but with God's help we are able to overcome Satan. To the unbeliever though, it's an impossible task. I'm sorry, but what I'm going to tell you may be very hurtful as it concerns Andrew's faithfulness."

Anne broke out in a cold sweat. She sat there mesmerized, hardly able to breathe.

"As you probably know, young Mark tends to be a bit of a problem for us here."

"I'm well aware that Mark has lots of hang-ups," Anne interjected, her voice full of fear, "but what has that got to do with my marriage?"

"Well last night after supper, Mark got into a squabble with his cabin leader and as Fritz had gone to town for supplies, I was called on to intervene. I took him back to my room and was trying to counsel him. We didn't seem be getting anywhere until he started talking about his mom. He told me something about his mom and Andrew that was truly shocking."

"A few days back, you mentioned that Andrew was spending an awful lot of time with Mark. Maybe he has ulterior motives. Mark thinks the world of Andrew, but seems really upset with his mom. I asked him why he was having trouble with her and here's his story. He and Andrew got home from their trip quite late. Mark wasn't sure, but he thought he must have been sleeping. At any rate, he thinks Andrew carried him into the bedroom. Apparently Mark woke up because he had to go to the bathroom. The lights were on in the front room and through a crack in the hall door he made himself privy to quite a scene. He saw his mom put her arms around Andrew, kiss him and push herself down on top of him. Mark left then for fear of being caught. He said he'd seen his mom doing this before with other men and it bothered him."

Anne sat in stunned silence, a look of terror playing across her face.

As she continued, Becky kept stroking the back of Anne's hand. "After taking Mark back to his cabin, I was in a real quandary. I prayed about it for a spell and then phoned Pastor Bob for his advice. After talking to Pastor Bob about the incident and your marital problems, I spent several more hours in prayer. This morning I felt strongly led of God, that painful though it would be, it was my duty to tell you."

"Oh my God, how can this be?" Anne replied, tears spilling down her cheeks. "But why, Becky, why did you divulge our private conversation about my marriage to anyone else? At least you should have asked my permission before talking about my personal life."

Becky put her arm around Anne. "I'm sorry. I guess I was over-zealous in trying to protect you. I consider you a very close friend. You know me well enough to know my intentions were good. You're right though, I went too far. Without question I should have checked with you first. Will you forgive me?"

"Yes of course," Anne blurted out between sobs. "Will you promise me you won't be talking about this to anyone else?"

Becky nodded.

With tears streaming down her face, Anne got to her feet. "Please Becky, could you leave me alone for a while? I have to try to work this all out."

"I'll be in my room any time you want to talk to me," Becky said, heading for the door. "As I've told you countless times before, you just can't trust most men."

Anne threw herself across her bed. As she lay there crying; the picture of her mother in the hospital bed in London kept flashing through her mind. "Will I have to go through the same thing Mom did?" she moaned. "I know Andrew and I had become more distant, but I thought things were on the mend. Is this the end? Where did we go wrong? Am I to blame? I've got to phone Andrew," she said aloud, getting to her feet. "I've got to get to the bottom of this."

"Maybe I should phone Pastor Bob and Nora first," she muttered, halfway to the pay phone. "It might be best to get their advice before I talk to Andrew."

Anne went to the camp pay phone and got Pastor Bob and his wife Nora on the line. Trying hard to control her sobbing, Anne blurted out Becky's story.

"Our heart goes out to you," Bob said. "I wish that Becky had taken the advice Nora and I gave her last night. We told her it would be best not to broach the issue with you at camp. We said it would be better for Nora and me to contact you and try to get to the bottom of it once you were back home."

"God only knows how terrified I am," Anne responded, her voice quivering. "Oh Dear Lord, what can I do?"

"Try to stay calm. Things may not be as grim as Becky painted them. We have to remember that Becky's source was an emotionally disturbed ten-year-old lad. Without question, Becky was over-zealous and Nora and I will be talking to her about that. I realize she's just the assistant youth pastor now, but she was the full-time youth pastor for several months and will no doubt again become full-time youth pastor when Nora and I step down in September. She should be using a bit more prudence."

"Becky and I have worked closely in church activities since she came. The other day I confided in her on a few of the problems Andrew and I are having in our marriage. I wish now I would have tried to talk it out with Andrew or the two of you."

"For some time now I've meant to speak to you about Becky," Nora interjected. "Bob, I and some of the other church members are not happy with what appears to be her strong bias against men. As Bob said, we will be talking to her now."

"From my point-of-view, Becky and I are just good friends. Without question she wants to protect me. I'd have to say you're right though, Nora. Anytime she talks about men, she puts a negative slant on it."

"Now to take action," Bob continued. "You mentioned that you intended to contact Andrew. If you think it would be better to do it in person, you can take the church Jeep and drive home, or have Andrew come out to see you."

"I've got my car here so I'll take it. It's less than an hour's drive home. Thank you for your advice. It's helped a lot. If all goes well, I'll be back to camp in the morning. Please pray for me."

"Our prayers are with you," Bob concluded. "Stay in touch. That means Nora and I want you to feel free to phone us at any hour if you need to talk."

It was a beautiful evening with a gorgeous sunset turning the whole sky crimson as Anne started out for home, but she hardly noticed it. "Dear Lord, help me through this," she kept repeating, tears streaming down her cheeks.

By ten PM Anne was pulling into their driveway. Panic gripped her chest when she noticed that Andrew's car wasn't there.

"Oh Dear God, is he at June's?" Anne moaned as she walked to the door. "I guess if I'd used my head I'd have phoned first. Just what would I have said to him though? 'I hear you've been fooling around on me.' Dear Lord, help me through this awful mess and give me strength if it's bad news."

"That man of mine," Anne muttered trying the front door and finding it unlocked. "How many times have I told him that he should lock the door when he leaves?"

"Anyone home?" she called out, still hoping against hope that somehow Andrew would miraculously make an appearance.

There was only silence. Then as Anne whispered, "please Lord, I need your help," she heard the sound of the toilet flushing.

"That you Anne?" Andrew shouted from the bathroom.

"I'm so glad you're home," Anne replied, her voice quivering. "I thought you were gone since your car isn't here. We've got to talk."

"The car's in the backyard. I just finished washing it. You've been crying," Andrew continued, striding across the room and taking Anne in his arms.

Anne gently pushed Andrew back and repeated firmly, "we've got to talk. I've heard from reliable sources that there's something going on between Mark's mom and you. I just can't take it," she cried hysterically. "What's happening to us?"

Anne slumped into the armchair, curled up in a ball and cried uncontrollably. Andrew knelt beside her and tried to hug her. Again, Anne pushed him away.

"Alright. Have it your way," Andrew said sternly, sitting down across from her. "Do we want to get to the bottom of this or not?"

"I guess so," Anne whimpered, "I'm just so terrified that I might be losing you. I know things have been a little strained between us for the last year or so, but as of a few weeks ago I thought things were turning around. I don't know what's happening, but I want you to know that I still love you dearly."

"I still love you dearly too. As to what's driving us apart, I'm confused, but it certainly isn't Mark's mom. If I had to make a guess, I'd venture to say it's got something to do with this church thing. Maybe doubling up on going to church kept us closer. If you'll remember, it was Fritz, your youth pastor and my priest who suggested we should attend their respective churches exclusively. I'm about ready to bail out of the whole church thing. I dare say my priest is no better than Fritz. From what I observe, they're both more concerned with their egos than they are in really living as compassionate Christians."

"Right now I really could care less about the church thing," Anne replied after pausing to gain control. "I just want to know what's going on with Mark's mom and you. If you love me as you said you do, why have you turned to her?"

"Hold it, hold it!" Andrew hollered. "I'm not having a damned affair with Mark's mom. I freely admit I got a little too close to Mark, but there's nothing going on between June and me, not in the past and certainly not now."

"Then try to explain your way out of this," Anne said sarcastically. "Mark saw what was going on in their front room between you and June the night you guys got back from your trip. He was coming back from the bathroom and the door from the hallway into the front room was ajar. From what Mark told Becky, you and this June slut were all over each other."

"Oh my God," Andrew replied, very subdued. "Now I can see where you're coming from." He got up, softly placed his hand on Anne's shoulder and continued. "It would have helped if Becky had kept her nose out of things, but based on what she no doubt told you that Mark saw, I can understand why you're upset. It's obvious that Mark didn't see it all. I should take some responsibility for what happened, but it's sure not what you're thinking. Yesterday, I talked the whole thing about Mark and his mom over with my supervisor. He reinforced what I had finally figured out. I was trying too hard to become close to Mark, almost like I wanted to be his father. As you're aware, I still have my hang-ups in this area. My motives were honourable, but I over-did it."

"Now about June; I don't know how much Mark saw that night, but as I just said, he obviously didn't witness it all. I mean, I had no idea this woman had the hots for me. One moment we're talking and the next thing I know she's kissing me madly and sort of pushing me down and trying to lie on top of me."

"You're saying you never had any idea before this that she had feelings for you?" Anne asked in disbelief.

"So help me God! I was totally and I mean totally flabbergasted. You remember me saying she kept a slovenly house and that she didn't exactly keep herself all that clean?"

Anne nodded intently.

"Well, after I untangled myself from her, I said, 'this isn't going to work, June. I'm married and not about to do anything to screw up my marriage.' I mean, really dear, June's got a fairly good body, but her face would stop a clock and it wouldn't hurt if she'd brush her teeth once in a while and use a bit of underarm deodorant. Anyway, that's about it. I got up to leave and told her I'd be back on Sunday to pick Mark up to take him to Bible camp."

"When I talked to my supervisor, he suggested it might be best if I let someone else in the office take over on Mark after he gets back from camp. Considering what has gone on, that's what's going to happen. I suppose if I'd have had any brains, I'd have told you about it the night it happened, but I thought it would hurt you. You, poor dear, have had a rough go of it. I'm sorry you had to go through all this, but maybe it's our wake-up call. I think we'd better start working on us, rather than always reaching out to help someone else. That means my work as well as your church involvement."

"I'm just so relieved you weren't cheating on me," Anne said as she rushed into Andrew's waiting arms. "Thank you so much for remaining true to me. I was terrified I was going to have to go through the same ordeal my mom did. You're right about 'working on us,' though. There's no question in my mind that we've been drifting apart for quite some time. We've got to somehow try to get the glow back."

"I have an idea for starters," Andrew whispered holding Anne tight. "Maybe we should start by sleeping on it."

"It's nice you're not sending me back to camp to sleep all by myself," Anne replied, smiling coyly. "I'll have to be back early in the morning though."

"I'd have to be awfully hard-hearted to send you back," Andrew said seductively, taking Anne by the hand and leading her into the bedroom.

"That was so beautiful, Dear," Anne whispered, after they made passionate love. "I can't think of a better first step, but we both have a lot of thinking to do on how to get our marriage back to what it used to be."

"Yes you're right," Andrew countered and then slyly added, "Maybe I should come out to see you tomorrow evening. If we could be as friendly with each other again as we were tonight, that would be a good second step."

"It's an idea," Anne replied, snuggling close to Andrew. "We'll have to see, we'll have to see."

CHAPTER TWENTY-SIX

Anne and Andrew awoke to heavy fog. After an early breakfast, Andrew was off to work while Anne was on the road back to camp. As she drove along in the heavy mist she whispered over and over again, "Thank you, Lord, for keeping Andrew true to me."

Just before Anne got to camp the sun broke through. Every blade of grass and every leaf sparkled like diamonds in the sunlight. Anne felt really positive for the first time in over a year. As her thoughts returned to last night's intimate encounter with Andrew; her face flushed. "I must try to avoid Becky," she thought as she stepped out of the car.

At eight AM Anne phoned Pastor Bob and Nora to tell them that Andrew and she had resolved the issue.

Anne managed to keep her distance from Becky until they were doing their joint supervision of the beach in early afternoon.

"You were gone last night," Becky said, coming up beside her. "I wanted to see how you were making out so I stopped at your room a bit after nine. Cora said you weren't in and must have left before she got off work. I thought maybe you had gone for a walk, but then I checked in the parking area and noticed your car was gone."

"I slipped home last evening."

"I spent many hours on my knees last night praying for your welfare," Becky continued, placing her hand on Anne's shoulder. "The Lord finally gave me peace and assurance that he'll be there for you if your marriage fails. If you need to talk more about it, I'll always be here for you."

"Listen, Becky. Andrew and I resolved the June incident last night and it's not what you had me believe it was." Anne reached up and removed Becky's hand. "Mark didn't see it all. I'll talk to you about it later. We'll have to remember that this is a kid's camp. I think we should be concerning ourselves about them, rather than always talking about my marriage."

"I was just trying...."

"I'm sorry," Anne said, cutting Becky off in mid-sentence. "Like I said yesterday, this is not the time or place to be talking about it. We'll discuss it when we get back from camp. I'm not upset with you. I'm just so glad that Andrew remained true to me."

Anne turned and walked to the other side of the beach. Becky took a step to follow, but then turned back to watching the kids. Once the supervision was over, Anne wanted to be by herself so stopped in at the office and picked up the keys for the guest cabin.

Throughout the day Andrew's thoughts were on Anne. George, Andrew's supervisor was out of the office for the day, but left a memo for Andrew to meet him for coffee in Red Deer on Saturday morning. After work, Andrew grabbed a bite to eat and then headed to camp. His mind was abuzz with how they could make their marriage better. He was so preoccupied that he drove right by the camp turnoff. As Andrew backed up, he was becoming aroused as he relived making love to Anne the night before. "I wouldn't mind an encore performance tonight," he thought as he pulled into the parking lot.

"Hey there," a voice called out.

Andrew looked up to see Anne running towards him. As they walked hand in hand, Andrew leaned down and whispered in Anne's ear, "I've been thinking about you all day."

"And I've been thinking about you all day too. I told Fritz that you'd be spending the night so we're going to use the guest cabin. It's no fancier than the other cabins, but we'll have privacy. There's a hotplate and I can make some tea."

It was hot and muggy in the cabin. While Anne started making the tea, Andrew took off his shirt and pants. There was a loud knock at the door. Andrew grabbed his pants and went scuttling for the bedroom.

It was Fritz.

"Sorry for the short notice, Anne, but on the spur of the moment we've decided for staff and counsellors to get together for a social hour. A local businessman from across the lake brought his pontoon boat over and took the young folk out on the lake for a ride. They'll be gone for couple of hours."

"I don't know," Anne began hesitantly.

"Sounds like a good idea," Andrew called out. He opened the bedroom door, strode across the room towards Fritz and extending his hand. "Maybe you'd let me tag along. How are you doing, Fritz?"

"Good to see you again, Andrew," Fritz said, moving his hand in Andrew's direction.

"Good to see you too. We'll be over in a minute or two. I just have to get my shirt on."

As soon as Fritz left, Anne turned to Andrew. "I think you're a bad boy. Correct me if I'm wrong, but didn't you give Fritz one of your special extra firm handshakes?"

"Not really," Andrew replied with a chuckle, "just my regular firm handshake. Fritz may not be my favourite minister, but I really don't have an axe to grind with him. Now Becky, that's different, but then you can't go around crushing women's hands."

"Are you really all that keen on going to some boring staff get-together? I'm certainly not in the party mood, especially if it involves watching some movie or the like. Maybe we should go for a walk instead."

"I feel about the same way, but I told Fritz we'd be over, so let's give it a try. Anytime it gets too much to bear we can always leave."

They just stepped inside when Fritz announced, "We're going to be informal tonight. I have a movie here that we might find interesting. The movie has received rave reviews from our church head office. It's a Christian movie with the rather startling title, 'Too Late.' The storyline is that through salvation there's a heaven to be won and a hell to be shunned. What do you say we take a look at it?"

Five minutes into the movie, Andrew whispered in Anne's

ear, "This stuff is pretty strong propaganda. Maybe your suggestion of a walk isn't all that bad an idea after all."

"Yes, let's go," Anne whispered back, taking Andrew by the hand and heading for the door.

"Men," Becky muttered under her breath as she glanced up and saw Andrew and Anne leaving. "Why does he have to come out here and interfere?"

Once Andrew and Anne got to the beach they both kicked off their shoes. Despite the early morning fog, it had turned into a gorgeous day. They scuffed along in the warm sand, hand-in-hand, drinking in the beautiful surroundings, not saying a word. Andrew would stop when he found a flat stone and see how many times he could skip it on the water. Anne would occasionally try, but didn't seem to have the knack for it. The sandy beach went on for close to a mile and then turned into large boulders. Andrew found a rock big enough for both of them to sit on. It was still warm from the sun. They sat down close to each other and dangled their feet in the water.

"Know something? I'm glad I'm here with you and not with Becky," Anne said, snuggling even closer to Andrew.

"And I'm glad you're not Becky," Andrew responded, chuckling. "If Becky were here I'd have to deal with a woman who doesn't like men. It was a dumb, dumb, dumb thing for her to spread some half-baked rumour. In a different vain, we must be careful not to blame Becky, or for that matter, June, for all our problems. They contributed a bit of course, but we have to take a lot of the responsibility on our own shoulders. Our marriage was under stress long before they came on the scene."

"I was thinking just about the same thing this afternoon.

Like your mom said to us, we were spreading ourselves so thin looking after others that our marriage took a serious slide. It became a vicious circle. The more I got involved with the church, the more you got involved in your work. The more you focussed on your work, the more I turned to the church."

"Anyway, I'm glad we smartened up soon enough," Andrew interjected. "Now turn around towards the sun and close your eyes. I have a little something for you."

As Anne turned around facing the setting sun, Andrew draped a necklace around her neck. "You can open your eyes now," he whispered in her ear.

"Andrew, it's my old agate," Anne cried out. "You've made it into a necklace. It's so beautiful!" Holding the agate up to her eye she continued, "Just look at the sunlight shine through it."

"It really was more than just an omen for us that our marriage would be blessed," Andrew added softly, fingering the smooth gem. "The Lord led me to it when I asked for a sign that we'd be together. When we displayed it on our mantle place, it was a pronouncement of our everlasting love. Then of course you let Becky talk you into believing it was an idol and you moved it somewhere out-of-sight."

"Yes, I know," Anne said sadly. "It's strange that I allowed my thinking to become so warped by her. I mean, yes, we were friends, but she was bitter about her dad, bitter about her ex-husband, bitter about most men and sort of bitter about life in general. Now that I really think about it, she was using subtle means to try to get me to turn against you too. The mistake I made was going along with her thinking instead of using my own God-given common-sense; never again. When we get back from camp, I'm going to have a long talk with her. I'll be kind, but straight."

By the time Anne and Andrew got back from their walk, the staff party was over and the kids had returned from their boat ride.

Andrew and Anne went to the guest cabin and Anne made another pot of tea.

"We'd better turn in early," Anne said after they finished their tea. "Tomorrow will be a full day as it's the last day of camp. There's a program in the afternoon and in the morning I have two classes to rehearse."

Anne flipped back the covers and hopped into bed.

"Now, what about the chance of an encore for last night's performance?" Andrew asked.

"Why not," Anne replied impishly, "why not."

"Come look at this," Andrew called out as he stood looking out the cabin window next morning. "I haven't seen a sunrise like this in a coon's age."

"Oh it's simply gorgeous!" Anne exclaimed, joining Andrew at the window. "I can't ever remember seeing such a beautiful sunrise and look, the whole sky is crimson from horizon to horizon. You'll have to pardon me again for always looking for signs, but I think God sent this sunrise to tell us that He's renewing our marriage."

"Could very well be," Andrew replied, pulling Anne close. "How about starting our renewed relationship with something to eat?"

After breakfast, while Anne was busy working with the kids preparing for the afternoon closing program, Andrew headed to Red Deer to meet with his supervisor for coffee.

"I'm concerned for you and wondering how you're holding in there after the Katrina and Mark incidents," George began. "Both of them are pretty heavy stuff, but back to back, now that's a real whammy."

"I think I've learned more in the last three weeks than in the three years before that. You warned me about the dangers of getting too close to one's clients. I guess I had to find out the hard way that I can't resolve all the pain in this world single-handedly. Unfortunately, I didn't tell Anne about the June incident when it happened. Poor girl found out about it second-hand. Thank God it's all been straightened out now. Anne and I are doing well. This was our wake-up call. We're both determined to slack off some."

"That's good to hear. You haven't taken your holidays yet and you need the break. I'm not about to twist your arm, but I'd say the sooner the better. Does Anne have any commitments in the next while?"

"Not that I'm aware of."

"Talk it over with your wife and if it works out for her, take the next two or three weeks off. You see, Andrew, when I first started out in this line of work I too thought I could solve all the world's problems. It took me some time to find that all-important balance. I think both you and Anne have finally found that happy middle ground."

They had just started the program when Andrew got back to the camp. As he walked into the sanctuary he noticed that Anne was sitting in the front row with her class. He slipped into a back seat. On a slip of paper he hurriedly wrote:

Miss Anne:

Would you be at all interested in going to the Oregon Coast with the author of this note for a second honeymoon? The sooner the better, preferably tomorrow.

Love, Andrew

Andrew folded the paper and beckoned to an usher. "Could you please take this note to Mrs Anne Ogilvy? I believe she's in the front row."

"Oh, Yes, Yes, Yes!" Anne cried out in glee to the usher. "Could you tell the gentleman who sent this note that I'd love to accept his offer?"

With a shrug of his shoulders and a most bewildered look on his face, the usher strode back to Andrew and relayed Anne's message to him.

"You wouldn't be the gentleman who offered to take me to the Oregon coast?" Anne asked with a smirk, as she came up beside Andrew at the close of the program.

"I'm the lucky guy alright. Have you got your bags packed, Miss Anne?"

After the program Anne and Andrew met with Pastor Layman and his wife Nora in the guest cabin.

"I talked to Becky this morning regarding the June incident," Anne said. "Things have been resolved with her and I'm happy to say we're still friends. I think we mended all the broken fences. If there's blame to be levied for Andrew's and my problems, the two of us must take most of the responsibility."

"We're happy things turned out so well for you," Nora said. "God has certainly answered our prayers. It's good to see the two of you pulling onside again."

CHAPTER TWENTY-SEVEN

As Anne's Sunday School class was in recess for the summer break, Sunday morning she and Andrew indulged themselves by sleeping in. They decided to 'tent it' on their holiday as they had done on their honeymoon. They had done most of the packing the night before, so by mid-afternoon they were on the road. Anne wanted them to retrace the route they had taken down to the Oregon coast and by nightfall they were getting into the Coal Branch. They'd passed through a couple of thunderstorms and seeing the sky still looked ominous, they took a motel for the night just on the outskirts of the small village of Coalberg. Little did Andrew realize that they were spending the night less than a mile from where his biological mother had lived as a girl.

"A few nights ago we talked a bit about starting a family," Anne said as they were getting ready for bed. "Have you thought any more about it?"

"Yes I have. As I said before, there's no sense waiting till we are financial secure before we begin. If we wait that long, the equipment needed to do the job might be worn out. And then there's always the chance we'll have forgotten how to use it. For what it's worth, I'm willing to gird up my loins and be ready when you're ready. How about us celebrating our third anniversary the same way we did the night we were married?

It might be just a practice run, but as they say, 'practice makes perfect.'"

"No one can fault you on not being consistent," Anne chuckled, taking Andrew by the hand and leading him into the bedroom.

After a late breakfast they were on their way. By mid-afternoon, Andrew and Anne crossed the border into northern Idaho and were passing through a sparsely populated section. The light rain that had been falling was letting up. Anne was curled up on the front seat sleeping. Andrew descended a steep river valley and crossed a bridge. Ahead, the road curved before starting up the other side of the river bank. Just as he starting into the bend, he saw an old man in a red coat and cowboy hat, standing on an approach at the left side of the road, waving his hand. Andrew hit the brakes, pulled across the road onto the approach, stopped and rolled his window down.

"Having trouble?"

"Yeah, I'm afraid that old goat of a pickup of mine has finally cratered. I'm back off the highway a mile or so. The miserable old bastard blew her motor. My name's Roper, Steve Roper."

"You'll need a lift then," Andrew replied.

Before the old man could reply, the sound of squealing tires forced Andrew's eyes back on the road ahead. Coming down the hill and into the corner a speeding semi-trailer truck was bearing down on them. The tractor trailer was whipping from one side of the road to the other, skidding on the wet pavement. It was completely out of control. The huge truck shot past them with only feet to spare. Miraculously, before the truck collided with anything, the driver got some control and managed to get across the bridge with a minimum of scraping to the sides of his trailer. He shot up the escape lane on the other side of the river and finally stopped.

****

Close to a thousand miles to the northeast, as Andrew and Anne headed down towards the bridge, Sister Maria was in her room meditating. Suddenly, she felt that mysterious, strong urge to pray for her son and as in the past, a person close to her son. She dropped to her knees at the side of the bed. Just as Andrew and Anne were crossing the bridge, she was earnestly praying for their welfare. She had no insight as to what was amiss, but as on previous occasions prayed fervently until the burden lifted. A few minutes later a feeling of peace enveloped her and she went back to her meditation.

****

"Man alive, that was too close for comfort," Andrew exclaimed turning back to Steve.

There was no one there. The old man had vanished.

"Oh my God, what happened to that old man?" Andrew exclaimed. "What the devil is going on here? We were between him and the truck so the truck couldn't have taken him out."

The sound of the careening truck woke Anne. "What's happening?" she asked, sitting up with a start.

"We were just a hair's breadth from getting wiped out by a semi!" Andrew exclaimed. "I don't get it. I just crossed the bridge when I saw this old man standing on the other side of the road. He was waving so I pulled over here and stopped to see what he wanted. He said his name was Steve Roper. I just started to talk to him when I heard this truck barrelling down on us. The truck nearly hit us. I was watching the truck and when I turned to talk to the old man again, he was gone. It was just like he vanished into thin air."

Andrew and Anne made an extensive search around their car, but failed to find any signs of the old man. They then drove back across the bridge and met the truck driver trotting down the road to meet them.

"I hope no one is hurt," he cried out. "I lost the brakes on the tractor and trailer. That's why I was all over the road."

"No, we're okay, but I'll bet your trailer missed us by no more than two feet," Andrew replied. "If I hadn't pulled off the road my wife and I would have been history."

"Thank God I didn't meet you or anyone else coming down the hill. Things were happening so fast I couldn't tell whether I hit you or not. I've contacted the sheriff and a tow truck on my radio. They should be here pretty soon."

Andrew and Anne turned their car around and drove back to the approach, while the truck driver checked for damage on the bridge.

Hearing a door slam, Andrew glanced in the rear-view mirror. An old sheriff with well-worn features was slowly walking up to the car. Andrew and Anne got out of their car to meet him.

"It looks like we've had a bit of a close one here, folks. I trust no one was hurt."

"It was too close for comfort, but we're okay," Andrew replied. "There's just a little damage to the truck trailer. The truck driver is checking the bridge out now."

"I was just a couple or three miles down the road when I got the message on my radio. I'd best go talk to the truck driver. I'd be much obliged to you if you'd stick around for a few minutes. It would help if I could get a statement from you. I've radioed our highway maintenance department. They'll be here within the hour to check things out."

After the sheriff attended to the truck driver, he drove back to Andrew's and Anne's car and had them sit in with him.

"Before we make out a statement, there's something awful strange going on here," Andrew said. "I wouldn't mind talking about it and I hope you don't think me goofy."

"Go ahead," the sheriff said, glancing up from his paper work.

"You see, my wife and I were heading south. We just crossed the bridge when I saw this old man standing on the approach of the intersection waving his hand. Over there," Andrew pointed. "I stopped to see what his trouble was. He said the motor in his pickup had just cratered back off the highway about a mile. Anyway, we just started talking when I heard this semi barrelling down the hill. The truck went screeching past and when I turned back to the old man, he was gone. Just plumb vanished into thin air! Without question, if I hadn't pulled off the road and stopped to talk with him, we'd have been wiped out by the truck. We've done a pretty thorough search around where the truck passed us, but no sign of the old timer."

"Looks like old Steve is at it again," the sheriff muttered, shaking his head. "Was he wearing a cowboy hat and red coat?"

313

"Yes, that's him."

"You people are the fifth in the last ten years or so to report talking to the old man at that spot. According to what I've been told, the ghost, or whatever you want to call it, is the spitting image of Steve Roper, an old timer who used to live in the area. He always says a few words, usually tells them his name and then disappears into thin air."

"You see, it was in late November, back maybe something like twelve years ago. Old Steve Roper was coming home from hunting when his pickup broke down about three quarters of a mile from the highway. Steve was a real odd one. His neighbours claimed he was a clairvoyant. I guess he was married once, back about forty years ago. He did a bit of logging over the years and a whole lot of hunting, some of it legal, some not. Anyway, the day he died he had walked out to the highway after his truck broke down. The roads were very icy that day. He was standing on the shoulder of the road, about where you saw him. Some young hooligans, high on booze, going far too fast, lost control of their car and slammed into him. Steve was instantly killed. If you want to go over to where you talked to him, you'll see the cross on the edge of the road marking the spot where he died."

"His sightings seem to sort of follow a pattern. He talks about being broke down, where he lives, sometimes gives them some sort of a message and then vanishes. Hard to say how many people have seen him who haven't reported it, or even stopped. The first time it happened I reported it to the State police authority in Boise. They thought it quite a joke; said we must have been high on mushrooms or the like."

"You say he's given some people messages?" Anne interjected. "Does anything ever come of those messages?"

"Nothing you could prove I suppose, but then come to

think of it there was Bob Cassidy. That was six or seven years ago. When Bob reported it to me he said old Steve waved him and his wife down at this same spot. After shooting the breeze with them for a minute or so he said 'you're going to need a boat' and then, just like that he disappeared. Bob thought it quite a lark. They had a small farm down on the river flats a few miles east of here. Three weeks later we got six inches of rain over a day and a half at the same time the snow was melting up in the mountains. The river flooded and washed their house away. Sort of makes you think, doesn't it?"

"Of course I have to make out a report on this incident and get your input. Maybe you could add a bit about seeing and talking to old Steve. I have written statements from most of the others who told me about their experience with old Steve's spirit. Just in case someone up the ladder gets to thinking I've gone loco, I'll have these signed reports for backing."

After getting the written statements from Andrew and Anne, the sheriff was on his way.

"What do you make of it all?" Anne asked as Andrew led her back over to the spot where he had encountered the spirit.

"I'm not sure, but one thing I know for certain. If I hadn't pulled over to talk to the old man, you and I would be dead. I mean, it was so close. The whole thing really blows your mind. Maybe it's like finding the agate. Who knows? Could God have used the spirit of old Steve to save us from being killed?"

"I would venture to say the Lord did just that," Anne replied. "There's no sense letting this spoil our holiday though. None the less, it is pretty mind-boggling."

They walked up to a small cross on the shoulder of the road. The faded writing on the cross read:

Steve Roper
Rest in Peace

They got into their car and were on their way. As the miles slipped by, their near-miss, Steve's sighting and his sudden disappearance weighed heavy on Andrew's mind. Over and over he kept saying to himself, "what does it all mean?"

CHAPTER TWENTY-EIGHT

Andrew and Anne crossed Idaho into Washington and by nightfall were at the Columbia River. They found a campground with a panoramic view of the river valley. Andrew got their little propane stove going. While Anne made supper, he pitched the tent. In the growing darkness they watched the tugboats pulling barges on the river, going up and down stream till they melded with the horizon.

By eight AM they were on the road again. After reaching the ocean they followed the coast highway, 101. Anne's wish was for them to follow 101 down the Oregon Coast to the Redwoods in northern California as they had done on their honeymoon.

"I'm thinking of passing a new law," Anne said as they started down 101. "This time around, Mr Ogilvy, Mrs Ogilvy insists that we stop and see all and I mean all, 'points of interest' instead of going full bore past them. As I recall, that's what we did on our honeymoon."

"You wouldn't be referring to my practice of picking up speed whenever I saw a 'point-of-interest' sign coming up would you?" Andrew responded with a chuckle.

"You've got it and to put teeth in the law, there's a

possibility, faint though it may seem, that certain bedroom privileges might have to be curtailed if you drive past too many of them."

"I see your point," Andrew quickly replied, smiling. "With teeth in it like that, it might be a real concern what with us wanting to start a family. You look on your side. I'll look on my side."

Most nights Andrew and Anne camped as near to the beach as it was safe and as on their honeymoon were lulled to sleep by the relentless roar of the surf.

Andrew was somewhat embarrassed by the slow pace they were moving at, but Anne prevailed. Slowly but surely they were inching their way down the coast. They spent many hours lying in the sun, many more hours walking the beach looking for elusive agates. At the cheese factory in Tillamook, they stocked up on enough cheese and chocolate to last them the rest of the trip, if not the rest of the year.

When they got to the Redwoods in northern California, it was Andrew's turn to drag his feet. For two days they wandered the Redwood groves, marvelling at the beauty of the immense trees.

Finally time dictated that they start heading back home. Towards evening, as they were backtracking along Highway 101, Andrew hit the brakes.

"Hold it," he said, pulling over on the shoulder. "Do you recognize that hill off to the right? It's the same hill we climbed on our honeymoon, isn't it?"

"It is, Dear. Remember standing up there gazing at the coastline stretching north and south to the horizon?"

A grown-over trail led off the road to the base of the hill. Although it looked like it hadn't been used for years, Andrew managed to follow it with the car.

"I've got an idea," Andrew said. "It looks like it will be a beautiful night so what say we park here, pack our sleeping bag and air mattress up to the top of the hill and sleep there."

Andrew set up the stove for Anne and while she made supper, he packed their sleeping gear up to the top of the hill. Once supper was finished, they locked the car and headed up the hill.

The sun was just setting and the ocean was a huge mirror. Andrew and Anne lay in their double sleeping bag, staring out at the ocean until the mirror turned dark grey and the stars came out.

"If my calculations are right, this might be the opportune time to start on the family," Anne whispered, snuggling close to Andrew. "I trust you didn't tire yourself too much carrying all our gear up to the top of the hill."

"I may be a little tired, but not that tired," Andrew replied, caressing Anne.

"That was a super way to celebrate climbing our hill again," Andrew said, pulling the tarp over the sleeping bag. They were soon asleep.

As day was dawning, Andrew slipped out of the sleeping bag without waking Anne. Unbeknownst to Anne, some time back he had a small bronze plaque made up to commemorate their third anniversary. Taking his hatchet and the plaque, he walked the hundred odd yards to the small grove of redwoods. Andrew chose a four foot diameter tree that looked out on the spot where they slept. Up about six feet off the ground he trimmed down one of the ribs on the bark to make a flat surface. He had drilled two holes in the plaque. Holding the plaque in place and using the back of the hatchet, he drove in two spikes attaching the plaque firmly to the tree. Taking his battery powered dremel, he etched in an addendum on the plaque.

By the time Andrew got back, Anne was stirring.

"You snuck out of bed on me."

"Yes, I had a little thing I had to do. Get your clothes on and come take a look."

Anne dressed and followed Andrew to the tree he had attached the plaque to. With Andrew's arm around her, she read:

TO ANNE OGILVY and (?)
THIS PLAQUE PLACED IN HONOUR OF ANNE OGILVY
LOVE OF MY LIFE
GIRL OF MY DREAMS
BEST FRIEND AND LOVER
YOUR HUSBAND OF THREE YEARS
ANDREW

"Thank you so much, Darling," Anne whispered, tears slipping down her cheeks. "You're such a wonder. Just when I think I've got you all figured out, you come up with something like this. I'll cherish this memory as long as I live. It's so thoughtful of you to add the question mark. Who knows, maybe at this very moment a small being is starting to grow in my body."

Torrential rain started in the afternoon, forcing them inland to the safer four-lane highway. When they stopped at a motel for the night, Andrew phoned home. There was bad news from the Lodge in Rocky Ridge. His mother had another mild heart attack and had been hospitalised for a few days. It now became urgent for them to get home as quickly as possible.

Sunday afternoon, Andrew and Anne arrived back home and headed straight out to Rocky Ridge to visit Edith.

"I was wondering for a spell if I'd ever see you two again," Edith began, tears staining her cheeks. "I guess it wasn't time for the Good Lord to call me home though. The doctor feels I'm holding my own, but he said with my heart being as weak as it is, the next attack would be very grave."

Andrew and Anne highlighted their trip to Edith and their new commitment to keep their marriage on track.

"While you were on holidays, I did a lot of thinking about the money we have laid away in investments from the sale of the old house," Edith said as Andrew and Anne were getting ready to leave. "It's foolish for you to be paying rent on your house when there's enough money to buy you a place. I'm not taking any of the money out anymore because I don't need it. It would be good for you to get a place of your own. Maybe, if the Lord spares me, I could come and visit you in your new home. That would make me so happy."

With Edith's blessing, Anne and Andrew began looking for a house. They had long dreamed of an acreage that would have a view of the mountains and still be close enough to Innsburg for an easy commute for Anne. While Andrew was at work, Anne spent many days with real estate agents looking for their dream acreage. Of the few properties that were available, nothing seemed to catch their fancy. Finally Anne struck pay-dirt. Her school principal had accepted a new teaching position in the Peace River Country. He and his wife had already made an offer on a house in Grande Prairie.

They were eager to sell their acreage as quickly as possible and priced it accordingly.

The acreage was located on a south western slope three miles west of Innsburg. The first time Anne laid eyes on the property, she fell in love with it. The house was a five year old bungalow with an undeveloped basement. A full-width veranda on the west side of the house gave a breath-taking view of the mountains. On the main floor there was a large open kitchen-living room, three bedrooms, a bathroom and a utility room. Andrew felt that by developing the basement they would have all the room they needed once they had a family. Outside was a double-car detached garage and a large storage shed. There was a bluff of trees on the northwest edge of the property with the garden plot on the southeast corner.

The price for the property was a bit more than the value of Edith's and Andrew's investments. To cover the difference, Andrew and Anne took out a small five year mortgage for $4000.

On the fifteenth of August, Andrew and Anne moved into their new home. Saturday, Andrew picked up his mom and brought her out for a visit. Edith was now confined to a wheelchair and though in constant discomfort with her arthritis, was game to make the trip.

"You will never know how happy I am that you have your own place," Edith said after a tour of the grounds and house. "It's good to see that money put to good use."

"Andrew and I are so grateful to you for making it happen," Anne replied. "I can't think of a kinder gesture."

"We have some more good news too, Mom," Anne

continued. "I found out yesterday that I'm pregnant. The baby should arrive sometime in April."

"That's the news I've so longed to hear. What a day! First seeing your new home and then finding out I'll soon be a grandmother. God has been so good to me. I know my health is fragile, but with God's help, I'll do everything in my power to be here to see my first grandchild."

The Sunday after they moved into their new house, Andrew and Anne began attending the United Church in Innsburg. Anne taught until Christmas and then took maternity leave. Both Andrew and Anne were happy in their new home and in his spare time Andrew worked at finishing off the basement.

Edith was holding her own and although still suffering a lot with her arthritis, spent several weekends and Christmas at the acreage.

Despite the occasional bout of morning sickness, Anne was thoroughly enjoying her time off work. She was now able to keep in closer contact with Edith and usually phoned her every day. Towards spring, Edith began slipping again. Plans were for her to spend Easter at the acreage, but on Good Friday, her heart started acting up again and her doctor had her admitted to the hospital.

After Easter Sunday service, Andrew and Anne drove out to be with Edith for the day. Although very weak, she was resting comfortably.

"Ever since I was admitted to the hospital, I've been praying non-stop that I'd be able to see the baby. After that, God can take me any time he sees fit."

"If the doctor is right, the baby should be here in two

weeks or so," Anne said as they were leaving. "When I deliver, if you can't travel, we'll bring the baby out here for you to see."

"I'll be so looking forward to that," Edith said. Andrew and Anne hugged her goodbye and headed out.

On the eighteenth of April, Anne went into labour while Andrew was at work. She contacted Andrew's supervisor, but Andrew was out making a visit. Her bag had been packed and ready to go for a week. Anne had contingency plans with a neighbour lady to drive her to the hospital if Andrew wasn't available. The neighbour dropped over and when a contraction ended, they headed for the hospital. The supervisor finally contacted Andrew and he rushed to Anne's side.

Anne's labour was on and off for most of the day, but by nine PM the contractions were becoming much stronger and the doctor was called. At eleven, with Andrew by her side, Anne delivered a baby boy. Both mother and father shed tears of joy at the birth of their son. They named him Roy Andrew.

It was a beautiful spring morning when Anne and baby Roy were discharged. The previous evening, Andrew checked with his mom's doctor.

"In her frail condition, it would be far better to bring the baby out here. In all honesty, I don't think your mother would survive the trip."

In the early afternoon, Anne, Baby Roy and Andrew headed out to the hospital in Rocky Ridge to see Edith. She was very weak, but her mind was still lucid.

Tears flowed down the old lady's face as Anne laid the

little boy in her arms. "What a thrill," she whispered, "my first grandchild. What have you named him?"

"We've named him Roy, after his grandfather," Andrew responded. "Roy Andrew Ogilvy will be his handle. I guess I was named after my father so the baby will be named after both his grandfathers."

With Edith's condition steadily deteriorating, Andrew drove to Rocky Ridge every day after work to spend a couple of hours with her. Ten days after Roy's birth, Andrew got a call from the hospital that his mom's body functions were starting to shut down. By the time he got to the hospital, she was drifting in and out of consciousness.

At ten PM she surfaced. "Thank you for coming, Son," she whispered, reaching for his hand. "I had such a beautiful dream last night, or maybe it was this morning. At any rate, I saw Roy. He was standing there with that big smile of his. He reached out his hand to me and then he disappeared." As Andrew held his mother's hand tight, she slipped back under.

A half hour later, with Andrew still holding her hand and a peaceful expression on her face, Edith breathed her last and slipped into the next dimension.

Andrew sat by his mom's bedside for a long time, holding her hand and weeping. Finally, he called the nursing station and went to phone Anne. At the sound of Anne's voice he again lost control.

"Your mom's gone?" Anne asked quietly.

"A few minutes ago," Andrew blurted out. "She was such a good mother."

"Indeed she was. She was the closest one to a saint of anyone I've known. If you'd like, I can phone your supervisor. He'll want to know."

"It would be nice if you could," Andrew said, pulling himself together. "I'll be home in an hour or so."

Andrew made arrangements with the hospital staff to have the funeral home pick up the body and then headed for home. Several times he'd have to pull over to the shoulder of the road as the tears blinded his vision.

Anne greeted Andrew at the door and held him close. Andrew broke down. Anne cried with him.

"She was such a wonderful Mom to me when I needed one so badly," Andrew said, trying to gain control again. "I so desperately needed to belong to a family and she made it happen. I'll never forget the warm feeling I got when she showed me the form she'd made out for my adoption."

"And I'll never forget how lovingly she accepted me. Really, she's been more of a mother to me than my real mother."

Over the next couple of days, Andrew and Anne were busy with funeral plans. Although Father Bernard had retired, he said he'd be honoured to take the funeral. Anne contacted her own family, but none could make it. Anne's father was recovering from prostate surgery and her mother felt she had to stay with him. Rachel was in South America on a missionary project.

Despite Anne's reservations, Andrew felt he had to do his mom's eulogy.

"It will be the last thing I'll be able to do for Mom. I just have to do it. People will understand if I break down."

Father Bernard was a great one for telling stories. In his opening remarks he told the incident of Edith praying for a miracle so she'd be financially secure enough to adopt Andrew. "It was going to have to be a big miracle, because Edith's finances were anything but robust. Her faith was so strong that God rewarded her in the strangest answer to prayer I've ever witnessed. A forgotten investment that her husband, Roy, had made in some small company down in the states years before, surfaced when the company was bought out by a larger one. When the books of the small company were reviewed, Roy's old investment came to light. The money Edith received was enough that she was able to adopt Andrew."

As Father Bernard began telling the story, Andrew's resolve to keep a firm hand on his emotions vanished and he started weeping. By the time he was called on for the eulogy though, he had again gotten a grip on himself.

After reading the formal part of the eulogy, Andrew put his notes aside.

"As most of you know, I was a foster child. The fall I turned thirteen some pretty rough things happened to me. Doctor Bell and his wife rescued me from a very abusive home. Through them, Mom and I met. Edith was the Mother I'd so longed for. I'll never forget it. A few months after I came to stay with her, she used her mother's prize gold broach to back a small loan to get enough money to buy me a school jacket." After pausing a moment to collect himself, he continued. "I don't know if you can understand what her sacrifice and kindness meant to me. Barring none, the happiest moment of my life was the afternoon she showed me the application for..." Andrew covered his face with his hands and fought for control. Many of the audience wept. Finally he blurted out, "...the application for my adoption. I was going to have a real mother rather than a foster one. Throughout the years she was always there for me, supporting me when I had relationship problems and when I was perplexed with career choices. She was such a compassionate lady. Not only did she finance Anne's folks' trip from Africa to our wedding, she provided the money for us to buy our house."

"Thank you, Mom, for being the best Mother in the world." Turning to the casket, he whispered, "Goodbye Mom." With tears streaming down his face he made his way back to his seat.

The love and support from family and friends helped Andrew with the pain of losing his mom. Nonetheless, within a few days he was on one of his real downers. Anne was proactive with this bout of depression and insisted that Andrew make an appointment with a new psychiatrist who had just moved to Red Deer. After getting Andrew to fill him in on his history of depression, the doctor did blood work. He finally persuaded Andrew to start taking an anti-depressant medication. It took some time for the medication to take effect, but it would prove a godsend for Andrew. Although he occasionally had his not-so-good days, he would never again hit the lows he used to experience.

CHAPTER TWENTY-NINE

Roy was growing fast and a great joy to both his mom and dad. By the time he celebrated his first birthday, Anne was again expecting. In the third month of her pregnancy, she had a very startling dream. She dreamt that when she delivered, the baby's face was undefined, almost as if it was out of focus. When she had her three-month check-up, Anne mentioned the dream to Dr Bright and asked if everything was normal.

"Three months is a little too early to detect a lot of abnormalities, but at this point everything appears normal. It's quite common for pregnant women to have scary dreams about their unborn baby."

Although she worried constantly about what the dream could mean, for the time being she decided not to share it with Andrew.

A week after Anne got her six-month check-up; Dr Bright phoned her and asked her and Andrew to come to the clinic the next afternoon. When Andrew got home from work, Anne told him of her dream. In light of the phone call from Anne's doctor, both were apprehensive.

The next afternoon they sat holding hands in the waiting room, both very much on edge.

"I'm afraid we have some bad news," Doctor Bright began when he saw them in his office. "Maybe there was something to your dream after all, Anne. I'm sorry, but we don't think your baby's brain is developing properly. In my view it's difficult to say whether the pregnancy will last full-term. If it does, there's a chance the baby will be stillborn. From the tests we've done, I'm suspicious your baby has anencephaly, a condition where only the lower part of the brain develops. I'm going to suggest we make an appointment for you to see a specialist in Red Deer. I might add it's quite common for parents to have their babies institutionalized if they're severely challenged and go to term. Most of these babies that survive birth won't live long."

"What you do with your baby should it go to term and survive birth will be your decision. I'll remain neutral. If you're in agreement Anne, I'd like to refer you to Doctor Blais. He's the specialist in Red Deer I had in mind."

When Andrew and Anne got home from the doctor's office they sat holding hands. Not a word was spoken as they stared off into space.

"Doctor Bright mentioned something about it possibly being a genetic problem," Andrew said, breaking the spell. "Not knowing much about my background, I suppose that's a possibility. Are you feeling as numb as I am?"

"Pretty much. What's going over and over in my mind is the question, why us?"

"Perhaps because God knows we're strong, Anne, or because He knows this will make us stronger. I don't imagine I have to ask you if we are going to look after the baby, should it survive birth."

"There's no question in my mind. After carrying the baby in my body for nine months, I won't be giving it up. I don't care how challenged the baby is."

"I'm with you on that. It may be a heavy load, but I know we'll manage."

The next week Anne and Andrew met with Doctor Blais. After examining her, reviewing all the data Doctor Bright had provided him and doing more testing, he met Anne and Andrew in his office.

"I'm happy you could come with your wife," Doctor Blais began, extending his hand to Andrew. "Doctor Bright has no doubt prepared you for some of the possibilities if your baby survives birth. We don't know whether the abnormality is related to a genetic disorder and at this point it's really academic. Your baby is a boy and if your little fellow lives, he could be very mentally challenged. The ultrasound shows that though the lower or primitive part of the brain is developing, the cognitive part of the brain appears to be very restricted in its development. This indicates to us the baby has anencephaly. In layman's terms, although the lower part of the brain that controls heartbeat and breathing is developing, the little fellow may not be able to think."

"Doctor Bright advised me that you would be looking after the baby if he doesn't succumb before birth or during the birthing process. Although in this day and age this isn't expected of you, I highly commend both of you for making this decision."

"Because these births can at times be difficult, Doctor Bright has suggested that if at all possible, you should deliver here in the Red Deer Hospital."

With Anne's due date approaching, both she and Andrew

were becoming most apprehensive. They both tried to steel themselves for the worst. As near as could be determined, her due date would be the first week in November.

November fourth at seven AM, Anne's first contraction came. Andrew bundled up Roy, dropped him of at their neighbour's place and then drove Anne to the hospital in Red Deer. Anne's contractions were sporadic for most of the day. At four in the afternoon, Doctor Blais decided to induce the birth.

Andrew was by Anne's side at seven when the baby was born. It was an easy delivery as the baby was less than five pounds. Despite having steeled himself, Andrew was shocked when he first saw the baby. The head was small, the forehead sloped and the eyes very bulged. What Andrew found most startling was that the infant lay there in a lethargic state and didn't move his limbs.

In honour of Anne's grandfather they named their baby boy Rob.

The baby was cleaned up and checked out by Doctor Blais. After Anne was back in her room, the nurse brought the baby in to her. As she held her tiny deformed boy to her breast, there were tears in her eyes.

"He doesn't seem to want to nurse like Roy did," she said, her voice breaking. Andrew patted the back of Anne's hand and was about to reply when Doctor Blais knocked and came in.

"Why won't he try to nurse?" Anne asked.

Dr Blais came over and placed a hand on both Anne's and Andrew's shoulders. "I know this is a very traumatic time for the two of you. My heart goes out to you. The reason the little guy doesn't move or nurse is that for all intents and purposes he's really not conscious as we understand the word. Although his lower brain and organs are developed, as I surmised, he suffers from anencephaly. The thinking part of his brain has not developed. This may sound heartless, but with your permission, we will carefully monitor him. If we detect he's in pain, we'll sedate him. Advanced as we've become in the medical world, I'm sorry, but there's nothing else we can do."

"Will he die then?" Anne sobbed.

"I'm afraid so. It is just a matter of time. From my experience, little ones born as challenged as your little fellow will only last from a few hours up to maybe a day or so. Would you be more comfortable having him here in the room with you?"

"I'd like that."

"I'll have the nurses arrange that then. My heart goes out to both of you. Do you have any other questions?"

Both Andrew and Anne shook their heads. Andrew walked Doctor Blais to the door. With tears in his eyes Andrew whispered, "Thank you," and shook the doctor's hand.

"The little guy just seems to be sleeping," Anne said to Andrew as she held little Rob. "Even though he'll only last a few hours it's comforting to be able to hold him."

After talking it over, they decided that as Roy was so young, it would be best if he didn't see his brother. At eleven, Andrew kissed Anne and sleeping Rob goodnight and went home.

At ten the next morning, Andrew stopped to see Roy for a few minutes and then headed to the hospital.

When Andrew met Anne, she was very upbeat.

"Little Rob lay on my chest all last night," she said, her face beaming. "Towards morning I had the most wonderful dream. I was with Rob and he was maybe about four years old. He had curly blonde hair and the deepest blue eyes. We were running and playing in this big opening in a forest. There were lots of wild flowers and a huge old pine tree in the middle of the meadow. We were skipping and laughing as we came up to the big pine. He took me by the hand and said, 'don't cry, Mommy, it's so beautiful where I'm going.' Then he was gone."

Andrew did not reply. He sat holding Anne's hand, tears in his eyes. Throughout the day, Andrew and Anne took turns holding their son. At ten-thirty in the evening Andrew was heading for home. He had just stepped into the hall when he heard Anne call his name. Andrew rushed back into the room.

Rob was convulsing on Anne's chest, his little arms flailing about. His tiny little hand grasped his dad's finger. With a shrill, high-pitched cry, he breathed his last and passed back into the meadow.

After the nurses took the little body away, Andrew phoned to check on Roy. He then got the nurses to bring in a cot and he spent the night with Anne.

They had a small funeral with just a few close friends attending. Anne's dream would be of great comfort to her and Andrew for years to come.

Anne was relieved that Andrew didn't experience the post-funeral depression he had gone through in the past. There was no question, his medications were working.

On the advice of her doctor, Anne returned to her teaching job a month after Rob's death. As the months passed by, Anne and Andrew were agonizing over whether they should try for another child. Doctor Bright felt it would be safe, but again arranged an appointment for them to see Doctor Blais.

"Nice to see you folks again," Doctor Blais said, ushering Anne and Andrew into his office. "My heart goes out to you over the loss of your baby. If I remember correctly, your little boy only lived a day. A few hours after he was born I had to leave for a conference. What brings you here this time?"

"It's been six months since we lost Rob," Anne said. "We're worried about our chances of having another deformed baby should I get pregnant again. Doctor Bright has assured us that our chances of having a normal baby are very good. We just wanted your opinion."

"Doctor Bright is right. Statistically there is only a very slight chance of you having another abnormal youngster. The checks we did on you, Anne, with your last pregnancy, showed that from all indicators you are a normal, healthy woman. There were no abnormalities that we could detect in your family. Bear in mind the background check we did was only on you. With Andrew, it was limited since we couldn't do a check on his biological family. With every pregnancy there is a slight chance of abnormalities cropping up. It's almost a law of nature, as it's the same in the entire animal world. Usually, if the abnormality is severe the foetus won't go to term. That's nature's way. As with your son, the odd time they do go to term and survive birth. You already have a healthy son. Doctor Bright says he's a very bright, normal little boy. My advice from both a medical and personal point-of-view is to go for it."

Three months later Anne found out she was pregnant.

Despite the words of assurance from the two doctors, Anne worried constantly whether or not the baby would be normal. One night two months into her pregnancy she was having another sleepless night. She envied Andrew sleeping peacefully by her side. Suddenly, Andrew sat up.

"I was just dreaming about Mom. We were back on the old acreage, walking on one of the trails in our wood lot. It had rained in the night and everything smelled so fresh. Mom looked even younger than she did when I first came to stay with her. She stooped over, picked a wild rose and held it out to me. I could see the little droplets of water on the delicate pink pedals. 'Look how perfect it is,' Mom whispered. Then, just like that she vanished."

"Like you, I've been doing my fair share of worrying. I'm sure there's a message in the dream telling us to leave our worries about the pregnancy in God's hands."

"Yes you're right. We'll both have to make a concerted effort to do just that. I've started to really get down with all the worrying I'm doing. I'm going to have to smarten up."

The next four months were much more worry-free for both Anne and Andrew. Whenever a pang of worry did surface, they'd go back to Andrew's dream of his mom and the perfect rose for solace. Anne's six-month check-up went well. It was going to be a girl and everything appeared normal.

As they were driving back to the acreage that evening, the setting sun turned the whole sky scarlet. "There's our sign again," Anne called out. "As I've said countless times before you'll have to pardon me for always looking for signs. I really believe in them though. Just look at that magnificent sky. I'm sure God's telling us that we're going to have a healthy baby."

As Anne neared her due date, even though Doctor Bright assured them that their baby girl would be healthy, she and Andrew slipped back into the worry mode.

Saturday morning at five AM, Anne went into labour. By six, Anne and Andrew were in the hospital. At ten the contractions were becoming very intense. Doctor Bright arrived and Anne was taken into the delivery room. Twenty minutes later, with Andrew standing by her side, Anne gave birth to a perfect baby girl. Doctor Bright was triumphant. Once the baby was cleaned up and Anne was back in her room, the nurse laid the baby on Anne's chest. Within minutes the little girl wiggled up to Anne's breast and started nursing contentedly.

Although Anne shed a few tears when Doctor Bright announced that the baby was perfect, Andrew maintained his decorum. Once the baby was nursing, he excused himself, went to the bathroom and wept with fervour.

In honour of grandmother and mother they named their little girl Edith Anne. The night Anne and baby Edith came home from the hospital Roy was very quiet and seemed preoccupied.

"Will my sister go to be with God like Rob did?" He asked, climbing onto his daddy's knee. "I sure hope she doesn't cause I'll have no one to play with then."

"Your baby sister is very healthy and will grow up just like you," Daddy assured his son.

"That's good. Can I carry her, Mom? I'm big now."

After a few months, Roy was allowed to carry-haul his sister around the house under strict supervision from his parents.

"We've sure come a long way from the day we first met at Miss Cathy's office," Andrew said as he and Anne sat on the couch in the front room one evening.

"Yes we sure have," Anne replied as she glanced over at Roy half-carrying, half-dragging his sister over to his mother. "For a while it didn't look like we'd ever get together, but the Almighty prevailed and here we are, a complete family."

CHAPTER THIRTY

After Edith's one month celebration party, the family retired to the front room. Roy was sitting on Daddy's knee while Edith nursed contentedly in Mommy's arms.

"When Mom passed on, I started to get this nagging feeling I should try to find my biological mother," Andrew said. "With all the stress of wondering about how we'd cope with Rob, it got shifted to the back burner. Now that Rob's gone and little Edith is doing well, the nagging feeling is starting to build again."

"You should go for it," Anne replied. "Over the years you've talked about it a few times, but you said you weren't quite ready to pursue it. You have my full support. I'd imagine your biological mother would still be alive, but if you leave it much longer, who knows?"

About the only information Andrew had was that his mother came from southern Alberta, that he was named after his father and that his dad had died in the war. After numerous letters and phone calls he had made no progress.

"I wonder if you're tackling this the wrong way," Anne suggested one evening to a very frustrated Andrew. "Up till now you've been concentrating on getting information on your mother. Why not try your dad? You know he died in the Air Force and what his first name was. Also, you know the last name of the first couple who adopted you."

"It's worth a try, I guess. So far I've been batting zero. What's there to lose?"

Assuming that his dad was also from southern Alberta, Andrew contacted the Royal Canadian Legion and explained the dilemma he was in. The Legion provided him with a list of all servicemen killed in World War Two from all points south of Red Deer. Over the next two weeks, Andrew spent all his spare time checking all the Andrews who had died in the war. He was amazed at how common the name Andrew was. Into the third week he'd short-listed it to three or four possibilities. He finally zeroed-in on an Andrew Carpenter from Lethbridge who had died in action in 1943. His father had been Alvin Carpenter. After a number of phone calls he traced an Alvin Carpenter to an old folk's home in Calgary. When he contacted the matron, she advised him it would be best to see Alvin in person as he was quite deaf.

On Saturday afternoon, he drove to the old folk's home to check out his lead. Alvin was in his late eighties and although nearly blind and deaf, his mind was still sharp. He was fairly tall, quite stooped and had a mat of white hair.

Andrew met Alvin in his room. He told Alvin he was an orphan and looking for his biological family.

"I lost my son, Andrew, in 1943," Alvin began in a shaky voice. "His plane was shot down on a bombing run. He was my only son. He was just twenty-two." There were tears in Alvin's eyes and he had to stop to regain his composure. "He had a girlfriend. Maria Turnbull was her name. It was such a hard time for all of us. She found out she was pregnant a few weeks after my son went overseas. As her home life was poor, she stayed with my mother and me until the baby was born. It was a boy and she gave him up for adoption. Maria went into a convent. We didn't know anything of the adoptive parents. As I recall, Maria had wanted her son named Andrew, after his father. I don't know if they honoured that. Could you come a little closer? My eyesight is very poor."

"Grandpa!" Andrew cried out, dropping down close to the old man. "I'm Andrew, your grandson."

"Oh my God," Alvin whispered. "You are my grandson! You're the spitting image of your dad."

Andrew embraced Alvin and they both wept.

"It's a long story," Andrew continued. "I was adopted at birth, but when my parents divorced and my mother got hooked on drugs, I ended up in an orphanage. I was in a succession of foster homes. Some were good and some bad. At thirteen I had just been in a very abusive foster home when a doctor took me under his wing. He didn't locate my parents, but found out my dad was in the Air Force and died in action. From what the doctor was told, my adoptive parents honoured my mom's wish and named me Andrew, after my dad."

"There's no question in my mind that you're Andrew's son. You look so much alike. As I said, your mom stayed with us throughout her pregnancy with you. I'll piece it together for you as best I can."

For the next hour or so Alvin told the story of Andrew's death, Maria's pregnancy, baby Andrew's birth, his adoption and finally Alvin's marriage to Joy. "I should have stayed in closer touch with your mom, but Joy had problems in that area. Before we married, she was quite uncomfortable with Maria. I hoped that after we married, her attitude towards your mom would change. Unfortunately it didn't turn out that way. As time slipped by she became more and more negative towards her. When my mom passed on and then Joy's dad died, we moved to Nova Scotia to be near Joy's mom. I feel guilty for not having stayed in contact with your mom, but it was a constant battle with Joy and I guess I took the line of least resistance. I have to be honest with you. I was too weak to go against my wife's wishes. After your mom became a nun, I lost all track of her."

"Joy and I had a fairly decent life together. You know, we had a few ups and downs, but nothing we couldn't overcome. After Joy's mom passed on and we'd retired from teaching, we moved back to Alberta. We came to the lodge together five years past. Before we moved into the lodge, I wanted to try and look your mom up, but Joy was against it. She passed away a little over two years ago."

Andrew and Alvin highlighted their respective lives to each other for several hours. When the supper bell rang, Andrew got up to leave. He promised to visit his granddad again soon.

"I found my grandpa," Andrew blurted out when Anne met him at the door. As Anne held him, Andrew continued. "It's got to be one of the happiest days of my life." While they ate supper, Andrew reiterated to Anne what Alvin had told him. "You have no idea the difference it makes to start finding your roots. My birth mother became a nun, so it shouldn't be too hard to locate her. I've got a couple of days coming to me at work. I'll book off work Monday and see if I can find her."

Monday morning, Andrew drove to the retirement home where Father Bernard was staying to get his assistance in attempting to locate his mom. After two hours on the phone, Father Bernard and Andrew hit pay-dirt. There was a Sister Maria who taught close to thirty years in a Catholic Church school in the native village of Wasp Lake in northeast Alberta.

Her birth name was Maria Turnbull. She had recently been diagnosed with cancer at the Cross Cancer Clinic in Edmonton and was in grave condition in the University Hospital in Edmonton.

Tuesday morning, Andrew was on the road to Edmonton to meet Sister Maria. When he got to her ward, the head nurse introduced him to Maria's doctor. Doctor Parliament was a small wiry man. Although he was bald, he had a full red beard with streaks of white starting to show.

"Father Bernard and you talked to me yesterday," he said, shaking Andrew's hand. "Sister Maria is critically ill. Earlier this morning I asked her if she was up to a visit from you. I told her that you talked to an Alvin Carpenter and had reason to believe you were Andrew, her biological son. When I mentioned the names Alvin Carpenter and Andrew, she started to cry. She said that she had given a baby boy up for adoption when she was seventeen and longed to meet him again."

"A gentleman here to see you, Sister," Doctor Parliament said, ushering Andrew into Maria's room.

Lying in bed, propped up by pillows was a small, frail lady, her blonde hair starting to turn white and her pretty face contorted in pain.

Time froze as they made eye contact.

"Oh my Lord! Oh my Lord!" she cried out. "My baby boy, my baby Andrew! Thank you, Lord, for bringing my boy to me before I die! You look so much like your dad. I've waited so long for this moment, so long."

Andrew rushed to his mom's bed, dropped to his knees

and wrapped his arms around her. Mother and son hugged each other, totally lost in indescribable joy.

"You're the one! You're the one!" Andrew exclaimed between sobs. "You came to comfort me in a dream the night I tried to kill myself. It was you, Mom! It was you! I remember it so clearly. You laid your hand on my shoulder and said, 'My Andrew.' I was thirteen then. That was many, many years ago."

Time seemed to stand still as mother and son shared their respective lives. A number of times nurses came in to suggest that Maria should rest, but she shooed them away.

"If you'll bring my purse over to me, I'll show you a picture of your dad and me taken a week or so before he left for overseas."

She reached in her purse, came out with a well-worn snap photo case and handed it to Andrew. He opened the case and stared at the three photos, completely transfixed. One was of a baby, one a tall, dark young man and a blonde girl in her late teens and one of a middle-aged couple.

"This is me as a baby and the young couple are you and Dad?"

"That's right," Maria softly replied. "Every night since the day I gave you up for adoption, I held your photo in my hand and asked God to shield you in his arms."

"I can't believe this!" Andrew cried out after looking closer at the photo of his dad. "It's him! It's him! Dad was the priest who counselled me when I was agonizing over whether I should take my last year of seminary and become a priest. He has the same birthmark over his left eye that the counsellor had. You remember, I just told you about going to see him."

Maria nodded. "Yes I remember. God does sometimes work in strange ways. How your dad or I came to comfort and counsel you when you were so in need is a mystery that only God knows. We'll never know how often the angels have interceded on our behalf."

"And who is the older couple?" Andrew asked.

"Those are my parents, your grandparents."

"Maybe I should leave now, Mom," Andrew said, getting to his feet. "I think we're both on overload. What a morning!" Andrew bent over and kissed his mom on her forehead. "I'll phone every night and bring Anne and the kids to see you on Saturday if you're feeling up to it."

"I'll look forward to your phone calls and another visit. The Lord has been so kind to me. He's given me a reason to live now."

As Andrew got to the door, he glanced back into the room. There his mom lay, a small frail lady, hands clasped in prayer. Heading out the door he heard her sigh, "Thank you, Lord, for bringing my darling boy back to me."

Andrew was very upbeat after visiting his mom. He was overcome with emotion when Anne greeted him at the door. "It was awesome, just awesome. You see, the priest who counselled me in Regina was just the spitting image of the picture of my dad, even the same birthmark over his left eye. The lady in white who came and comforted me in a dream the night after I attempted suicide looked like the early picture of my mom. I thought that finding my granddad was the highlight of my life, but visiting with my birth mother, well, there's no way I can describe how I feel."

Anne held Andrew in her arms.

"I've finally found my roots," he cried. "I've finally found my roots."

Each evening Andrew phoned his mother for a few minutes. Doctor Parliament had advised that because of Maria's weakened condition, it would be best not to tire her out with lengthy phone calls.

Doctor Parliament was making his rounds Saturday morning when Andrew, Anne and the kids arrived at the hospital to visit Maria. The doctor stopped to talk with Andrew.

"I don't want to get your hopes up too high, but your mom is doing much better than she was before you visited her. Is it the start of a remission? It's too early to tell. As you probably know, there's far more we don't know about cancer than we know. It often seems if people give up on life, they don't last long. Conversely, if they have a strong will to live, the cancer will sometimes mysteriously go into remission and they can live for years. We know that close contact with family is very therapeutic, so within reason, the more contact you can keep with your mother, the better."

Maria was sitting up in bed when Andrew, Anne, Roy and Baby Edith came into her room. Anne was carrying Edith, while Roy was holding onto his dad's hand. Without uttering a word, Maria reached out her arms to Anne and Baby Edith. Anne rushed to the bed and embraced Maria. They held each other and wept.

"Are you my real grandma?" Roy asked, sidling up to his mom, baby sister and Maria. "I had another real grandma, but she had to go to heaven because her heart got too sick."

"Yes I'm your real grandma too," Maria responded, wiping the tears from her eyes and holding Roy close. "You see, I had your daddy as a baby just like your mom had you and little Edith. I was very young then and your daddy's father was killed in the war. When your dad was born I couldn't look after him, so your daddy went to stay with another Mom and Dad. Has your dad ever told you about that?"

"He said that sometimes he had nice homes, but sometimes the mommies and daddies were bad and very mean to him," Roy stated earnestly. "When I grow big, I'm going to go and give those bad people a good hit for being mean to my daddy. Mommy said you are a good grandma. If you come to our house you can even sleep in my bed with me."

"I would love to do that," Maria replied, eyes aglow. "For a four-year old boy you're sure talkative and very husky."

"I'm really, really strong too," Roy continued, flexing his arms tight until he vibrated. "I can even carry our dog. When I get big I'm going to be strong like my daddy. He lifts weights. He's as strong as a bear."

"This is the first baby I've held on my lap since I held my little Andrew," Maria said turning back to Anne and Andrew. "God only knows how it hurt to hand my baby over to the nurse for the last time. God is so good though," she continued, her face aglow. "I gave up my baby and God so richly rewarded me. I have a handsome son who is as strong as a bear, a beautiful kind daughter-in-law, a perfect little granddaughter and a grandson who's not only strong enough to carry a dog, but kind enough to share his bed with me."

It was time to go. "Are you going to come live at our house?" Roy asked as they headed to the door. "Maybe Mommy could cook you some porridge and soup and make you better."

"What a nice offer, Roy. I love both porridge and soup."

Andrew, Anne and the kids were soon on the road home. "I want my new grandma to come to live with us," Roy stated time and time again.

"We'll have to see," was Mom's consistent reply.

CHAPTER THIRTY-ONE

When they visited Maria the next weekend, they were amazed at how she had improved. "The doctor says my tumours have shrunk to less than half the size they were two weeks ago," she said, her face beaming. "I'm confident God is giving me this remission. He's sparing me so I can enjoy my family and maybe he has work for me to do yet."

On their fourth weekend visit, Doctor Parliament saw Andrew while on his rounds and asked to see him in his office in the afternoon. While Anne looked after the kids, Andrew stopped in to see the doctor.

"In my years of practice I've seen a number of terminal cancer cases go into remission, but without question, I've never seen such a rapid turnaround as your mother is experiencing. You saw for yourself how weak and emaciated she was when you first visited her. Now, she's off pain killers and has gained twenty pounds. Not only that, we can't detect any sign of tumours. Would you and your wife be able to look after her for a bit? Yesterday, she mentioned something about going back teaching. I'd be just as happy if she'd agree to convalesce for a month or two before she did that."

"We have plenty of room. Anne and I would be delighted to have Mom stay with us for as long as she wants."

Sunday afternoon, the doctor discharged Maria from the hospital on the condition she stay with Andrew and Anne and see him on a weekly basis for the next six weeks. Andrew and Anne were happy to have Maria with them. Her health steadily improved and each day, weather permitting, she, Roy and Rover went on long walks. Roy wanted Grandma to sleep in his bed with him. Mommy told him she'd have to sleep in her own bed because his bed was just too small. They remedied the situation by moving Roy's bed in beside Grandma's in the guest room.

Once in their bedroom for the night, Maria had many Bible stories to tell Roy. Not only would she tell them, she'd have Roy help her act them out. Roy and Grandma were fast bonding.

Maria couldn't have been happier. Her health was improving and for the first time in over thirty-three years she had the love and support of family.

"I would really like to see Alvin," Maria began one evening. "I owe him and his mother, Rose, so much. If at all possible, I'd like to drop down for a visit."

When Maria phoned the old folks' home the matron told her that a flu epidemic was sweeping the lodge and Alvin was under the weather.

"Because of your health issues, I strongly advise against a visit at this time," the matron said. "The last thing you need is to come down with the flu."

"You're right," Maria replied. "I'd love to see him, but I must take care of my health. I'll stay in touch."

"I can't tell you how much it means to me to be so looked

after by my family," Maria said a few evenings later. "It's kind of strange. I've felt so well of late I wonder if maybe I'm starting to play hooky from life. I'll forever be indebted to you for the kindness you've showed me, but shouldn't I be getting back in the saddle? Last week Doctor Parliament said he was very pleased with my recovery. I'm not that old yet. Maybe I should be getting back to work."

"You're more than welcome to stay here indefinitely," Andrew replied, "but much as Anne, the kids and I love having you near, we won't stand in the way of you doing what you feel you have to do."

"If you do go back teaching, Andrew and I want this to be your second home," Anne added. "We insist that you stay in close contact."

"It's a three hundred mile trip to your school," Andrew continued, "but we're thinking of trading our car in on a little diesel model. The Volkswagen Rabbit is supposed to be on the market later this year. They get something like sixty miles to the gallon. If I get one of those and you go back teaching, there'll be no problem picking you up for weekends and holidays."

After Maria's two-month check-up, Doctor Parliament met her in his office. "Well, Sister, you've done it, or perhaps the Almighty and you have done it. I'm giving you a clean bill of health. I should temper that optimistic outlook with a bit of caution. In our experience, when cancer goes into remission, in the majority of cases it does return. You might have a five-year window, ten or even a twenty year remission period. In some instances the person eventually dies of other causes, but on average, you should know that the cancer does return. If any problem crops up let me know, otherwise I'd like to see you in six months."

That afternoon Maria contacted her school, told them she'd made a complete recovery and would be available to fill her old position in another week.

Roy was not at all pleased that he'd be losing his roommate and did his best to talk his grandma into staying. Despite his lobbying, Maria and Andrew were packed to leave Saturday morning. As his grandma hugged him goodbye, Roy was looking quite doleful. "I'm going to sleep beside your bed till you come back," he said as Grandma got into the car.

It was a dull, early winter day when they pulled out of Innsburg. By the time they got to Red Deer, it started snowing. They drove through snow all the way to Wasp Lake. All but the last ninety miles of the road to Maria's school were paved and by late afternoon they arrived at the school compound.

The school compound was about a half mile out of the village. On one side of the compound were a two-room school and a house for the teachers. In the middle of the compound were the two old dormitories and a kitchen. Next to the dormitories there was a large church and the church rectory. To the north and west of the compound was forested area. It was getting dark, but Maria took Andrew on a tour around the grounds.

"A lot has changed since I started to teach here. Back then most of the kids stayed in these dormitories. Now we're a separate school, but the kids live on the reserve or in the village and are bussed to school."

After touring the compound, Maria and Andrew walked back to her duplex for tea. "For many years, Sister Flo taught with me and shared this house. Then a number of years back, she was needed elsewhere and the church moved her on. The church decided to make a duplex out of the house, but the last few years the other teacher has lived in the village."

"Yes life goes on, but for me, the sun has finally come out from behind the clouds," Andrew said. "I don't know if you felt this way before, Mom, but until we found each other I had a kind of empty feeling in part of my soul. At the same time, for years I was afraid to look for you in case it would be a disappointment."

"For me it was just about the same. I always prayed for you, but I still felt somewhat guilty for giving you up. Just before I got sick I wrote in my diary that I must try to find you this year. I've kept a diary ever since I entered the convent. One of these times it would be good for you, Anne and me to go through the diaries together. I'm really curious about something. Over the years I'd be doing my normal thing, when suddenly, I'd get this unbelievably strong urge to pray for you. It would be interesting to see if we could correlate these times with what was happening to you at that specific moment. I bookmarked the pages when these incidents occurred. At any rate, I guess we were both ready to find each other. Thank God you were able to take the initiative."

"Changing the subject, Mom, when we first met, you showed me a picture of my grandparents. You told me both of your parents had problems, but you didn't tell me much more. What's their story?"

"It's a very heavy story. I was an only child. My mother suffered postpartum depression at my birth and never recovered from it. When I told her I was pregnant with you she tried to kill herself and had to be permanently institutionalized. She died about fifteen years ago. Dad was an alcoholic and drank himself to death. He died a couple of years after Mom died. I went to both of their funerals. It was so sad since they were like strangers to me. Up until their deaths, I constantly prayed for them. I always felt so helpless that other than praying, there was nothing more I could do for them. I guess both of them are with their Maker now and that gives me comfort."

After tea, Maria walked Andrew to his car.

"We'd love to have you spend Christmas with us," Andrew said. "I'll come to get you when your school is out for the holidays."

"My, my, that will be so nice to spend Christmas with my family," Maria responded. "School is to be out on December the twentieth, if I remember correctly. I've just got to look up Alvin again. I must make a concerted effort to contact him over the holidays."

It was very late when Andrew got home, but Roy was still up. His mother had been unsuccessful in getting his co-operation in moving his bed back to his own room. After a short family conference, the parents acquiesced to the young one's insistence that he be allowed to be the guardian of Grandma's room. His old room would become the new guest room.

The twentieth of December dawned -20 Fahrenheit, but by seven AM Andrew was on the road to his mom's school. Throughout the week up to the Christmas break, Maria was almost as excited as her students.

"You'll never know what this means to me," Maria said as they pulled onto the highway. "My last thirty or so Christmases have been down times for me. There would be friends welcoming me to their homes, but as you put it before, there was always that gnawing empty spot in my soul that only family can fill."

"Yes, it will be so good for us all to spend Christmas together. I dropped down to Calgary last weekend to see

Alvin. On Christmas morning, I'll pick him up and bring him to our place for the day. He said that so many good things were happening to him and how happy he'd be to see you again."

"That will be wonderful. The Christmas after I gave you up for adoption I spent with Alvin and his mother, Rose. It was a sad time for us all. I was feeling so low, not having my baby. Rose had just been admitted to extended care because of failing health and all of us were feeling the pain of spending the first Christmas without your dad. In spite of all our heartaches, we spent such a blessed day together supporting each other."

Roy was delighted to have his grandma back for a visit and insisted on carrying her bags into their bedroom. As Andrew had to work till the twenty-third, Anne, the kids and Maria drove to Red Deer the next day to do Christmas shopping.

Early Christmas morning, Andrew and his mom left to pick up Alvin in Calgary. When they arrived, Alvin was sitting on a bench, just inside the lodge front door.

"Dad," Maria called out, bending down and placing her hands on Alvin's shoulders.

"Maria," Alvin replied, peering closely at his daughter-in-law, his face aglow. He struggled to his feet, eyes glistening.

"What a wonderful present for an old man at the end of his life," Alvin blurted out, hugging Maria. "First finding my grandson and then my daughter-in-law. God is good. Please forgive me for not staying in touch with you, but it was so hard to go against Joy."

"I understand," Maria responded. "The important thing is that by no small miracle we're together now."

On the way back to Innsburg, Alvin and Maria never stopped talking.

Roy was jealous of all the attention his grandma was paying Alvin and did his level best to be involved in their conversations.

"I can honestly say that this has been the happiest, most blessed Christmas I've ever had," Maria said, as they were eating supper. "Six months ago, I thought I'd be spending Christmas on the other side, but thankfully, God had different plans."

Let's drink to this happy time," Andrew said, opening a bottle of wine. He poured Roy a glass of fruit juice and all the adults a glass of wine.

"To family," he called out. Everyone toasted the happy occasion.

After they finished supper, Andrew drove Alvin back to the lodge. By the time he got back home everyone was in bed. As he crawled into bed beside Anne, he whispered, "what a day. It makes one realize the truth in the scripture that says, 'It's more blessed to give than to receive.'"

The holidays slipped by too quickly and soon it was time for Andrew to drive Maria back to her school and everyone else to get back to their schedules.

Every month to six weeks, Andrew would drive up and get his mom for the weekend. In mid-winter, Andrew took delivery of his small diesel car. The cost of the trips was now a third of what they had been. Maria's medical check-ups continued to show she was cancer-free.

During the school summer break, Maria spent July and August with her family, accompanying them when they took a two-week vacation to Vancouver Island. She and Andrew dropped down to see Alvin a couple of times. In September, Anne returned to her teaching job.

For Thanksgiving, Andrew and Anne had both Maria and Alvin home for the holiday. They were looking forward to the family being together for Christmas again, but the Almighty had different plans. On November twenty-eighth, Alvin dropped dead of a massive heart attack while eating breakfast.

Andrew drove up to get his mom and the two arranged the funeral. As Alvin had no close church affiliation, the lodge Chaplin took the service.

Andrew attended to the formal part of the eulogy and then introduced his mom.

"Years ago, Alvin and his mom, Rose, opened their hearts and home to a sixteen year old girl from a dysfunctional family who was so in need. I was that girl. At the time, I was pregnant with Andrew. It was a very difficult time for me. The day after I found out I was pregnant we got news that my boyfriend, Andrew's father, was killed in action. I owe so much to Alvin and his mom. Fate saw to it that Alvin, my son Andrew and I would be separated for many years, but God in his compassion allowed us to get back together as a family a year or so ago. I looked on Alvin as my dad. God rest your soul, Alvin........."

CHAPTER THIRTY-TWO

The years passed. Maria continued to be a very integral part of Andrew's and Anne's family. Andrew continued picking up his mother for weekends several times during the year. She always spent Christmas, Easter and the summer holidays with them. As Maria's old friend, Flo still taught school, she'd usually spend a week with Maria during the summer break at Andrew's and Anne's. Roy and Edith were so grateful to have their grandma close at hand. Maria planned to teach until she was sixty and then retire to live with Andrew, Anne and the kids. Maria's health remained very robust and at her eight-year check-up, Doctor Parliament told her that she may well be in that small percentage of people whose cancer never returns.

In October of the ninth year of Maria's cancer remission, Andrew had a vivid dream about his mom. At the start of his dream he was talking with her and she seemed quite robust. He lost sight of her for a moment. When he noticed her again, Maria looked as frail as she was when they first met. Andrew awoke in a cold sweat. Although the dream haunted him, he chose not to share it with anyone.

That Christmas, despite her good report from the doctor, Maria was feeling tired. She attributed her tiredness to her heavy work schedule as she was teaching a very big class.

Maria thought it of little significance, so did not mention it to the family during the holiday. Once back at Wasp Lake, her run-down feeling continued. She was now spending most of her weekends resting. The last weekend in February, Andrew picked her up. She was now having a little discomfort in her lower abdomen.

Finally, she mentioned her condition to Andrew. On Andrew's insistence, Maria phoned the cancer clinic in Edmonton and made an appointment for Monday morning. Before they left, Maria made arrangements for a substitute teacher to fill in for her for a day or two. Throughout the weekend, Maria insisted they not talk about her condition.

Maria went through extensive tests on Monday. The hospital would have her results by the end of the week and contact her. Although Maria maintained a positive mind set, she had prepared herself for bad news if the cancer had returned.

"We are very concerned for you," Doctor Parliament began when he contacted Maria on Friday. "We have discovered some cancerous cells. Though as yet there are no tumours, we must assume that the cancer is returning. If you're not in great pain, I'd like to see you in a month's time. If you start to experience real pain, come in at once."

Maria postponed her check-up till the Easter break in early April. The news was not good. The tests showed several small tumours growing in her lower abdominal region. Doctor Parliament suggested they start on chemotherapy immediately.

"I don't think so," Maria replied. "Many years ago, if you'll remember, my cancer looked terminal. God saw fit to give me several more very good years. I'm going to leave my health in His hands. Over the last several months I've prayed about my health. Will God again give me another remission, or will He call me home this time? That decision is in His hands, not mine."

"I admire your courage and will honour your wish, Maria. I will supply you with painkillers, but if the pain gets to the point it's becoming unmanageable, I'd like you to admit yourself to our hospital again."

"I'll do that, Doctor. If it be God's will, I would so like to finish the school year."

Over the next month and a half Maria's tiredness became chronic and her discomfort escalated to real pain. The first weekend in June, Andrew rented a small motorhome from a neighbour. He, Anne, Roy and Edith made the trip up to Maria's school as she was in too much pain to make the trip down to Innsburg.

The weekend was a time of closeness for the family. When they first met, Andrew, Anne and the kids were all shocked at how much weight Maria had lost. About all she could keep down now were a little yogurt, dry toast and weak tea. After supper on Saturday Maria gathered her family around her.

"This may well be the last time you see me alive in this world. I have asked God to spare me until the end of the school year. I want you to know I'm not angry with God for allowing the cancer to return. I just have so much to be thankful to Him for. God has rewarded me with close to nine wonderful years with my family. Never in my wildest dreams did I imagine this would happen when I was so low. I guess, like the Apostle Paul I can say, 'I have fought the good fight.' I'm so looking forward to seeing Alvin, Rose and my beloved Andrew again."

Without saying a word, Andrew, Anne, Roy and Edith all hugged Maria.

After attending Mass with Maria on Sunday morning, Andrew and the family hugged her goodbye and headed for home.

Maria's health continued to deteriorate. The last week of school, she was unable to keep anything down except weak tea.

Andrew or Anne phoned every night. If all went as planned, Andrew would again borrow the motorhome after school was out and take his mom to the University Hospital.

The last day of school, Maria managed on sheer willpower. At the end of the day she hugged all her pupils' goodbye and using her walker, slowly dragged herself back to her house. Once she got home from school she phoned Anne and suggested it might be best for them to leave as soon as possible in the morning.

Maria made herself a pot of tea, took her painkillers and lay down to rest. She prayed and meditated for some time, but was in too much pain to fall asleep.

"What's that?" she murmured. "It's nearly dark. Did I drift off? Am I awake or am I dreaming? It sounded like someone calling my name."

"Maria, I've come for you," she heard again.

Startled, Maria looked to the foot of her bed. She could not believe her eyes. There stood her Andrew, looking not a day older than when he left for overseas.

"Andrew, what are you doing here?" she asked in bewilderment.

"Go to the old pine tree in the meadow. I'll meet you there."

As quickly as Andrew appeared, he disappeared.

Heavy tree cover bordered the north side of the compound. In the northwest corner, a foot trail led into the bush to a small meadow where an old gnarled pine tree stood. Over the years, in summer, Maria would often walk out to the pine tree to pray.

Hardly daring to believe what she'd just experienced, Maria pulled on her coat and slowly headed outside.

It was a beautifully warm, moonlit night, with a soft wind. Maria was in much pain as she attached a note to the door. She was trying hard to fathom Andrew's visit. With the use of her cane, she hobbled along the uneven path. She was very weak and had to stop several times to rest.

Then as Maria was entering the meadow, she felt something warm on her left hand. She glanced over in amazement. Andrew was walking hand-in-hand with her. When Maria looked over towards the old pine, she couldn't believe her eyes. A young girl was sitting with her back against the old tree.

"God have mercy," she exclaimed. "I don't understand. She looks just like I did when I was young. What on earth is going on?"

"Come closer," Andrew said, leading Maria ever closer to the tree.

"But I don't understand. I'm so old and in such pain and you and this girl look so young."

"Come closer, Maria."

Suddenly, things were a blur for Maria. Where one second ago she was in terrible pain, now she was feeling no pain. She looked down at her hands in wonderment. Her hands were the hands of a young girl!

"How can this be? Look at the tree trunk, Andrew. The young girl has vanished and there's an old woman in her place. Oh my stars! She looks like me, but how can this be?"

"Your old body has been replaced with a new one. That's what happens when you die."

"Have I died then?"

"Yes, you have," Andrew whispered.

As Andrew held Maria close, they were enveloped by light. It grew in intensity until they both shone. Suddenly, the light was gone and with it, Andrew and Maria.

CHAPTER THIRTY-THREE

As they had to make an early start, Andrew, Anne, Roy and Edith went to bed early.

Andrew was uptight and it took him some time to fall asleep. Shortly after dozing off, he had a most vivid dream. He saw the youthful figures of his mom and dad in each other's arms, standing beside an old pine tree. They appeared be enveloped in a bright light. Suddenly they vanished.

Andrew awoke with a start. He woke Anne and told her of his dream. Even though it was getting late, Andrew felt strongly that he should phone Father Menard. The Father lived in the church manse in the compound. When Andrew got Father Menard on the phone, he was still up watching the news.

"I'll go over and check on Sister Maria and then get back to you. I talked to her this afternoon. She's in a lot of pain and is expecting you around noon tomorrow."

"What's this?" Father Menard said as he knocked on Maria's door.

A note read:

Dear Andrew and Anne,

My Andrew has come for me. We're to
meet at the old pine tree in the meadow.

Love, Mom

Father Menard was aware that Sister Maria often went to
the old pine tree to pray. He went back to the manse, got a
flashlight and headed down the path to the meadow.

As he neared the pine, he saw a figure sitting up against
the base of the tree.

"Dear Lord, it's Sister Maria," he said, his voice breaking.
He squatted down to check on her vital signs.

"The poor dear has gone to be with her Lord," he whispered,
tears slipping down his cheeks. "Till we meet again then,
Sister," he added, patting her forehead.

In a few minutes he was back on the phone with Andrew.
Anne got on an extension.

"You were on the mark, Andrew," Father Menard said, his
voice trembling. "The Lord did call your mom home. She left a
note on her door that she'd gone to the pine tree in the meadow
to meet Andrew, whatever that meant. She often went there
to pray. I found her body leaning up against the pine. As the
old saying goes, 'Our loss is heaven's gain.' I imagine you'll be
coming up to make funeral arrangements."

"We'll be there sometime tomorrow afternoon, Father."

Anne went to Andrew, held him in her arms and they both
wept. After a cup of cocoa they went to bed.

Andrew and Anne arose early to break the news of Grandma Maria's passing to Roy and Edith. Both were heartbroken.

"I'm just going to miss my grandma so much," Edith sobbed. "I thought she'd get healed again."

"It's kind of hard to take," Roy added, wiping the tears from his eyes. "I guess though, Grandma's got no more pain and she's with Grandpa now. She told me lots of times how she couldn't wait to see him again."

After an early breakfast, they were on the road with their neighbour's motorhome.

In late afternoon they arrived at the compound. It was Maria's wish that she be buried as simply as possible. They were quite a distance from a large town and seeing Maria's death was of natural causes, Andrew decided not to have a funeral home involved. Felix White Fox, one of Maria's old students, offered to build the casket and by late Saturday afternoon he had it finished. It was a simple plywood box. Anne bought a comforter from the local Hudson Bay Store to line it. Several of the boys and men dug the grave, while the older ladies prepared the body. On Saturday evening, Flo arrived just before the viewing took place in the church.

Father Menard requested that Andrew, Anne, Roy, Edith and Flo be allowed to view the body first.

"Thank you so much for including me with your family, Andrew," Flo said. "Although your mom and I were sisters of the church, we were as close to each other as birth sisters." With tears in her eyes she patted Maria's forehead and whispered, "Goodbye Maria. I'll see you again in heaven."

Andrew placed his hand on his mom's folded hands. Though tears were sliding down his cheeks, there was a smile on his face. In his mind's eye stood the youthful figures of his mom and dad with their arms around each other in front of the old gnarled pine tree.

On Sunday, after Mass, Andrew and Anne were going through Maria's effects and loading them into the motorhome. They had found Maria's current diary and were cleaning out her small deep freeze. At the bottom of the freezer, Andrew found a small canister containing what looked like some old books.

"Look what I found," Andrew called out. "Here are Mom's old diaries. Let's take a look at them. Years back Mom said that someday the three of us should go through her diaries, but I guess we never got around to it. She told me about the times she had these sudden strong urges to pray for my welfare. We both were curious if there was a correlation between these times and the times I was in crisis. She told me she bookmarked the times of prayer, so they shouldn't be too hard to find."

Andrew and Anne sat on the bed and put the diaries in chronological order.

"I'll go through the bookmarked entries and see if they ring a bell for you," Anne said. "Here's a marker in her first five year diary."

Felt the sudden urgent need to pray for my baby's welfare in class this morning. Sister Louise allowed me to go to my room. I prayed for my son until the burden lifted.

Andrew looked at the date, his eyes filling with tears. "This has got to be the time I was put in the orphanage."

"Here's another. By the date you would be twelve, I believe."

Felt this sudden strong urge to pray for my son.
Had a vision of a boy lying in bed in a dark room,
crying. I prayed till the burden lifted.

"That probably is about when I went to stay with Arthur, Dorothy and Dieter," Andrew added.

"This entry is about eight months later."

After supper, I felt a powerful urge to pray
for my boy. This time the feeling was extremely
strong. I prayed for several hours.

Andrew reached over and took the diary. "Oh my God!" he gasped, fighting for control. "I can't believe this. This was on the same evening I attempted suicide."

"God was protecting you," Anne whispered, putting her arm around Andrew.

"This one would be shortly after you're eighteenth birthday."

Felt the strong need to pray for my boy again.
Strangely, I felt the need to pray for another
friend of his.

"Could this be about the time I told you I was planning on becoming a missionary?"

"That would be right around that time," Andrew replied, shaking his head in wonderment.

"This last one was when we were on our second honeymoon down the Oregon coast."

While meditating, I felt this unbelievably strong urge to pray for the safety of my son and another person. I prayed earnestly for about ten minutes or so and the burden lifted.

"Good gracious," Anne cried. "This was on the day the big truck nearly hit us."

"It's so amazing how Mom's prayers protected both of us over the years," Andrew added. "It makes you conscious of the power of prayer."

The funeral was held Monday afternoon. Several of Maria's friends from Innsburg drove up. Father Menard led the service while Maria's old friend, Flo, did the eulogy. After Flo finished, Father Menard gave those in the audience whose lives had been influenced by Maria the opportunity to say a few words. Andrew and Anne gave a tearful tribute to Maria. They shared the reading of the diaries and the power of her prayers in their lives. Many of her old friends and students told how much Sister Maria had influenced their lives for the good.

At the lunch following the funeral, Father Menard approached Andrew.

"I have a favour to ask. I would be so honoured to have a small keepsake of your mother's. We've known each other for so many years. She was such a Godly saint."

"That she was, Father. Anne and I would be happy to do that for you. Do you have anything in mind?"

"Would it be going too far to ask for her cane?"

"Not at all, not at all, but do you have any idea where it might be? Anne and I have gone through all her belongings and we've yet to run across it."

"When I went out to the pine tree in the meadow the evening she passed away, I believe her cane was leaning up against the tree."

"Anne and I will go for a walk out to the old pine and get it for you. It would be nice if we could get away for a bit and I'd like to see the spot where Mom used to go to pray."

Hand-in-hand they started down the path to the old pine. As they were coming up to the meadow, Anne stopped Andrew. "There's something strange happening here. I'm getting this strong feeling of déjà vu."

"That's it! That's it!" she exclaimed as they came into the meadow. "I can hardly believe my eyes. I was in this meadow before, in my dream with Rob the night he lay on my chest."

Slowly they walked to the old pine.

It had been a very still day, without a cloud in the sky, yet when Andrew touched his mom's cane; they heard the muted rumble of thunder off in the distance.

When they turned in the direction of the sound, an amazing sight met their eyes. Three figures were approaching them from the far side of the meadow. There was a tall man, a blonde woman and a child. The figures were very bright and seemed to be floating rather than walking.

"What is it?" Anne whispered, clutching Andrew's arm.

As the figures came closer Andrew exclaimed, "My God, it's Mom, Dad and..."

"The little one is Rob!" Anne interrupted. "He looks exactly the same as he did in the dream."

The three spirits stopped and hovering a few yards from them. The light surrounding the spirits grew increasingly brighter until it was almost too much for the eyes to bear. While Andrew and Anne watched in amazement, the spirits were totally engulfed by the huge ball of pulsating brilliant light. There was another distant muted clap of thunder and suddenly, the light and the spirits were gone.

Andrew and Anne clung to each other in silence, trying hard to assimilate what they just witnessed.

"I'm so overcome," Anne finally whispered. "I've been in this meadow before and now to see the Spirits of your folks and our little Rob. I feel we're on holy ground."

"We are indeed," Andrew replied, shaking his head in wonderment. "Mom, Dad and wee Rob's Spirits knew how much it would mean for us to see them. I have such a feeling of completion. They're together at last."

ABOUT THE AUTHOR

Michael Parlee was born and raised in the Peace River Country of northwest Alberta. He spent most of his adult life farming and operating a land clearing business in the area. Complications from a work-related accident forced him into early retirement in the late 1990's. Sitting around twiddling his thumbs was driving him stir crazy. He had always wanted to take a stab at writing so he began his first novel, 'Tanya'. He published Tanya in 2006. He's still being bitten by the writing bug. 'Son of Sister Maria' is his second book. He will shortly publish 'Grandpa's Magic Beard,' a children's book. His fourth book, 'You Must Forgive to Live' is nearing completion and he's well into his fifth book, 'The Parlee-Hudz Connection,' the Parlee family history. Michael lives in Bowden, Alberta with his wife Pauline.

His e-mail address is mpparlee@shaw.ca

ABOUT THE COVER ARTIST

Eldon Walls was born and raised in central Alberta Canada. He is a skilled mural artist having painted over 10,000 square feet of murals in the Alberta towns and cities of Strathmore, Leduc, Airdrie, Coronation, Nordegg and Calgary. Presently he is painting a mural in the town of Trochu. In addition to murals, Eldon does Cowboy Cartoon art. He has been commissioned to do art work in the form of caricatures for special occasions such as birthdays, anniversaries and retirements.

Eldon shows another aspect of his talent in doing Book Covers. In addition to the cover for 'Son of Sister Maria,' he has done the cover and illustrations for 'When Cowboys Come to Play' by Jeramy McNeely and 'From Cowboy's Office Window' by Tom King.

Eldon will soon be working on the book covers for two more books that Michael Parlee has written.

To see more of Eldon's work, go to his website www.eldonwalls.com

CPSIA information can be obtained at www.ICGtesting.com
Printed in the USA
LVOW081759280412

279473LV00001B/14/P